Dark Nights, Bright Lights

Buchreihe der ANGLIA/ ANGLIA Book Series

Edited by
Lucia Kornexl, Ursula Lenker, Martin Middeke,
Gabriele Rippl, Hubert Zapf

Advisory Board
Laurel Brinton, Philip Durkin, Olga Fischer, Susan Irvine,
Andrew James Johnston, Christopher A. Jones, Terttu Nevalainen,
Derek Attridge, Elisabeth Bronfen, Ursula K. Heise, Verena Lobsien,
Laura Marcus, J. Hillis Miller, Martin Puchner

Volume 50

Dark Nights, Bright Lights

Night, Darkness, and Illumination in Literature

Edited by
Susanne Bach and Folkert Degenring

DE GRUYTER

For an overview of all books published in this series, please see
http://www.degruyter.com/view/serial/36292

ISBN 978-3-11-057862-1
e-ISBN (PDF) 978-3-11-041529-2
e-ISBN (EPUB) 978-3-11-041562-9
ISSN 0340-5435

Library of Congress Cataloging-in-Publication Data
A CIP catalog record for this book has been applied for at the Library of Congress.

Bibliographic information published by the Deutsche Nationalbibliothek
The Deutsche Nationalbibliothek lists this publication in the Deutsche Nationalbibliografie;
detailed bibliographic data are available on the Internet at http://dnb.dnb.de.

© 2015 Walter de Gruyter GmbH, Berlin/Boston
This volume is text- and page-identical with the hardback published in 2015.
Printing: CPI books GmbH, Leck

♾ Printed on acid-free paper
Printed in Germany

www.degruyter.com

Acknowledgements

Edited collections of essays always represent a collaborative effort. In the case of the present volume, the editors have a particularly large group of people to thank for making the publication possible.

First and foremost, we would like to thank our contributors, not just for the chapters they have written for the collection but for their patience when we were slow to move forward and their alacrity when we asked for speed. To the editors of the Anglia Book Series, especially Gabriele Rippl, Martin Middeke, and Hubert Zapf, we would like to express our gratitude for the inclusion of the title in the series as well as for their invaluable support and help. At De Gruyter Mouton, we would like to thank Ulrike Krauß, Katja Lehming, and Olena Gainulina for their lightning-fast responses whenever yet another question occurred to us. Thanks are also due to Franz Mutschler, postgraduate student at the University of Kassel, for assisting us in the proofreading process and for his comments. Our particular thanks go to Melanie Schrage-Lang, doctoral candidate at the University of Kassel, for her invaluable contribution to the project. She tirelessly tackled typos in first, second, and third drafts, formatted manuscripts, made many valuable comments and suggestions, and never once lost her patience.

We would also like to thank the members of the transdisciplinary research consortium 'Verlust der Nacht' (Loss of the Night) in Germany. Their research efforts into the effects of artificial light at night immediately fascinated us when we heard about them. We acknowledge the conferences, workshops, and discussions organised by the consortium as a major source of inspiration.

Finally, without the support and tolerance of our families and spouses this collection would not have been possible. The volume is dedicated to them.

Mannheim and Kassel, June 2015   Folkert Degenring and Susanne Bach

Table of Contents

Folkert Degenring and Susanne Bach

Introduction: Dark Nights, Bright Lights

Vincent van Gogh, in a letter to his brother in 1888, wrote about Arles in southern France that the "town here is *nothing*, at night everything is *black*", and, should he ever see Paris again, he looked forward to painting "the effects of gaslight on the boulevard" (qtd. in Brox 2015: 22; emphases in the original).

What ailed the painter so much had been a given for most of humanity's history: the prevalence of natural darkness at night. According to Christian faith, God created "two great lights; the greater light to rule the day, and the lesser light to rule the night" (*King James Bible*, Gen. 1:16). This lesser light, i.e. the moon with her cycle ranging from new to full, was the main source of night time illumination for a very long time, indeed. This is true not only if one considers the prehistory of *homo sapiens* but for much of recorded history as well. Artificial light sources were sparse and expensive – and oftentimes also dangerous to use and to keep. For a long time, lamps and candles, for example, constituted a constant fire hazard, they stank and smoked, and due to their usually being made of animal or vegetable fat, i.e. valuable resources, were costly and readily available only to the rich (cf. Brox 2015: 13). This situation would change only gradually, and it is relatively recently that the public and private use of artificial light has become a matter of course. A matter of course, that is, in some societies. The globe, as composite images shot from space show impressively, is unevenly lit at night, and while it is true that it is no longer solely the rich who can afford to light the night indiscriminately, the presence of illumination is not just indicative of population densities but also correlates with the global distribution of wealth.

This is the case not just for individuals and their homes but also for social bodies and public space. Indeed, it is quite difficult to separate private and public space when discussing night time illumination. For one, light does not stop at property boundaries and spills indiscriminately from one area into the other. And historically, too, private property and the lighting of public spaces were intimately linked: according to Jane Brox, house owners in the larger European cities were ordered in the 1600s "to hang a lamp or place a candle on their street-facing windowsills" (15). After some time, a more centralised organisation to complement and later replace individual citizens' efforts was needed, and city administrations organised the care of iron fire baskets in which fires were kept burning in the streets at night.

City illumination has come a long way since the times of fire baskets. It is not just the lighting technologies which have changed in the course of time, however, but attitudes towards night time illumination as well. Historically, the increasing brightness of the night has elicited surprisingly ambivalent and sometimes contradictory responses, considering that the new sources of light were frequently hailed as beacons of progress and modernity. On the one hand, for example, in 17th-century Cologne the authorities predicted a steady rise in "drunkenness and depravity" (qtd. in Brox 2015: 18) should the fear of darkness vanish as a consequence of increasing illumination; on the other hand, in 21st century Britain, the public "believes that domestic floodlighting has a high security value" (Morgan-Taylor 2015: 164). And when the first gas-fuelled street lamps made their appearance in London in 1807, their light was perceived "as natural and as pure as daylight" and shedding "a warmth as purifying to the air as cheering to the spirits" (qtd. in Brox 2015: 20). Towards the end of the century, however, in 1881, Oscar Wilde's poem "Impression du matin" provokingly placed a prostitute underneath a "gas-lamp's flare" (1979: 1678), thus trying to stress the deception and artificiality of both and – most likely unwittingly – echoing the 17th-century concerns of Cologne's city authorities.

At the same time, the introduction of electrical arc street lights caused some to avert their eyes in horror and retrospectively glorify gaslight, like Robert Louis Stevenson in "A Plea for Gas Lamps":

> The word ELECTRICITY now sounds the note of danger. [...] [A] new sort of urban star now shines out nightly, horrible, unearthly, obnoxious to the human eye; a lamp for a nightmare! Such a light as this should shine only on murders and public crime, or along the corridors of lunatic asylums, a horror to heighten horror. To look at it only once is to fall in love with gas, which gives a warm domestic radiance fit to eat by. (Stevenson 1881: 295)

Today, brightly lit streets at night are only rarely met with derision, praise, or glorification: in many parts of the world street lights are simply taken for granted and receive little attention. Their discursive absence speaks for itself; their artificial light now seems a natural part of the night.

Light and Darkness in Language, Culture, and Society

Light and darkness are central parameters in nearly all areas of life; even some one-celled creatures follow a circadian rhythm (cf. Melbin 1987: 1). The cycle of light and darkness thus has an existential function and "orchestrates the behaviours of nearly every living thing" (Mizon 2012: 3). Given this importance, it is not surprising that light and darkness and associated aspects feature more or less centrally in many mythologies and cosmogonies: the sun and the moon as sources of light are often directly or indirectly deified, for example (ibid.).

Greek cosmogony, for instance, sees the goddess Nyx, literally 'Night', as the mother of the gods and goddesses associated with fate, sleep, and dreams but also with strife, deceit, blame, retribution, doom, and death (cf. Bronfen 2013: 30). Day, night, light, and darkness prominently feature in the biblical book of Genesis as well, of course:

> In the beginning God created the heaven and the earth. And the earth was without form, and void; and darkness was upon the face of the deep. And the Spirit of God moved upon the face of the waters. And God said, Let there be light: and there was light. And God saw the light, that it was good: and God divided the light from the darkness. And God called the light Day, and the darkness he called Night. And the evening and the morning were the first day. (Gen. 1:1–5)

The Bible, cultural historian Elisabeth Bronfen argues, knows two kinds of darkness: the primordial darkness which represents the opposite of light, on the one hand, and on the other, the illuminated darkness of the earthly night (2013: 45). While it is true that light is privileged in Genesis since God calls it good, the night in turn is not explicitly labelled as evil. Indeed, the biblical night is not characterised by a complete lack of light. On the fourth day, after the creation of heaven, earth, the seas, and the plants,

> God made two great lights; the greater light to rule the day, and the lesser light to rule the night: he made the stars also. And God set them in the firmament of the heaven to give light upon the earth, and to rule over the day and over the night, and to divide the light from the darkness: and God saw that it was good. (Gen. 1:16–18)

Since night and day were created together, night should be thought of as different from the primordial darkness (cf. Bach and Degenring 2015: 48).

Given the importance of light in mythology and cosmogony, it does not come as a surprise that language itself should bear testimony to light and darkness as vital and cultural forces; certainly this is the case in the European context. In English, for example, there is a wealth of expressions that relate to light, darkness, and vision. An argument can be 'lucid' or 'opaque', 'I see' denotes understanding, and new knowledge is considered 'enlightening' while 'being kept in the dark' means being kept ignorant. Indeed, the term 'Enlightenment' denotes a historical period during which the development of the natural sciences in the modern sense of the word picks up speed and the rational understanding of the world assumes cultural primacy – or at least that is how the period is constructed in retrospective. In contrast, the general understanding of the Middle Ages as the 'Dark Ages' suggests that the period as a whole was defined by a mix of superstition, ignorance, and irrationality which, from today's enlightened perspective, implies an almost nightmarish quality (cf. Bach and Degenring 2015: 46).

This is a distorted image, of course, as any historian (and in all likelihood most laypeople, too) will readily point out. But while the rich and long cultural history of light and darkness is much more complex, and their symbolic and metaphorical meaning is much more ambivalent, things are indeed much more clear cut in everyday language: many, if not most, expressions associated with light imply 'good', while many, if not most, expressions associated with darkness imply 'bad'. And it is these everyday expressions, these 'metaphors we live by' (cf. Lakoff and Johnson 1980), which are a profound and powerful factor in the shaping of our worldview, including our views of the past. Language and culture do not, of course, exist in isolation from one another but are intimately linked and constantly influence each other. So when it appears to us only right and proper that the devil has earned himself the byname 'Prince of Darkness', or that in Plato's famous allegory of the cave light is the arbiter of perception, understanding, and knowledge, we are dealing with prime examples of interlocking cultural and linguistic phenomena. And much as culture and language cannot be entirely separated, light and darkness as physical phenomena cannot be separated from social aspects, either. In most societies, illuminating the night equals exerting influence on working conditions, recreation, rest, and sleep (cf. Bach and Degenring 2015: 48).

The sociologist Murray Melbin, for example, has argued that the development of lighting technologies and their widespread availability has led to what he calls the 'colonization of the night' (1987). Thus, in medieval European cities, the lack of night-time illumination forced "blacksmiths [to] lay down their bellows and goldsmiths ceased beating out metal" (Brox 2015: 14), and after curfew only midwives, priests, doctors, and watchmen were supposed to walk the streets at night, together of course with shady characters like prostitutes and criminals (cf. 15). Nowadays, night shifts are a given not only in factories, but in medical and emergency services, law enforcement, the service sector, and the entertainment and leisure industry as well: today, New York is far from being the only 'city that never sleeps'. It could be said, then, that light at night has created a new sort of space (cf. Binder 2015: 9) that affects behaviour (cf. Ginthner 2004: 2). What this might mean is perhaps best illustrated by an analogy. As Robert Wilson, the famous US theatre scenographer, explains: "Light is the most important part of the theatre …. How it reveals objects, how objects change when light changes, how light creates space, how space changes when light changes …. I paint, I build, I compose with light. Light is a magic wand" (qtd. in Holmberg 2005: 121). The power of light to construct and define space is not limited to the theatre, of course, even though theatre practice has changed most dramatically (so to speak) in the wake of changing lighting technologies since the early modern period (cf. Koslovsky 2011: 108). And what is true for theatre space is true for other illuminated spaces as well. Since "local space is not a static reality, but is continually produced and redefined" (Edensor 2015: 89), light can create new experiences of public space (cf. Nye 2015: 31), it can 'create' space (by illumination), and it can 'create' time (by appropriating the night).

In those parts of the world where 'nocturnalization' (Koslofsky 2011: 2 *et passim*) has been completely adopted conceptually, natural darkness has become a rarity. From sunset to sunrise, modern cities are brilliantly illuminated, and in urban areas it has become impossible to glimpse any but the very brightest stars at night. It could be argued that the ubiquitous and easy availability of artificial light has another major consequence beyond the increasing rarity of entirely un-illuminated darkness: artificial illumination has paradoxically become invisible and goes unnoticed most of the time. This is not universally true, however. Increasing light levels affect astronomy, for example, and astronomers have been amongst the first to label unwanted light at night 'light pollution'. But light at night is not just a phenomenon that affects astronomers, as Travis Longcore and Catherine Rich have pointed out in an overview article in *Frontiers in Ecology and the Environment* in 2004:

> Ecologists have long studied the critical role of natural light in regulating species interactions, but, with limited exceptions, have not investigated the consequences of artificial night lighting. In the past century, the extent and intensity of artificial night lighting has increased such that it has substantial effects on the biology and ecology of species in the wild. We distinguish "astronomical light pollution", which obscures the view of the night sky, from "ecological light pollution", which alters natural light regimes in terrestrial and aquatic ecosystems. Some of the catastrophic consequences of light for certain taxonomic groups are well known, such as the deaths of migratory birds around tall lighted structures, and those of hatchling sea turtles disoriented by lights on their natal beaches. The more subtle influences of artificial night lighting on the behaviour and community ecology of species are less well recognised, and constitute a new focus for research in ecology and a pressing conservation challenge. (Longcore and Rich 2004: 191)

That is not to say, however, that in recent years concerns over the level of light at night have not been voiced publically, for example by the International Dark Sky Association (IDA). Founded in 1988 by David L. Crawford and Tim Hunter "to address the growing problem of light pollution", and, according to their home page, "the only non-profit organization fighting to preserve the night", the IDA claims:

Once a source of wonder—and one half of the entire planet's natural environment—the star-filled nights of just a few years ago are vanishing in a yellow haze. Human-produced light pollution not only mars our view of the stars; poor lighting threatens astronomy, disrupts ecosystems, affects human circadian rhythms, and wastes energy to the tune of $2.2 billion per year in the U.S. alone. (IDA 2014)

Evidence that the topic is receiving increased attention may also be found in the efforts of the collaborative research consortium 'Verlust der Nacht' (Loss of the Night) in Germany,[1] which investigated astronomical, biological, ecological, economical, historical, medical, and technological dimensions of light at night. The consortium's homepage makes clear, however, that their coordinated interdisciplinary research effort is, to this date, unique:

Because light has positive connotations with security, wealth and modernity, humans tend to illuminate their environment intensively. Although artificial light provides countless advantages to humans, it also has its dark side. Over the last decades, light pollution, the pollution of naturally dark skies by artificial light, has intensified, without regard to its potential impacts on humans and the environment. While some scientific investigation of light pollution and its effects has taken place, it has been narrowly focused within astronomy or the effects on single organisms. To date, there has not been a wide ranging interdisciplinary investigation. (Verlust der Nacht 2013)

It is nevertheless fair to say that outside of the field of lighting engineering and technology development, academic interest in critical perspectives on night time illumination has been relatively rare. It is also true that ground-breaking publications have existed for some time – for example Wolfgang Schivelbusch's seminal historical study *Disenchanted Night: The Industrialization of Light in the Nineteenth Century*,[2] to name but one. However, light-related research has remained a marginal area of interest in most disciplines. Some recent publications have begun to partially remedy this investigative lack, but many, if not most, research questions are still left open and need to be addressed by the sciences and the humanities. This is true for literary studies, too, and the present volume is one of the few collections that specifically examine the role and function of artificial and natural light and the illuminated night in Anglophone literature.

---

1 The authors of this introduction are associated members of the research consortium and explicitly wish to express their gratitude to the members of 'Verlust der Nacht' for imparting valuable facts and knowledge, for lively discussions and thought-provoking conferences.
2 Translated from the German original, *Lichtblicke: Zur Geschichte der künstlichen Helligkeit im 19. Jahrhundert* (1983).

Light, Darkness, and Illumination in Literature

Of course this should not be understood to imply that no previous work on the imagery of light and darkness has been done, or that the work is far from noteworthy. Shakespeare studies, for example, have long debated the lighting traditions and conventions of the Elizabethan stage, as is evident in Alan C. Dessen's article "Night and darkness on the Elizabethan Stage: Yesterday's Conventions and Today's Distortions" (1978), or Robert B. Graves' monograph *Lighting the Shakespearean Stage, 1567–1642* (1999). Other scholars, like Hugh Magennis in "Imagery of Light in Old English Poetry: Traditions and Apparitions" (2007) have examined the imagery of light as a Christian symbol in Old English poetry, or the connection between darkness, light, religion, and the environment in 20th century poetry, as in the case of John Powell Ward's "Darkness and Light: Poetry, Religion and the Environment" (2003). The symbolic treatment of light and darkness, night and day in the works of individual authors like Robert Louis Stevenson has been examined – e. g. in Linda Dryden's "City of Dreadful Night: Stevenson's Gothic London" (2006) – just like the connection of entire genres with light-related imagery, for example in Kenneth Vye Bailey's "Bright Day – Dreadful Night: Metaphoric Polarities in Fantasy and Science Fiction" (1992). Sometimes individual authors have been examined in connection with very specific forms of lighting, as J. G. Keogh has done with Edgar Allan Poe and gaslight in "The Crowd as No Man's Land: Gas-light and Poe's Symbolist Effects" (1984); and in William Brevda's 2011 monograph *Signs of the Signs: The Literary Lights of Incandescence and Neon* the role of electric and neon signs in American literature is discussed. Additionally, in 2013, literary scholar Elisabeth Bronfen focussed on a related topic, i. e. the night in philosophy, the arts, and literature, in her cultural history, *Night Passages: Philosophy, Literature and Film.*[3]

Despite these research efforts, it is surprising that light and nocturnal illumination in literature have received so little attention to date, given their prevalence in culture and society. This does imply a pertinent question, however: why *should* literary studies deal with the topic at all, and not just leave it to disciplines like engineering, biology, zoology, medicine, ecology, history, economy, psychology, or sociology? Literature has always been a means of cogitation and evaluation. It is capable of expressing subjective and individual experiences while at the same time commenting on social states and collective processes. It can offer futuristic scenarios, explore alternative worlds, or give access to a ver-

---

[3] Translated from the German original, *Tiefer als der Tag gedacht: Eine Kulturgeschichte der Nacht* (2008).

sion of the past. It can shed light on current trends, deliberate theories, and offers an experimental space, especially for those examinations which in reality cannot or should not be undertaken. It predicts, warns, plays with ideas, offers alternatives, challenges, and it can conduct experiments without being bound to the necessarily strict codes of the sciences. This appears to be the case no matter from which theoretical angle literature is examined; and while the literary construction of reality and extraliterary reality cannot simply be equated in the sense that one can be considered the mirror of the other, they can be correlated in meaningful ways. Literature is thus a medium that allows a deeper understanding of extraliterary phenomena, as the following chapters demonstrate.

In the collection's first chapter, "City Nights, City Lights in London Literature of the 1890s", Paul Goetsch discusses the role of London nights in late Victorian literature. The 1890s can be described as a transitional phase during which aspects of the late Victorian and the modern period coincide, and as a time during which anxieties triggered by the state of the Empire, international competition, and modernisation come to the fore. Goetsch argues that during this phase, many writers employed "darkness-light imagery and references to the lighting of the city to articulate their views of London" (15), and identifies typical approaches taken in realist-naturalist novels, imperial and urban fantasies, and city poems of the 1890s. The chapter focuses on the latter, but Goetsch takes care to develop connections between the poetry and contemporary prose fiction, reconstructing the general mood of the decade by highlighting parallels and differences in themes and approaches. Many writers of the 1880s and 1890s tend to associate London with fog, smog, the night, and darkness, suggesting the city to be a dangerous place. They seem, to a certain degree, to ignore the changes in public lighting and the brightening of the city at night in the course of the decade. Paul Goetsch shows that some poets respond quite well to these changes and embrace artificial light, especially in the well-lit entertainment sections of London, interpreting "the partial illumination of London as a chance of pursuing pleasure, turning night, as it were, into day, and escaping temporarily from Victorian respectability" (31).

In the following chapter, "'The Hours of the Day and the Night Are Ours Equally': *Dracula* and the Lighting Technologies of Victorian London", Maria Peker examines Bram Stoker's seminal novel and thus another text that stems from the final decade of the 19th century. Similarly to Goetsch, albeit from a different angle, Peker argues that this was the decade during which London nights became gradually disassociated from their traditional connotations of danger and terror. Paradoxically, the period also witnessed the revival of a genre that was obsessively preoccupied with the night, darkness, and the horrors hidden within it: the Gothic. Peker suggests that it is not merely a coincidence that many of the novels which today are considered amongst the greatest examples of the Victorian Gothic were written during the time of transition from gas to electric lighting, but intimately connected with the technological changes that altered the perception of urban space at night. Gaslight "becomes part of the Gothic code and, in the economy of the city, it ceases to represent an unambiguously progressive element, which used to create the impression of modernity and feeling of security just a couple of decades before" (39). In Stoker's novel not only Dracula but also his antagonists, the Crew of Light, use both obsolete and modern means of lighting, which questions simple interpretations of the novel as a struggle between a supposedly enlightened modernity and an archaic and superstitious past.

In "'Light of Life': Gender, Place, and Knowledge in H. G. Wells' *Ann Veronica*", Jarmila Mildorf examines one of Wells' works which today might be less well known than his science romances, but which caused a scandal upon its publication: set in a time when walking alone during the night was still unacceptable and morally marked off as deviant behaviour for a woman, the novel shows the eponymous character as she explores the city of London after having run away from her secluded suburban home. Drawing on the novel's portrayal of London as 'splendid' during the day and 'threatening' and 'sinister' during the night, Mildorf explores the role of light and darkness in creating London as atmospheric setting, scene of action, and visual field in the novel, arguing that the usage of light and darkness in "Wells' presentation of London illustrates the gendered experience of cityscapes [...], especially in a Victorian moral climate" (68). However, and less conventionally, the quality of the light also reflects Ann Veronica's mood, "and her perception of places changes with the changed time of day, for example" (ibid.), adding an innovative element to the novel's treatment of light and darkness; ultimately, "it is the experience of London in twilight that brings to Ann Veronica's awareness her own gendered position and the immoral side and danger of the previously idealised cityscape" (69).

Richard Leahy, in "The Literary Realisation of Electric Light in the Early 20th Century: Artificial Illumination in H. G. Wells and E. M. Forster" examines Wells from a different perspective: his chapter draws attention to artificial light in literature against the background of an emerging capitalist mass society and the rapidly changing perceptions of electric light around the turn of the century. Before the new lighting technology became firmly established, Leahy argues, authors like Wells and Forster employed it as a symbol that connoted authoritarian or even totalitarian structures. However, when the public became more familiar with the new technology and the possibilities it offered, sentiments shifted, and so did its representation in literature: the "increasing adoption of electric light in the cities and towns of this period, and the improvement in its technology and delivery, humanised its literary presence in the early years of the 20th century. [...] It [now] helped with individual characterisation rather than creating a sense of mass alienation" (87).

Questions revolving around the individual and a sense of alienation also inform Laura E. Ludtke's contribution, "Public and Private Light in Virginia Woolf's *Night and Day*". Light as a symbol and metaphor is central to the text, and its usage is a highly complex and multi-faceted one. The increasing levels of illumination at the time when Woolf began writing the novel brought about a re-conceptualisation of private and public space, and associated phenomena and themes like the 'chance encounter' or 'surveillance' inform *Night and Day*. Adapting Baudelaire's notion of the *flâneur*, Ludtke's reading considers the female experience of urban space in the novel from the perspective of the *flâneuse* and establishes a parallel between the shifting boundaries of public and private and the shifting relationship of night and day brought about by artificial illumination: "At night, the characters become more self-aware and self-reflective [...] and come to realise that the complexities revealed by these artificial lights correspond more accurately to the reality to which they ascribe than to what is seen in the 'cold light of day'" (95).

With "Serenading the Night in Benjamin Britten's Opus 31", Robert Gillett and Isabel Wagner add a musicological dimension to the collection. In 1943, Benjamin Britten set to music six texts, the anonymous "A lyke-wake dirge", and poems by Charles Cotton, Alfred Lord Tennyson, William Blake, Ben Jonson, and John Keats. The original collective title for these settings was 'nocturnes' – a designation for musical 'night pieces' – but later changed to "Serenade for Tenor Horn and Strings". Gillett and Wagner trace the ways in which Britten's serenade can be read as a kind of essence or compendium of the night. The selection of texts that inform the serenade thus touches on many of the themes associated with the night: light, darkness, and shadow; sleep, dream, and nightmare; death, damnation, and redemption; rest and peace; moonlight and the uncanny; sex and sexuality, especially dangerous and dissident sexuality; love and tenderness, albeit attenuated and indirect; and suspended, projected, and hypothetical violence. In short, it "exemplifies the anguish of night in a terrifying shamanic journey; and it synaesthetically conveys different intensities of light through vivid musical effects" (126).

Lars Heiler's chapter, "Darkness Visible: Night, Light, and Liminality in Arthur Conan Doyle's *The Hound of the Baskervilles* and Jed Rubenfeld's *The Death Instinct*", straddles a span of over a century and provides a bridge between the two historical foci of the collection, i. e. the period around the turn of the 19th and the 20th century, respectively. Heiler discusses two texts which at first glance have only little in common: Doyle's classic detective story and Rubenfeld's postmodern historical thriller. Nevertheless, there are striking resemblances between the two works. Both explore the well-rehearsed topos of human duality which they locate in spatial divisions, but also in realms of light and darkness. In addition, both associate light with order and darkness with chaos, and link this opposition to the work of the detective, whose performance can be measured by how well he negotiates this division. What is more, the historical and cultural differences between the production contexts of both novels allow Heiler to explore "how the representation of lighting and darkness in Doyle's and Rubenfeld's texts produces forms of liminality and potentiality, which are reflected in a number of spatial, psychological, cultural, scientific, and technological transitions; how, in other words, the dialectics of the Enlightenment is underpinned by the dialectics of illumination" (129).

In "The Blackout of Community: Charlotte Jones' *The Dark*", Stella Butter considers light and darkness in terms of their symbolic and metaphorical content as well as in terms of the effect they can have on the stage. Her analysis of the play also draws attention to the profound impact the presence or absence of readily available illumination has on a community: the direct and immediate effect of a power cut on the social interaction of those who are affected by it. Drawing on the works of sociologist Zygmunt Bauman and philosopher Peter Sloterdijk, Butter describes Jones' play as an exploration of community in contemporary Britain in which the metaphoric qualities of light and darkness are connected with lighting levels of the stage and the psychological landscapes of the characters, but also with the audience itself: "*The Dark* is notable for the full use it makes of theatrical lighting so that the audience members can themselves experience how lighting contributes to creating a specific (atmo)sphere within the playhouse" (161). Butter's analysis thus demonstrates in exemplary fashion the various analytical levels on which artificial light in a play can be assessed, and eloquently argues for the consideration of light as an actant in its own right.

Murat Sezi's chapter, "Genre, Gender, Mythology: Functions of Light and Darkness in Terry Pratchett's *Feet of Clay* and *Thud!*", discusses two of Pratchett's popular Discworld novels, which parody and subvert not only aspects of the fantasy genre, but also of other genres integrated into them; in the case of the two novels at hand, those are the detective story and the police procedural. Sezi points out that the night and darkness are of considerable significance in all three genres, and that their combination almost necessitates the night as a mood-invested space and sphere of action in the novels. They continue the artistic, literary, and philosophical tradition associated with light and darkness, Sezi argues, but also infuse them with new meanings. Thus, light and darkness are not only a part of the fictional mythologies presented in the novels but also "a strategy repeatedly used in the novels [...] in order to defamiliarise, in the most literal sense taking that which is familiar and presenting it to the reader in a novel and creative way" (180).

Susanne Bach, in her chapter "Twenty Thousand Lights Hanging From the Ceiling: Ecocatastrophe in Karen Thompson Walker's *The Age of Miracles*", discusses a text written in fantasy's sister mode, i.e. science fiction. Walker's dystopian coming of age novel describes a world in which, due to the Earth's rotational deceleration, the length of days and nights is steadily increasing. This alteration affects all forms of life, from micro-organisms to human beings. Some species are doomed to die, other, more adaptable species thrive; but life on Earth is fundamentally altered. Days eventually last up to six weeks and due to radiation intensity the sun quickly harms and kills. Society splits up into those who live by the now arbitrary 24-hour clock and others who live by the new days' length. Bach describes Walker's novel as a speculative inquiry and as a fictitious litmus test, probing into the psychological effects natural and artificial light have upon the human mind and body, as well as into the sociological, medical, cognitive, linguistic, and economic consequences of an extreme and up to now unheard of form of 'light pollution'.

The notion of light constituting a form of pollution is also under scrutiny in Folkert Degenring's chapter. In "On Behalf of the Dark? Functionalisations of Light Pollution in Fiction", he traces the historical development of the concept of light pollution and examines various definitions that look at the phenomenon from astronomical, ecological, cultural, medical, and legal perspectives. Approaching the topic from a qualitative as well as a quantitative angle and employing both close and distant reading methodologies, the chapter looks at a sample of literary texts explicitly referring to the concept, prominent examples being Mark Haddon's *The Curious Incident of the Dog in the Night-Time* (2003), Ali Smith's *The Accidental* (2005), or Monica Ali's *Alentejo Blue* (2006).

The chapters thus follow not only a roughly chronological order but also a thematic one. They trace the ambivalent and sometimes contradictory attitudes towards light and illumination that manifest themselves in literary texts and show the extraordinary variety and flexibility of the ways in which (artificial) light is invested with meaning in literature; and they do so with a broad range of methodological and analytical perspectives. In uniting the essays collected here, the volume aims to contribute to the understanding of just how profound the impact of light is on our lives, and to continue the investigation of an aspect of literature that not only enjoys a venerable tradition but that is constantly being renewed, remade, and transformed in artistic expression.

Works Cited

Bach, Susanne and Folkert Degenring. 2015. "From Shakespearean Nights to Light Pollution: (Artificial) Light in Anglophone Literature". In: Josiane Meier, Ute Hasenöhrl, Katharina Krause, and Merle Pottharst (eds.). *Urban Lighting, Light Pollution and Society.* New York, NY: Routledge. 46–65.

Bailey, Kenneth Vye. 1992. "Bright Day – Dreadful Night: Metaphoric Polarities in Fantasy and Science Fiction". *Foundation* 54.1: 36–51.

Binder, Beate. 2015. "Introduction". In: Josiane Meier, Ute Hasenöhrl, Katharina Krause, and Merle Pottharst (eds.). *Urban Lighting, Light Pollution and Society.* New York, NY: Routledge. 9–12.

Brevda, William. 2011. *Signs of the Signs: The Literary Lights of Incandescence and Neon.* Lewisburg, PA: Bucknell University Press.

Bronfen, Elisabeth. 2013. *Night Passages: Philosophy, Literature, and Film.* New York, NY: Columbia University Press.

Brox, Jane. 2015. "Out of the Dark: A Brief History of Artificial Light in Outdoor Spaces". In: Josiane Meier, Ute Hasenöhrl, Katharina Krause, and Merle Pottharst (eds.). *Urban Lighting, Light Pollution and Society.* New York, NY: Routledge. 13–29.

Dessen, Alan C. 1978. "Night and Darkness on the Elizabethan Stage: Yesterday's Conventions and Today's Distortions". In: G. W. Williams (ed.). *Renaissance Papers.* Columbia, SC: Camden House. 23–30

Dryden, Linda. 2006. "City of Dreadful Night: Stevenson's Gothic London". In: Richard Ambrosini and Richard Dury (eds.). *Robert Louis Stevenson: Writer of Boundaries.* Madison, WI: University of Wisconsin Press. 253–264.

Edensor, Tim. 2015. "The Rich Potentialities of Light Festivals. Defamiliarisation, a Sense of Place and Convivial Atmospheres". In: Josiane Meier, Ute Hasenöhrl, Katharina Krause, and Merle Pottharst (eds.). *Urban Lighting, Light Pollution and Society.* New York, NY: Routledge. 85–98.

Ginthner, Delores. 2004. "Lighting: Its Effect on People and Spaces". *Implications* 2.2. <http://www.informedesign.org/_news/feb_v02-p.pdf> [accessed 10 May 2015].

Graves, Robert B. 1999. *Lighting the Shakespearean Stage, 1567–1642.* Carbondale, IL: Southern Illinois University Press.

Holmberg, Arthur. 2005. *The Theatre of Robert Wilson.* Cambridge: Cambridge University Press.

IDA. International Dark Sky Association. 2014. "About IDA". <http://www.darksky.org/about-us> [accessed 26 April 2015].

Verlust der Nacht. Interdisziplinärer Forschungsverband Lichtverschmutzung. 2013. "About us". <http://www.verlustdernacht.de/about-us.html> [accessed 26 April 2015].

Keogh, J. G. 1984. "The Crowd as No Man's Land: Gas-light and Poe's Symbolist Effects". *The Antigonish Review* 58: 19–31.

Lakoff, George and Mark Johnson. 1980. *Metaphors We Live By* Chicago: University of Chicago Press.

Longcore, Travis and Catherine Rich. 2004. "Ecological Light Pollution". *Frontiers in Ecology and the Environment* 2.4: 191–198.

Magennis, Hugh. 2007. "Imagery of Light in Old English Poetry: Traditions and Apparitions". *Anglia* 125.2: 181–204.

Meier, Josiane, Ute Hasenöhrl, Katharina Krause, and Merle Pottharst (eds.). *Urban Lighting, Light Pollution and Society*. New York, NY: Routledge.

Melbin, Murray. 1987. *Night as Frontier: Colonizing the World after Dark*. New York, NY: The Free Press.

Mizon, Bob. 2012. *Light Pollution: Responses and Remedies*. New York, NY: Springer.

Morgan-Taylor, Martin. 2015. "Regulating Light Pollution in Europe. Legal Challenges and Ways Forward". In: Josiane Meier, Ute Hasenöhrl, Katharina Krause, and Merle Pottharst (eds.). *Urban Lighting, Light Pollution and Society*. New York, NY: Routledge. 159 – 176.

Nye, David E. 2015. "The Transformation of American Urban Space. Early Electric Lighting, 1875 – 1915". In: Josiane Meier, Ute Hasenöhrl, Katharina Krause, and Merle Pottharst (eds.). *Urban Lighting, Light Pollution and Society*. New York, NY: Routledge. 30 – 45.

Schivelbusch, Wolfgang. 1995. *Disenchanted Night: The Industrialization of Light in the Nineteenth Century*. Berkeley, CA: University of California Press.

Stevenson, Robert Louis. 1881. "A Plea for Gas Lamps". *Viginibus Puerisque and Other Papers*. London: C. Kegan Paul & Co. 288 – 296.

The Bible. Authorized King James Version with Apocrypha. 2008. Eds. Robert Carroll and Stephen Pickett. Oxford: Oxford University Press.

Ward, John Powell. 2003. "Darkness and Light: Poetry, Religion and the Environment". *Scintilla* 7: 73 – 86.

Wilde, Oscar. 1979. "Impression du Matin" (1881). In: Meyer Howard Abrams (eds). *The Norton Anthology of English Literature*, Vol. II. 4th ed. New York, NY: W. W. Norton. 1678.

Paul Goetsch
City Nights, City Lights in London Literature of the 1890s

In 1901, Greater London had 6.5 million inhabitants. It was the largest city in the world, the seat of the British government, and, in Masterman's phrase, the heart of the Empire.[1] Though it had hardly begun to rival Paris as a centre of culture and popular entertainment (Eisenberg 2003), some contemporary observers esteemed it as a powerful symbol of modernity – "the apotheosis of modern life" (Ford 1995: 111). Other late-Victorian writers, however, responded ambivalently to the city. As Joseph McLaughlin argues, they revived an ancient literary trope according to which "the city is, and has always been, a place of darkness and light, sin and salvation, barbarism and culture" (McLauglin 2000: 1; cf. Williams 1973: 215–232). Julian Wolfreys goes a step further and maintains: "never before the end of the nineteenth century had a single sight or topography so effectively served as the focal point for an exploration and expression of cultural anxiety, as had London" (2004: 54). This anxiety had one of its origins in the rapid growth of the city and the fact that London continued to act as a magnet for people from the rural areas and immigrants from the colonies and other countries. Another cause of anxiety was modernisation, that is, the separation of the city's functions, the division between home and workplace, the segregation of the lower and upper classes, and the concomitant loss of a larger sense of community (cf. Lesser 1987). Other fears centred on the Empire, international competition, and colonial wars.

In the following study I discuss how writers of the 1890s used darkness-light imagery and references to the lighting of the city to articulate their views of London. Leaving aside those utopias that envision the destruction of modern London and a return to rural England (cf. Warwick 1999), I distinguish between typical approaches taken in realist-naturalist novels, imperial and urban fantasies, and city poems of the 1890s. My main focus is on the poetry.

---

1 Cf. Masterman (1973). For a comprehensive overview see also Ackroyd (2000); Baron (1997); Beckson (1992); Dyos and Wolff (1973); and Schneer (1999).

The Realist-Naturalist Approach

In 1888, Henry James wrote of London, "When a social product is so vast and various it may be approached on a thousand different sides and liked and disliked for a thousand different reasons" (James 1981: 8). He added, "One has not the alternative of speaking of London as a whole, for the simple reason that there is no such thing as the whole of it. [...] Rather it is a collection of many wholes, and of which of them is it most important to speak?" (18). James tries to solve this problem in *The Princess Casamassima* (1886) by contrasting different sections of the city with one another, thus revealing its social and cultural diversity and marking important stages in the protagonist's development. A similar approach is taken by earlier Victorian novels, for instance by Dickens' *Bleak House* (1852) and Walter Besant's *All Sorts and Conditions of Men* (1882), which propagates the education of the poor and appeals to the sense of responsibility of the middle and upper classes.

In the 1890s, writers more frequently dealt with one of the problem areas which the expansion of London had created. Typical locations were the East End (cf. Newland 2008), one of its slums or working-class quarters, and Southern London. Assuming that most of their readers were not familiar with these problem areas, the realists and naturalists focused on the living conditions of the workers, the poor, and the immigrants, analysed the causes and consequences of poverty, and worried about social and political unrest and degeneration. Their fear of crime was intensified by the Whitechapel murders of Jack the Ripper (1888).[2] Like some contemporary social studies, the realists made use of "the almost obligatory analogy between the urban poor and the 'uncivilized' peoples of truly foreign lands" (Nord 1987: 122) and acted as if they were explorers of a foreign region. In order to define their response to the problem area, they often resorted to metaphorical descriptions of the strange and sometimes uncanny environment and its atmosphere. In *A Child of the Jago* (1896), Arthur Morrison renders a night in one of the slums as follows:

> It was past the mid of a summer night in the Old Jago. The narrow street was all the blacker for the lurid sky; for there was a fire in a farther part of Shoreditch, and the welkin was an infernal coppery glare. Below, the hot, heavy air lay a rank oppression on the contorted forms of those who made for sleep on the pavement: and in it, and through it all, there rose from the foul earth and the grimed walls a close, mingled stink – the odour of the Jago. (Morrison 1969: 45)

---

2 For an overview cf. Walkowitz (1992).

Morrison alludes to hell, disease, and the suffering of the homeless sleepers on the pavement and thus prepares the reader for his conclusion that the Jago has been "for one hundred years the blackest pit in London" (ibid.).[3] In keeping with the oppressive midnight atmosphere, there are no street lamps to light up the darkness and relieve the gloom; the only source of light is a fire elsewhere causing a lurid, infernal glare in the sky.

Another popular technique was to give an account of what a sensitive outsider might observe on his or her walks or cab rides through London and the slums. In *The Sign of Four* (1890) Sherlock Holmes, Watson, and a female client take a cab in pursuit of Sholto. While Holmes, whose knowledge of the byways of London is "extraordinary" (Doyle 1986: 672), concentrates on their route, Watson worries about going to "an unknown place, on an unknown errand" (121) and responds to the environment imaginatively and emotionally:

> It was a September evening and not yet seven o'clock, but the day had been a dreary one, and a dense drizzly fog lay low upon the great city. Mud-coloured clouds drooped sadly over the muddy streets. Down the Strand the lamps were but misty splotches of diffused light which threw a feeble circular glimmer upon the slimy pavement. The yellow glare from the shop-windows streamed out into the steamy, vaporous air and threw a murky, shifting radiance across the crowded thoroughfare. There was, to my mind, something eerie and ghostlike in the endless procession of faces which flitted across these narrow bars of light – sad faces and glad, haggard and merry. Like all humankind they flitted from the gloom into the light and so back into the gloom once more. I am not subject to impressions, but the dull, heavy evening, with the strange business, upon which we were engaged, combined to make me nervous and depressed. (Doyle 1986: 120–121)

Later, when they reach Sholto's dark place in South London, Holmes calls the environment slightly unfashionable, stays calm and remains in command of the situation even when a native from India opens the door to them. Watson (who here represents the reader) is surprised and puzzled and compares "the questionable and forbidding neighborhood" to the "monster tentacles which the giant city was throwing out into the country" (122).

As the passages from Morrison and Doyle suggest,[4] the realists and naturalists draw upon the traditional antagonism between darkness and light. In order to create an atmosphere that expresses their view of London, they foreground the interactions between the time of day, the weather, especially the fog, the street lamps, and other sources of light. Often, the lamps in the bystreets of the resi-

---

3 Cf. Kirsten Hertel's study, *London zwischen Naturalismus und Moderne: Literarische Perspektiven einer Metropole* (1997): 180–181.
4 Wolfreys (2004) analyses a number of similar passages in novels by Collins, Gissing, Stevenson, and Wilde.

dential areas and in the slums struggle against the darkness and are too feeble to illuminate the streets sufficiently and rather produce strange, sometimes Gothic effects. Time and again in realist novels of the period, darkness seems to triumph over light in the problem areas of London and turn them into an underworld, as the titles of George Gissing's *The Nether World* (1889) and Jack London's *People of the Abyss* (1902) suggest.

In 1845 Disraeli criticised the division of British society into two nations, the rich and the poor. In 1891 Margaret Harkness, a writer of slum fiction, amended Disraeli by distinguishing between "two nations, *East* and *West*" (qtd. in Nord 1987: 123). With the West she associated "all that was bright, open, dazzling, and enlightened," with the East "all that was dark, labyrinthine, threatening, and benighted" (ibid.).

This distinction makes sense if one keeps in mind that not all slum novels are located in the East End. The distinction is nevertheless questionable, because there are some works that regard the city itself, and not just a particular problem area, as one of the dark places of the world.

Imperial and Urban Fantasies

In his book *In Darkest England and the Way Out* (1890), William Booth, the founder of the Salvation Army, mentions *In Darkest Africa* (1890), Henry Morton Stanley's account of his adventures in Central Africa, and asks his readers, "As there is a darkest Africa, is there not also a darkest England?" (qtd. in Keating 1976: 14). Joseph Conrad, for one, gives an affirmative answer. In *Heart of Darkness* (1899), Marlow compares the colonial exploitation of the Congo to the Roman conquest of Britain and uses light and darkness imagery to characterise London and the Thames:

> The sun set; the dusk fell on the stream, and lights began to appear along the shore. The Chapman lighthouse, a three-legged thing erect on a mud-flat, shone strongly. Lights of ships moved in the fairway – a great stir of lights going up and going down. And farther west on the upper reaches the place of the monstrous town was still marked ominously on the sky, a brooding gloom in sunshine, a lurid glare under the stars.
> "And this also," said Marlow suddenly, "has been one of the dark places of the earth." (Conrad 1960: 47–48)

While a number of writers wrote optimistic romances about imperialist adventures, others worried about the Empire, which in the last quarter of the nineteenth century had expanded rapidly and by 1900 was comprised of "13,000,000 square miles of subject territory, inhabited by nearly 320,000,000 persons" (Ford 1958:

20). The sheer size of the Empire, international competition, the conflict with Egypt, the South African War, and other events triggered fears of the decline and fall of the Empire, as did theories of evolution and degeneration. In this context, London served as a metonym for the Empire, the relationship between the West and the East, between civilisation and the jungle.

In several crime stories, for instance, the villains are either Englishmen returning from one of the colonies or immigrants who illustrate Conan Doyle's belief that London was "that great cesspool into which all the loungers and idlers of the Empire are irresistibly drained" (Doyle 1986: 4). Other stories deal with the theme of invasion and reverse colonialism, for instance Bram Stoker's *Dracula* (1897), Richard Marsh's *The Beetle* (1897), and H. G. Wells' *The War of the Worlds* (1898). While Wells' Martians are powerful enough to attack London in the daytime and put its inhabitants to flight, the main actions of the imperial fantasies by Stoker and Marsh take place at night. Both Dracula and the Beetle, the Transylvanian and the Egyptian monster, use the cover of night to pursue their plans of conquest and control. Dracula says of himself, "I seek not gaiety nor mirth, not the bright voluptuousness of much sunshine and sparkling waters which please the young and gay" (Stoker 1965: 33). He adds that he loves the shade and the shadow. Actually, Dracula, like the wolves near his castle, is a child of the night. It is in the night that he is active and looking out for prey. In the daytime he usually sleeps in a box or a coffin, which is why an important part of his invasion plan involves the placing of coffins in the suburbs surrounding London. Harker, who spends several nights talking to Dracula, feels exhausted by this "nocturnal existence" and wonders "whether any dream could be more horrible than the unnatural, horrible net of gloom and mystery which seemed closing around" (42) him. When he realises that he has unwittingly helped Dracula to prepare the invasion of England, he is deeply shocked and overcome by the desire to rid the world of the monster. He and representatives of several western nations at last succeed in killing Dracula (cf. Goetsch 2002).

According to Wolfreys, London was "the locus and agent, as well as provisional identity for monstrous otherness" (2007: 9). This is borne out not only by imperial fantasies but also by more strictly urban fantasies. A case in point is Robert Louis Stevenson's *Strange Case of Dr Jekyll and Mr Hyde* (1886). In this Darwinian story of the duality of man (cf. Goetsch 2005), Hyde represents the instinctual life which Jekyll has repressed for a long time. Those who see him are struck by his deformity and compare him to animals, especially to apes. His aggressive behaviour, when threatened, surprises even Jekyll.

For Peter Ackroyd, Stevenson's work is perhaps "the greatest novel of London fog," because its "fable of changing identities and secret takes place within the medium of the city's 'shifting insubstantial mists'" (Ackroyd 2000: 438). For example, an early-morning cab ride taken by Utterson, Jekyll's friend, is described as follows:

> Mr. Utterson beheld a marvellous number of degrees and hues of twilight; for here it would be dark like the back-end of evening; and there would be a glow of a rich, lurid brown, like the light of some strange conflagration; and here, for a moment, the fog would be quite broken up, and a haggard shaft of daylight would glance in between the swirling wreaths. The dismal quarter of Soho seen under these changing glimpses, with its muddy ways, and slatternly passengers, and its lamps, which had never been extinguished or had been kindled afresh to combat this mournful reinvasion of darkness, seemed, in the lawyer's eyes, like a district of some city in a nightmare. (Stevenson 1962: 20)

In *Dr Jekyll and Mr Hyde* the times of day and night appear to be as little stable as Jekyll-Hyde's identity and the London weather. Like the realist novels, the imperial and urban fantasies stress the power of darkness.

The Poets of the 1890s and the City

As Stange and others have shown (Stange 1968; Thesing 1972; Forsyth 1976), many early- and mid-Victorian poets were frightened of the rapid growth of London and eschewed writing about it. Others criticised urban conditions (cf. Lessenich 2013). In "Locksley Hall Sixty Years After" (1886), Tennyson complained about the exploitation of the workers and about urban crime and asserted that the city's "gleaming alleys" prevented further "Progress" (qtd. in Lessenich 2013: 718). In "City of Dreadful Night" (1880), James Thomson saw London as a dark apocalyptic world:

> Although lamps burn along the silent streets,
> Even when moonlight silvers empty squares
> The dark holds countless lanes and close retreats;
> But when the night its sphereless mantle wears
> The open spaces yawn with gloom abysmal,
> The somber mansions loom immense and dismal,
> The lanes are black as subterranean lairs. (qtd. in Lessenich 2013: 721)

In the course of the 1880s and 1890s urban poetry changed in several respects.[5] Writers like W. E. Henley and John Davidson discovered London types – workers, clerks, sandwich men, nurses and other ordinary people – for poetry and paid

---

5 For balanced accounts of the different directions taken by contemporary poetry, cf. Nünning (2002); Pfister (1983); and Thesing (1972).

attention to some of those features of city life – working conditions, class problems – which contemporary realists dealt with. Rudyard Kipling and other poets wrote patriotic poems about the Empire and some of its lower-class supporters. Other poets played down the power of darkness and the Gothic, phantasmagoric potential which the contemporary fantasists had tapped into, and instead regarded the city as stupendous, stimulating, and enjoyable. It is this group with its anti-Victorian and avant-garde bias which I am interested in.

Lionel Johnson argues in "London Town" (1891) that he prefers the city over the country and attributes a music of its own to the "tumult of the street" (Johnson 1982: 117). His paean to London climaxes in the lines:

> Here is a marvellous world of men;
> More wonderful than *Rome* was, when
> The world was *Rome*.
> See the great stream of life flow by!
> Here thronging myriads laugh and sigh,
> Here rise and fall, here live and die:
> In this vast home. (Johnson 1982: 117)

Similarly, Arthur Symons[6] asserts that immersing oneself in city life means forgetting the burden of individuality, at least temporarily. In the "Prologue" to *Days and Nights* (1887), Symons advises art-seekers to go "where cities pour / Their turbid human stream through street and mart [...]." He claims that "Art" stands "amidst the tumult" and is both calm and ruthless; it does not think of solutions to human suffering, but regards all the phenomena of city life as proper subjects of poetry (S 1: 3–4). In his 1892 review of Henley's *London Voluntaries*, he declares that "the test of poetry which professes to be modern" is "its capacity for dealing with London, with what one sees or might see there, indoors and out" (qtd. in Thesing 1972: 308).

The stance that Symons and other poets take here has been explained in terms of the influence of French writing, in particular that of Charles Baudelaire and Paul Verlaine (Clements 1985). Other explanations point to the aesthetic, decadent, and symbolist movements and to impressionism.[7] In what follows I will largely neglect such influences and instead discuss how the 1890s poems compare with contemporary prose fiction when dealing with darkness and light and related themes.

---

6 Quotations in the text preceded by S refer to Arthur Symons' *The Collected Works* [1924] (1973).

7 For an overview cf. Bristow (2005), as well as Munro (1970), Thornton (1983), Hönnighausen (1988), and Vadillo (2005).

London Lights

One poem that passes Symons' test of modern art is Richard Le Gallienne's
"A Ballad of London" (1895). The poet blends a fin-de-siècle sense of the transi-
toriness of things with a 'nineties hedonism and affirmation of life. At the beginning of the poem (A: 59 – 60)[8] he celebrates London as a place where one can
forget the night, because, paradoxically, the sun seems to shine at midnight:

> Ah, London! London! Our delight,
> Great flower that opens but at night,
> Great City of the Midnight Sun,
> Whose day begins when day is done.
>
> Lamp after lamp against the sky
> Opens a sudden beaming eye,
> Leaping alight on either hand,
> The iron lilies of the Strand.

The illusion that the day begins again at nightfall is produced by many *ersatz-
suns* – the lamps after lamps which are turned on and beam at the sky, the
rows of lamps on both sides of the Strand, the lanterns of the hansoms.

> Like dragonflies, the hansoms hover,
> With jeweled eyes, to catch the lover;
> The streets are full of lights and loves,
> Soft gowns, and flutter of soiled doves.
>
> The human moths about the light
> Dash and cling close in dazed delight,
> And burn and laugh, the world and wife,
> For this is London, this is life!

In the second part of the poem the poet, like the realists discussed above, shows
himself to be aware of the fact that at the root of London one can find suffering,
injustice, and corruption.

> Upon thy petals butterflies,
> But at thy root, some say, there lies
> A world of weeping trodden things,
> Poor worms that have not eyes or wings.

---

8 Quotations in the text preceded by 'A' refer to Robert K. R. Thornton (ed.), *Poetry of the 'Nineties'* (1970).

From out corruption of their woe
Springs this bright flower that charms us so,
Men die and rot deep out of sight
To keep this jungle-flower bright.

The poet also broaches the idea of the decline and fall of empires and suggests that Paris and London, the present flowers on the 'world-tree', may ultimately suffer the fate of such predecessors as Babylon, Sidon, Tyre, and Rome.

Paris and London, World-Flowers twain
Wherewith the World-Tree blooms again,
Since Time hath gathered Babylon,
And withered Rome still withers on.

Sidon and Tyre were such as ye,
How bright they shone upon the Tree!
But Time hath gathered, both are gone,
And no man sails to Babylon.

Not only Paris and London are doomed but also the delight London has given human beings.

Ah, London! London! Our delight,
For thee, too, the eternal night,
And Circe Paris hath no charm
To stay Time's unrelenting arm.

Time and his moths shall eat up all.
Your chiming towers proud and tall
He shall most utterly abase,
And set a desert in their place. (A: 59–60)

The imagery of the poem clarifies Le Gallienne's vision of London further. Like the city itself, London's lights are compared to the sun and the stars, to beaming eyes, and jewels of various kinds. They are beautiful and powerful enough to turn the night into an artificial day and London into a great flower opening at night.

What the poem celebrates is first of all the illumination of London at night, a theme taken up by other writers as well. Arthur Symons' poem "In the Temple" focuses on the conflict between darkness and light and stresses the stimulating effect of the "racing lights" which remind him of "festive nights" (S 1: 153). In the companion poem "In the Train" (1896), Symons' speaker observes that the darkness is broken by the lights from the streets and the buildings. This suffices to energise him and so enjoy the dazzling impression London makes at night:

> Night and the rush of the train,
>> A cloud of smoke through the town,
>>> Scaring the life of the streets;
> And the leap of the heart again,
>> Out into the night, and down
>>> The dazzling vista of streets! (S 1: 153)

According to Alice Meynell's "November Blue," the illumination of London by electric light makes a difference. In the first stanza she describes a dull November day which leaves the town "unheavened" because the blue sky is nowhere to be seen. In the second stanza she notes the effect of the electric lighting:

> But when the gold and silver lamps
>> Colour the London dew,
> And, misted by the winter damps,
>> The shops shine bright anew –
> Blue comes to earth, it walks the street,
>> It dyes the wide air through:
> A mimic sky about their feet,
>> The throng go crowned with blue. (qtd. In Vadillo 2005: 102–103)

As Meynell says in the epigraph of her poem, "The colour of the electric lights has a strange effect in giving a complementary tint to the air in the early evening" .This interest in colours and subjective impressions aligns Meynell with the Impressionists. Since 'blue' symbolises heaven, Meynell suggests "that London is at its most beautiful when divine (natural) light and human (artificial) lighting are united" (Vadillo 2005: 103).

The role of the visual is as important in Meynell's poem as it is in Graham Tomson's "London in October". Tomson (aka Rosamund Marriott Watson) trusts that the "glamour of the London street" will make her forget her doubts and sorrows and enjoy the "sensuous sheer delight / In the blue, lamp-hung night". She therefore closes her poem by dedicating herself to London:

> Thine are our hearts, beloved City of Mist
> Wrapped in thy veils of opal and amethyst,
> Set in thy shrine of lapis-lazuli,
> Dowered with the very language of the sea,
> Lit with a million gems of living fire –
> London, the goal of many a soul's desire!
> Goddess and sphinx, thou hold'st us safe in thrall
> Here while the dead leaves fall. (qtd. in Vadillo 2005: 152)

In real life, the illumination of London may have been more limited and selective than Tomson, Meynell, Le Gallienne, Symons, and other poets would have us believe. After all, gaslight still dominated in the 1890s and only slowly gave way to electric light, as the following data indicate:

1807   Pall Mall Street illuminated with gas
1817   Gaslights in London's Covent Garden theatre
1823   Gaslights in 52 British towns
1878   Electric light first employed on the Embankment, London
1883   First power station opened at Holborn Viaduct
1887   Five London theatres use electric light
1890   The Deptford power station built to supply London with electricity
1892   Electric advertising in Piccadilly Circus
1898   Electrification of the London Underground begins
1914   70 power stations operating within the metropolis.[9]

It may, however, be argued that the centres of entertainment preceded other parts of London in the degree of illumination. If so, Le Gallienne and Symons, if not Meynell and Tomson, chiefly praise the night life made possible, at least partly, by the lights of the city.

The variety of entertainments available in a modern metropolis includes the promise of sexual gratification. Le Gallienne's "A Ballad to London" alludes to this by rhyming "night" and "delight," by linking lights and loves, and by characterising human beings as moths, which, in dazed delight, seek the flames. Similarly, James Gould Fletcher eroticises the city lights by associating them with the "laughter from red lips" (Fletcher 1988: 125).

A more outspoken poem on sexuality is Alfred Douglas' "Impression de Nuit. London" (1899). In order to express the erotic allure of London night life, Douglas draws upon the same kinds of images as Le Gallienne and personifies London as a woman or rather a giantess who represents all the lights of the city and whose appearance resembles that of the Great Whore of Babylon of whom the Bible says, "the woman was arrayed in purple and scarlet colour, and decked with gold and precious jewels and pearls" (Rev. 17:4):

> See what a mass of gems the city wears
> Upon her broad live bosom! Row on row
> Rubies and emeralds and amethysts glow.
> See that huge circle like a necklace, stares
> With thousands of bold eyes to heaven, and dares
> The golden stars to dim the lamps below,

---

9 These data are based on Baron (1997), Ackroyd (2000), Rebske (1962), and Schivelbusch (1983).

And in the mirror of the mire I know
The moon has left her image unawares

That's the great town at night: I see her breasts,
Pricked out with lamps they stand like huge black towers,
I think they move! I hear her panting breath.
And that's her head where the tiara rests.
And in her brain, through lanes as dark as death,
Men creep like thoughts. ... The lamps are like pale flowers. (A: 61)

As the ending emphasises, London is a powerful seductress who reduces men to thoughts in her brain and makes them dependent on what she has to offer.

A Night on the Town

A number of poems deal with night life and its pleasures, and a frequently chosen topic is sex in the city. The favourite locations are the theatres and the music halls, and the favourite character types include actresses, singers, dancers, and prostitutes as well as men-about-town seeking sexual contact.

Arthur Symons, the self-appointed "spokesman of Decadence" (Thornton 1983: 134) whose *London Nights* (1895) violated the standards of Victorian respectability, once compared his life with a music hall (S 1: 179). In several of his poems he admires and desires music hall entertainers, attends their performances, and waits for them at the stage door. In one poem he shows himself to be convinced that the actress' eyes "gleam" for him across the footlights (S 1: 171). In another text dealing with a Parisian ballet he is led by the multicoloured lights and the movements of the dancers to believe that he is watching a "dance of phantoms," but then he insists that one of dancers addresses her smile only to him (S 1: 181). In "At the Cavour" (1896) he concentrates on the influence of the gaslight on people's mood; this time, however, he does not sentimentalise his own position and is aware of the fact that to speak of love in such an environment is part of the role everyone is playing:

Wine, the red coals, the flaring gas,
Bring out a brighter tone in cheeks
That learn at home before the glass
The flush that eloquently speaks.

The blue-grey smoke of cigarettes
Curls from the lessening ends that glow;
The men are thinking of the bets,
The women of the debts, they owe.

> Then their eyes meet, and in their eyes
> The accustomed smile comes up to call,
> A look half miserably wise,
> Half heedlessly ironical. (S 1: 119)

One of the poets who share Symons' fascination for the female performers in the music hall is Theodore Wratislaw. In the poem "At the Empire" (1896) he praises the luxurious promenade, the electric light, the carpets, the mirrors, and, above all, "the calm and brilliant Circes who retard / Your passage with the skirts and rouge that spice / That changeless programme of insipid vice" (A: 44).

In keeping with the importance of night life, some poems about the sunset look forward expectantly to the night. Arthur Symons asserts in an essay, "daylight never meant so much to me as the first lighting of the lamps" (S 5: 29). In "The White Statue" (1897), a poem on the Pygmalion theme, Olive Constance dreams that a statue she loves will come alive and declares: "I love you most at purple sunsetting" (A: 45). In "Sunset in the City" (1892) Richard Le Gallienne records the phases of the sunset and treats it as a grand mixture of colours, light, and darkness which transforms London magically:

> Within the town the streets grow strange and haunted,
>   And, dark against the western lakes of green,
> The buildings change to temples, and unwonted
>   Shadows and sounds creep in where day has been.

With the arrival of night, the magic of the sunset is gone, except perhaps for the couple of true lovers mentioned at the end of the poem:

> Within the town, the lamps of sin are flaring,
>   Poor foolish men that know not what ye are!
> Tired traffic still upon his feet is faring –
>   Two lovers meet and kiss and watch a star. (A: 62)

Whereas the sunset poems look forward to the night, the dawn poems look backwards and usually do not welcome the break of day. In Symons' "Heart's Desire" the speaker tells himself that the night was more divine than the early morning, although his sexual desire was not satisfied (S 1: 250). In her collection *A London Plane-Tree and Other Verse* (1889), Amy Levy prints two related poems on dawn. In "Borderland" the speaker is half awake, half dreaming. Believing that her lover has come, she spreads her arms in delight and hopes that the night will be prolonged. In the second poem, "A Dawn," she dreams again of her lover and wonders whether she will be able to face the grey and empty morning.

In "Impression du Matin" (1881) Oscar Wilde uses an impressionist approach similar to that of Le Gallienne in "Sunset in the City". Noting the changes of colour early in the morning that seem to transform houses into shadows and St. Paul's into a bubble, he creates a magical, harmonious atmosphere reminiscent of Wordsworth's "Composed Upon Westminster Bridge" (1802) and Whistler's painting "Nocturne in Blue and Gold: Old Battersea Bridge" (c. 1872–1875). He then registers the sounds of waking life, which disrupt the silence of the morning, and shifts the attention to the last witness to the past night, a prostitute, who is a product of the city and is as "hardened as its streets" (Bristow 2005: 158):

> The Thames nocturne of blue and gold
>   Changed to a Harmony in grey:
>   A barge with ochre-coloured hay
> Dropt from the wharf: and chill and cold
>
> The yellow fog came creeping down
>   The bridges, till the houses' walls
>   Seemed changed to shadows and St. Paul's
> Loomed like a bubble o'er the town.
>
> Then suddenly arose the clang
>   Of waking life; the streets were stirred
>   With country wagons: and a bird
> Flew to the glistening roofs and sang.
>
> But one pale woman all alone,
>   The daylight kissing her wan hair,
>   Loitered beneath the gas lamps' flare,
> With lips of flame and heart of stone. (Wilde 1967: 745)

That Wilde is not interested in a conventional moral response is indicated by his assumption that the daylight kisses the woman. Here, Wilde "sounds a distinctly decadent note and dramatically records both his fascination and ambivalence toward an all too common urban problem" (Thesing 1972: 295). Other works in which Wilde draws upon decadent and aesthetic motifs prevalent in the nineties include the poems "Impression" (1881), "The Harlot's House" (1885), "Symphony in Yellow" (1889), and the novel *The Picture of Dorian Gray* (1891).

Night and Day

As the examples have shown, some poets of the 1890s are fascinated by the night life of London and the freedom it entails. In "April Midnight" (1892), for instance, Arthur Symons celebrates roaming through the city with his partner:

> Side by side through the streets at midnight,
> Roaming together,
> Through the tumultuous night of London,
> In the miraculous April weather.
>
>> Roaming together under the gaslight,
>> Day's work over,
>> How the Spring calls to us, here in the City,
>> Calls to the heart from the heart of a lover!
>> [...] (S 1: 140)

A related sense of freedom characterises poems that deal with daytime excursions in London, whether on foot or by cab. In this context Ana Parejo Vadillo has demonstrated how women poets used the transport system to move around in the city and explore places previously avoided by middle-class women. In "A March Day in London" (1889), for example, Amy Levy's speaker paces the street all day long "with aimless feet" (qtd. in Vadillo 2005: 66). In spite of her weariness, she is driven on by fears which she cannot define, but which may originate in her being a Jew at a time when the "urban mobility of Jewish immigration, which mostly concentrated in the East End of London, was the cause of great anxiety, especially among the middle classes" (qtd. in Vadillo 2005: 66). In "A March Day" Levy eventually confronts her fears by generalising them:

> What is the thing I fear, and why?
> Nay, but the world is all awry –
> The wind's in the east, the sun's in the sky.

Then the beauty of the city reawakens her hope that her place is in London after all:

> The gas-lamps gleam in a golden line,
> The ruby lights of the hansoms shine,
> Glance, and flicker like fire-flies bright;
> The wind has fallen with the night,
> And once again the town seems fair
> Thwart the mist that hangs i'the air.

And o'er, at last, my spirit steals
A weary peace, peace that conceals
Within its inner depths the grain
Of hopes that yet shall flower again. (qtd. in Vadillo 2005: 67)

In "Ballade of an Omnibus," a poem following "A March Day" in Levy's poetry volume, she describes herself as a "wandering minstrel poor and free". This time, however, she is self-confident and boasts that in fine weather she will take a seat at the open top of the omnibus:

Some men to carriages aspire;
On some the costly hansoms wait;
Some seek a fly, on job or hire;
Some mount the trotting steed, elate.
I envy not the rich and great,
A wandering minstrel, poor and free,
I am contented with my fate –
An omnibus suffices me.

Like other poets of the 'nineties, she enjoys city life:

The scene whereof I cannot tire,
The human tale of love and hate,
The city pageant, early and late
Unfolds itself, rolls by, to be
A pleasure deep and delicate.
An omnibus suffices me. (Levy 2009: 735–736)

In one of her earliest publications (1907), young Katherine Mansfield personifies London as a woman and has her say the following:

In my streets [...] there is the passing of many feet, there are lines of glaring lights, there are cafes full of men and women, there is the intoxicating madness of night music, a great glamour of darkness, a tremendous anticipation, and, o'er all, the sound of laughter, half sad, half joyous, yet fearful, dying away into a strange shudder of satisfaction, and then swelling out into more laughter. The men and women in the cafes hear it. They look at each other suddenly, swiftly, searchingly, and the lights seem stronger, the night music throbs yet more madly.

Out of the theatres a great crowd of people stream into the streets. [...] Convention has long since sought her bed. With blinds down, with curtains drawn, she is sleeping and dreaming.

Do you not hear the quick beat of my heart? Do you not feel the fierce rushing of blood through my veins? In my streets there is the answer to all your achings and cryings. Prove yourself, permeate your senses with the heavy sweetness of the night. (qtd. in Kaplan 1984: 165)

Whether Mansfield had read many 'nineties poems or not, her statement may serve as a summary of several of the arguments which made some of the 'nineties writers break with Victorian attitudes and welcome London and its nights and lights as a literary subject.

Conclusion

As this survey of late-Victorian literature has shown, writers were not in agreement on how to respond to and evaluate urban reality. This is reflected by their use of the darkness-light polarity in general and by their references to the actual situation in London.

Dismayed by the rapid expansion of London, its slums, and living conditions, some realists and naturalists stress the symbolic darkness of the environment, its hellish or jungle-like character, and people's misery and hopelessness. When recording the presence of artificial light, they tend to describe it as a component of the general gloom or emphasise its ineffectiveness in the struggle against the night or the London fog. In urban Gothic fantasies, darkness may express a threat to human identity or allude to what Patrick Brantlinger in his book on *British Literature and Imperialism, 1830 – 1914* has called the *Rule of Darkness* (1988).

Some poets of the 1890s respond positively to artificial light and the well-lit entertainment sections of London. They are fascinated by the city's night life and like to take up aesthetic and decadent motifs and ideas. They break with early- and mid-Victorian norms of writing and move in the direction of modern poetry. It should, however, be noted that the High Modernists Ezra Pound and T. S. Eliot may owe less to Wilde, Symons, or Le Gallienne than to earlier Victorians like Browning, Tennyson, and James Thomson and to late-Victorian realists like John Davidson (cf. Barry 2011; Lessenich 2013).

To summarise, many literary works of the 1890s tend to associate London with night, darkness, bad weather, fog, or smog and thus suggest that the city is a dangerous or endangered space. They largely ignore the fact that the lighting of the city (thanks to gaslights and the introduction of electricity) had made some progress in the late-Victorian period. It was left to a small group of poets to interpret the partial illumination of London as a chance of pursuing pleasure, turning night, as it were, into day, and escaping temporarily from Victorian respectability.

Works Cited

Ackroyd, Peter. 2000. *London: The Biography*. London: Chatto & Windus.

Baron, Xavier (ed.). 1997. *London 1066–1914: Literary Sources and Documents*. Volume 3: *Late Victorian and Early Modern London 1870–1914*. Mountfield: Helm.

Barry, Peter. 2011. "London in Poetry since 1900". In: Lawrence Manley (ed.). *The Cambridge Companion to the Literature of London*. Cambridge, MA: Cambridge University Press. 180–187.

Beckson, Karl. 1992. *London in the 1890s: A Cultural History*. New York, NY: Norton.

Brantlinger, Patrick. 1988. *Rule of Darkness: British Literature and Imperialism, 1830–1914*. Ithaca, NY: Cornell University Press.

Bristow, Joseph (ed.). 2005. *The Fin-de-Siècle Poem: English Literary Culture and the 1890s*. Athens, OH: Athens Ohio University Press.

Clements, Patricia. 1985. *Baudelaire & the English Tradition*. Princeton, NJ: Princeton University Press.

Conrad, Joseph. 1960. *Youth. Heart of Darkness. The End of the Tether*. London: Dent.

Doyle, Arthur Conan. 1986. *Sherlock Holmes: the Complete Novels and Stories*. New York, NY: Bantam Classics.

Dyos, Harold J. and Michael Wolff (eds.). *1973. The Victorian City: Images and Realities*. London: Routledge & Paul Keegan.

Eisenberg, Christiane. 2003. "The Culture of Modernity: London and Paris around 1900". *Journal for the Study of British Cultures* 10: 171–186.

Fletcher, James Gould. 1988. *Selected Poems*. Ed. Lucas Carpenter and Leighton Rudolph. Fayetteville, AR: Arkansas University Press.

Ford, Boris. (ed.). 1958. *The Pelican Guide to English Literature, 6: From Dickens to Hardy*. Harmondsworth: Penguin.

Ford, Madox Ford. 1995. *The Soul of London: A Survey of a Modern City* (1905). London: Everyman.

Forsyth, Raymond A. 1976. *The Lost Pattern: Essays on the Emergent City Sensibility in Victorian England*. Nedlands: Western Australia University Press.

Goetsch, Paul. 2002. "Monsters in Fin-de-siècle Prose Fiction". *Monsters in English Literature: From the Romantic Age to the First World War*. Frankfurt/Main: Peter Lang. 284–307.

Goetsch, Paul. 2005. "The Savage Within: Evolutionary Theory, Anthropology and the Unconscious in Fin-de-Siècle Literature". In: Anne-Julia Zwierlein (ed.). *Unmapped Countries: Biological Visions in Nineteenth Century Literature and Culture*. London: Anthem. 95–106.

Hertel, Kirsten. 1997. *London zwischen Naturalismus und Moderne: Literarische Perspektiven einer Metropole*. Heidelberg: Winter.

Hönnighausen, Lothar. 1988. *The Symbolist Tradition in English Literature: A Study of Pre-Raphaelitism and Fin de Siècle*. Cambridge, MA: Cambridge University Press.

James, Henry. 1981. "London". *English Hours*. Oxford: Oxford Paperbacks. 1–29.

Johnson, Lionel. 1982. *The Collected Poems*. Ed. Ian Fletcher. New York, NY: Garland.

Kaplan, Sydney Janet. 1984. "'A Gigantic Mother': Katherine Mansfield's London". In: Susan Merrill Squier (ed.). *Women Writers and the City: Essays in Feminist Literary Criticism*. Knoxville, TN: Tennessee University Press. 161–175.

Keating, Peter (ed.). 1976. *Into Unknown England 1866–1913: Selections from the Social Explorers.* Manchester: Manchester University Press.

Lessenich, Rolf P. 2013. "City and Street". In: Bevis, Matthew (ed.). *The Oxford Handbook of Victorian Poetry.* Oxford: Oxford University Press.

Lesser, Wendy. 1987. *The Urban Tradition: Transformations of London as Reflected in Dickens, James and Conrad.* Ann Arbor, MI: UMI.

Levy, Amy. 2009. "Ballade of an Omnibus". In: Caroline Blyth (ed.). *Decadent Verse: An Anthology of Late Victorian Poetry, 1872–1900.* London: Anthem Press.

Marsh, Richard. 2004. *The Beetle* (1897). Ed. Julian Wolfreys. Peterborough: Broadview Press.

Masterman, Charles F. G. 1973. *The Heart of the Empire: Discussions of Problems of Modern City Life in England* (1901). Brighton: Harvester.

McLaughlin, Joseph. 2000. *Writing the Urban Jungle: Reading Empire in London from Doyle to Eliot.* Charlottesville, VA: Virginia University Press.

Morrison, Arthur. 1969. *A Child of the Jago* (1896). London: McGibbon and Kee.

Munro, John M. 1970. *The Decadent Poetry of the Eighteen-Nineties.* Beirut: American University of Beirut.

Newland, Paul. 2008. *The Cultural Construction of London's East End: Urban Iconography, Modernity and the Spatialisation of Englishness.* Amsterdam: Rodopi.

Nord, Deborah Epstein. 1987. "The Social Explorer as Anthropologist: Victorian Travellers among the Urban Poor". In: William Sharpe and Leonard Wallock (eds.). *Visions of the Modern City.* Baltimore, MD: Johns Hopkins University Press. 122–134.

Nünning, Ansgar. 2002. "'Subtle city of a thousand moods': Die Vertextung Londons in der urban poetry der Nineties im Spannungsfeld zwischen Naturalismus und Ästhetizismus". In: Monika Fludernik and Miriam Huml (eds.). *Fin de Siècle.* Trier: WVT. 177–206.

Pfister, Manfred. 1983. "Endzeit und Augenblick: Die Lyrik der Nineties". In: Manfred Pfister and Bernd Schulte-Middelich (eds.). *Die Nineties: Das englische Fin de siècle zwischen Dekadenz und Sozialkritik.* München: Francke. 358–376.

Rebske, Ernst. 1962. *Lampen, Laternen, Leuchten: Eine Historie der Beleuchtung.* Stuttgart: Franck.

Schivelbusch, Wolfgang. 1983. *Lichtblicke: Zur Geschichte der künstlichen Helligkeit im 19. Jahrhundert.* München: Hanser.

Schneer, Jonathan. 1999. *London 1900: The Imperial Metropolis.* New Haven, CT: Yale University Press.

Stange, G. Robert. 1968. "The Victorian City and the Frightened Poets". *Victorian Studies* 11: 627–640.

Stevenson, Robert Louis. 1962. *Dr. Jekyll & Mr. Hyde. The Merry Men and Other Tales.* London: Dutton.

Stoker, Bram. 1965. *Dracula* (1897). New York, NY: Airmont.

Symons, Arthur. 1973. *The Collected Works* (1924). New York, NY: Garland.

The Holy Bible. n.d. Oxford: Oxford University Press.

Thesing, William. 1972. *The London Muse: Poetic Response to the City 1850–1924.* Ann Arbor, MI: University Microfilms.

Thornton, Robert K. R. (ed.). 1970. *Poetry of the 'Nineties'.* Harmondsworth: Penguin.

Thornton, Robert K. R. 1983. *The Decadent Dilemma.* London: Edward Arnold.

Vadillo, Ana Parejo. 2005. *Women Poets and Urban Aestheticism: Passengers of Modernity.* Basingstoke: Palgrave Macmillan.

Walkowitz, Judith R. 1992. *City of Dreadful Delight: Narratives of Sexual Danger in Late-Victorian London.* Chicago, IL: Chicago University Press.

Warwick, Alexandra. 1999. "Lost Cities: London's Apocalypse". In: Glennis Byron and David Punter (eds.). *Spectral Readings: Towards a Gothic Geography.* Basingstoke: Macmillan. 73–87.

Wells, H. G. 1997. *The War of the Worlds.* Mineola, NY: Dover.

Wilde, Oscar. 1967. *Complete Works.* London: Collins.

Williams, Raymond. 1973. *The Country and the City.* London: Chatto & Windus.

Wolfreys, Julian. 2004. *Writing London.* Volume 2: *Materiality, Memory, Spectrality.* Basingstoke: Palgrave Macmillan.

Wolfreys, Julian. 2007. *Writing London.* Volume 3: *Inventions of the City.* Basingstoke: Palgrave Macmillan.

Maria Peker

"The Hours of the Day and the Night Are Ours Equally": *Dracula* and the Lighting Technologies of Victorian London

London's Lighting at the End of the 19th Century

The reign of Queen Victoria was famously the era of general progress in science and technology. Nowhere else was the power of industrial modernisation as glaringly obvious as in the great city of London, especially when the radical improvement of street lighting made it one of the most illuminated cities in the world. By the 1820s it had become the first capital to rely almost exclusively on gas for its public illumination; in the following years miles and miles of gas mains were laid, thousands of public gas lamps erected, millions of cubic feet of gas stored in huge gasometers.[1] Compared to the previous lack of systematic lighting and the dim sporadic flickering of solitary oil lamps and lanterns, streets flooded with gaslight dazzled urban dwellers and visitors to the city and it looked as if that uneasy discrepancy between the same space by day and by night, which had been felt acutely before, was finally erased. Artificial light seemed to have banished primordial shadows and darkness; it symbolised the power of reason and the advance of modernity, which turned the city into a rationally structured and controllable space. Enthusiastic visitors claimed that its most powerful tourist attraction was precisely this marvellous transformation of darkness into radiance:

> But it is really at night that London must be seen! London, magically lit by its millions of gas lights, is resplendent! Its broad streets disappearing into the distance; its shops, where floods of light reveal the myriad sparkling colours of all the masterpieces conceived by human industry; a world where men and women come and go all about you; all these things produce, the first time, a state of intoxication! (Tristan 1980: 2)

Quite emblematically, "gas lighting had converted London nights into day" (Nead 2000: 83) representing the victory of light and reason over the gloom of ignorance and backwardness.

---

1 For a more detailed discussion of statistical aspects of London lighting system cf. Schivelbusch (1995: 31).

Later in the century, however, gas lost the sense of overwhelming brilliance that had been attributed to it at the beginning and the fascination of novelty it once represented. The new technology of electricity made it seem dark and archaic. The advent of this new-fashioned bearer of light was glorified even in couplets sung in music halls:

> Oh have you heard the latest news of how the world's to be,
> Soon lighted up from pole to pole by electricity.
> The light of day will be eclipsed soon by the light of night,
> When all the Earth's illuminated by electric light.
>
> Chorus: Moonlight, limelight and the light of day,
> Silber [sic] light and candle light are not half so bright.
> Gas light, bude light[2] soon will pass away,
> All must take a back seat through electricity. ("The New Electric Light")

In 1873 a reporter for *Illustrated London News* rejoiced that "it is possible that all our streets in a few years hence may be nightly bathed in the glorious light of electricity, and the thousands of gaslights may then be replaced by two or three magneto-electric points set high above the housetops of London" (qtd. in "The New Electric Light"). Indeed, it was three years later that electric arc lamps were first installed in the West India Docks, and in 1879 the Embankment became the first London street to be electrically lit throughout. During this time, gaslight acquired something of a nostalgic value. Superseded by the ultra-modern power of electricity it began to seem old-fashioned if not hopelessly antiquated. At the end of the century Londoners started to perceive gaslight, which in comparison to the electric light seemed feeble and dim, as being divorced from its original task of dispelling darkness and creating comforting transparency of space. It did not, like electricity, illuminate the streets of the city to the degree of absolute clearness, but neither did it leave them in total darkness. The result was the mysterious dimness of London streets at night, which rendered familiar spaces exotic and mysterious. The night city lit by gas became surreal and strange.

Thus, the Victorians witnessed an unswerving progress of urban lighting, which was increasingly dissevering traditional associations of night with danger, criminality, and evil in general. The steady improvement of public illumination simultaneously meant the continuous betterment of safety and order issues, as

---

2 Invented by Goldsworthy Gurney, the bude-light "was effected by passing a stream of pure oxygen gas throught the wick of an oil lamp, whereby [as John Bethell asserts] a most intense and beautiful light was produced" (Bethell 1843 – 1844: 198).

the rate of criminality sank drastically during the night hours. Obviously, greater visibility in streets and alleys hindered felons from using open violence and had a reassuring effect on people who might otherwise have been fearful to appear in public spaces during late hours.[3]

Urban Gothic

It might therefore seem rather surprising that the end of the Victorian era, which coincided with the time electric light started to replace the then old-fashioned gas lighting, saw the re-emergence of Gothic fiction as one of the dominant genres in contemporary popular literature. Gothic code is to a great extent defined through a semiotics of darkness and night. Crimes and mysteries of traditional Gothic tales are usually hidden in the thick nocturnal shadows of medieval castles and solitary monasteries. Moonlit landscapes and feeble candlelight impotently struggling with surrounding threatening gloom belong as firmly to the set of Gothic conventions as dark underground rooms and tunnels (cf. Sedgwick 1986). The brightly-illuminated metropolis with its sparkling shop windows and brilliant pleasure gardens seems to be rather remote from these secluded and murky locations.

Despite these apparent incongruities, however, modern critics are unanimous in their opinion that it was precisely the urbanisation of Britain in the 19th century that triggered the revival of the Gothic. The shift from earlier remote locations to the modern urban environment is regarded as one of the most characteristic features of this second wave of Gothic literature. The city (most particularly, London) became one of the protagonists in the tales, frequently represented as a dark, menacing labyrinth full of uncanny and degenerate creatures. Gothic conventions, among which the issues of darkness, murkiness, and gloom took prominent place, were transferred from the traditional secluded rural settings to the great modern cities, symbolising the acute relevance of Gothic horrors for contemporary urban life. Hence the phrase 'Victorian Gothic' has now become virtually synonymous with 'Urban Gothic'.

The reasons why the late-century cityscape was so important for the re-emergence of Gothic fiction have been amply discussed in recent criticism.[4] In this

---

3 One sign that street illumination was perceived by Londoners as hindering criminal activities was the public demand, supported by many social reformers, to improve bad street lighting in East End streets after the Whitechapel murders. Cf. Rumbelow (1975: 123).

4 For a discussion of the close dependence of the genre on urban settings see Warwick (2007: 29 – 37); Spencer (1992: 197 – 225); Ridenhour (2013).

article I would like to focus on the aspect which is frequently casually mentioned but rarely directly addressed in the academic works on the subject, namely that of artificial lighting and its significance for the Urban Gothic. I suggest that it is not a coincidence that the time of the beginning transition from gas to electric public lighting was also the time in which the greatest Victorian Gothic novels were written. If, as Jamieson Ridenhour argues, "[t]he Gothic's primary characteristic is a tension between the present (i. e., the culture that produces a given work) and the past" (2013: 4), then in the Victorian Gothic it can be symbolically represented on the textual level sometimes as a direct clash, but more often as a complex interplay of primitive natural darkness, archaic means of lighting, and their neoteric successors, gas and electricity. What I intend to do in the following pages, using the Victorian Gothic classic *Dracula* (1897), is to demonstrate that the imagery of light and lighting appliances in the novel serves to contradict the interpretation of the tension Ridenhour is talking about in terms of a simple antagonism. My reading of the symbolism of light in the novel supports the argument of critics such as Glennis Byron who suggest that it would be wrong to read the interaction of the past and the present, archaism and modernity merely as a battle between good or light and evil or dark forces (2007).

The Ambiguity of the "Light-Dark" Opposition in the Urban Gothic Mode

In Ridenhour's dichotomy of past and present the second part can easily be replaced by the category "science". Indeed, science and the technological innovations that followed in its wake were crucial constituents of the concept of modernity in the 19th century. There is a long-standing critical debate about Bram Stoker's interest and investment in science and whether or not in his works modernity or technological progress is ultimately the winner in the battle with irrational and supernatural forces. Some critics interpret *Dracula* as an explicit proclamation of the indisputable power of science, technology, and modern reasoning abilities. Rosemary Jann, for example, suggests that the narrative contains a "celebration of the methods of rationalistic analysis and the technological manipulation of knowledge" (1989: 278). Others, like Carol A. Senf, see the presence of modernity in the novel as more problematic and ambiguous: "Stoker wavered in his confidence in the power of science and technology" (2000: 218 – 219). Whether or not he ultimately lined up on the side of materialist science, the interaction between the archaic powers of the supernatural and the modern efficacy of logic and reason is, obviously, central for the structure of his most famous novel. But although the dichotomy seems to be rather straightforward, the evaluation of science per se is far from being obvious in the text. Glennis Byron argues that in the novel "science is variously interpreted as the source of the vampire hunters' ability to defeat the Count, and the source of their helplessness and confusion in the face of supernatural forces" (2007: 49). There is (literally) a dark side to science in the novel and it is "not always unequivocally associated with the forces of good" (50).

Reflecting this ambiguity of science as both benign and malevolent power, both natural and artificial light are far from possessing only positive connotations in the text. In *Dracula*, as in many other Urban Gothic novels, the semiotics of darkness gives way or, more correctly, extends to include the semiotics of light. Gaslight in particular becomes part of the Gothic code and, in the economy of the city, it ceases to represent an unambiguously progressive element, which used to create the impression of modernity and feeling of security just a couple of decades before. Instead, I suggest that it starts to convey its anthropomorphic qualities onto the Gothic villain so that the villain and gas become metaphorically close. At the same time, in contrast to electricity, which by its panoptic power is at least supposed to banish even the slightest possibility of privacy in the public realm, gaslight creates spaces of peculiar freedom and resistance to the hegemonic structures: "[g]as lights darkness, whereas electricity annihilates it" (Nead 2000: 83). In the Urban Gothic gas becomes the alternative type of light, facilitating the transgressions of boundaries, which are impermeable during the day or in the penetrating electric light. Archaic night light, be it natural moonbeams or artificial gas illumination (which by the end of the century was already perceived as old-fashioned), de-marginalises liminal spaces and states, and thus creates a significant shift in the traditional balance of power. Though seemingly drawing on the familiar association of night with evil and horror, the Urban Gothic makes those negative connotations more complex. In these novels, night is the space of freedom and fluid identities. A period of interplay between artificial light and natural darkness, night is indeed the time when there is a possibility for identities, which are fixed in the daytime, to become fluid and unstable.[5] Night refuses to be colonised by illumination; instead, it appropriates or extinguishes it for its own aims.

Similarly, daylight or electric light, which may be supposed to represent the progressive element and create the transparency of space, which in its turn

---

5 This is true not only for supernatural creatures, but also for respectable gentlemen in other Gothic novels, such as Robert Louis Stevenson's *Strange Case of Dr Jekyll and Mr Hyde* (1886) and Oscar Wilde's *The Picture of Dorian Gray* (1891).

would mean safety and stability, rarely have an unambiguously positive value in the economy of the genre. Electricity fails in its task to turn night into day and does not help to eradicate horrors swarming in the dark urban labyrinths. And, rather paradoxically, the Gothic mode seems to question whether the transformation of night into day is, on the whole, beneficial. If night and night light (both natural and artificial) permit the investigation of alternative states, day fixes subjective consciousness firmly within the rigid grid of patriarchal discourse. Public safety can, therefore, only be bought by an individual's forswearing of his natural (the other word would be 'primitive') desires and pleasures. The Victorians believed that natural or physical desires, which were common to both humans and animals, were antagonistic to the ideal of rationality and culture.[6] They were that dark side of man's psyche which Freud later on defined as 'Id'. Light exposes the aberrancies from what was supposed to be the positive norm in society and permits to police these deviations. Thus an urban Panopticon emerges where an individual has to suppress his basic, instinctual drives in order not to threaten communal harmony.

Ultimately, it turns out that within the Urban Gothic mode it would be difficult to draw a strict line between such a seemingly self-explanatory set of oppositions as light and darkness, or to set up a taxonomy within one group of this binary. Thus, there seems to be an evident antagonism between natural or archaic light (emitted by the sun, the moon and the stars) and artificial or modern light sources (produced by gas or electricity). But gaslight can be interpreted both as a modern product of urban development if compared, for example, to candles in the medieval castles and as an archaism (or at least as being old-fashioned) if seen side by side with electric lighting. Electricity, in its turn, is at the surface believed to be the proof of the power of progress and technology but, as we will see, it may also fail in its battle with magical and primitive forces. Similarly, day is not always the realm of a positive set of values and is not always light, whereas night must not necessarily be evil and is rarely completely dark. Urban Gothic plays on this sort of imprecision and demonstrates the futility of attempts to establish an argumentative differentiation, which would be valid in all contexts. Bram Stoker's novel is a good example of these ambiguities.

---

6 In *Culture and Anarchy* (1869) Matthew Arnold discusses at length similar sets of oppositions. He associates the light, cultural, progressive and rational side with Hellenism, and the dark, barbaric, archaic, and physical side with Hebraism. Strong anti-Semitic undercurrents in Victorian intellectual thought are, of course, blatantly obvious in this dichotomy. Incidentally, Dracula's appearance is also frequently interpreted as typically Jewish.

The Symbolism of Light and Darkness in *Dracula*

On the whole, *Dracula* is a novel which is obsessed with the issues of both light and darkness. Indeed, the text is structured around the alteration of day and night, sunset and sunrise neatly puncturing the story. Every one of the three principal narrators in the novel – Jonathan Harker, Mina Harker and Dr Seward – keeps minute record of these liminal temporal stages. Transitions from day into night are, of course, crucial for the narrative because they correspond with the rise and fall of Dracula's power and for the most part the action takes place in the night hours when Dracula's might is at its peak. When Van Helsing is talking to his friends about their chances to win in this battle of good and evil he estimates their relative forces in terms of the ability of balancing precisely between transparency or visibility and obscurity. In his description of the vampire's abilities and limitations, he focuses on Dracula's manipulation of light and darkness:

> [h]e can come in mist which he create [...]; but, from what we know, the distance he can make this mist is limited, and it can only be round himself. He come on moonlight rays as elemental dust [...] He can see in the dark – no small power this, in a world which is one half shut from the light. [...] His power ceases, as does that of all evil things, at the coming of the day. Only at certain times can he have limited freedom. If he be not at the place whither he is bound, he can only change himself at noon or at exact sunrise or sunset. (Stoker 1998: 239 – 40)

In accordance with familiar cultural assessment, in his monologue Van Helsing evokes the traditional associations of darkness with archaism and light with progress and power of reason: "We have on our side power of combination – a power denied to the vampire kind; we have resources of science; we are free to act and think; and the hours of the day and the night are ours equally" (238). In another scene he compares Mina's typewritten account to the light dispelling the darkness of perplexity and confusion: "This paper is as sunshine. [...] I am daze, I am dazzle [sic], with so much light [...]. There are darknesses in life, and there are lights; you are one of the lights" (183). Quite predictably, the traditionally positive value of light as clarity and progress in Van Helsing's system of belief is opposed to the negative connotations of darkness as backwardness and superstition. Dracula, who is, appositely, an aristocrat and thus a member of an antiquated class system, represents this association between darkness and archaism in the novel. In accordance with this evaluation of light, artificial lighting is expected to take its place among the "resources of science" (238) mentioned by Van Helsing along with other technological inventions such as

Dr Seward's phonograph, Mina's and Jonathan's use of shorthand or train travel (all of which have been much discussed in recent criticism).[7] Van Helsing implies that by using illuminating technologies (such as the anachronistic electric flashlights, which I will discuss in more detail later) he and his associates can disperse darkness and thus master the domain of evil night. He implies that darkness only belongs to the realm of supernatural power and suggests that, by annihilating it (in both its literal and metaphorical sense) through the employment of, among other modern inventions, new lighting appliances, it is possible to conquer Dracula. On the other hand, by appropriating both day and night, both light and darkness to the power of reason and invention, Van Helsing articulates Victorian confidence in modernity and progress.

Thus, on the surface, there seems to be a traditional dualism between the brave and virtuous Crew of Light, with the sage Van Helsing as its leader, and the evil and dark Children of the Night, whose monstrous chieftain is Dracula himself. However, it would be misleading to trust this simple set of traditional connotations. Rather than being simply metaphorically close to the discourses of darkness and gloom, Dracula is also in many different ways interconnected with the domains of light and illumination. The Count cannot be simply banished into the realm of night; on the contrary, it is him who actually intrudes into the – seemingly adverse – sphere of light and rationality and who, moreover, appropriates the surprisingly anthropomorphic characteristics of modern means of city lighting. As I will illustrate later, it seems that both natural light (such as moonlight or candlelight) and artificial light (by gas or electricity) are in his power. Besides, it is important not to forget that, as Nina Auerbach puts it: "Stoker's Dracula could not shape-shift in daylight, but he walked around it freely" (1995: 120). Sunlight does not annihilate the un-dead in Stoker's novel; it just robs him of his ability to change his form. Thus, although Dracula's "power ceases, as does that of all evil things, at the coming of the day" (Stoker 1989: 240) (and this assertion also needs to be modified, as I will show later), he is not vulnerable to light per se. And, as I pointed out at the beginning, London night at that time was far from being absolutely dark. Artificial light, which in the 19th century city aimed at creating day at night, fails to fix Dracula in one form – on the contrary: it unexpectedly facilitates his transmutations. Hence, the apparent binary of good heroes fighting with the power of light against evil forces, whose realm is darkness and night, is more ambiguous than the superficial structure of the novel might suggest.

---

7 See for example Page (2011: 95 – 113); Punter (2007: 31 – 41).

Darkness, Light, and Artificial Illumination

Incidentally, in treating these subjects the text follows the general shift of the genre from classic Gothic to its urban successor. When Jonathan first meets the Count in his secluded castle, the narrative keeps playing on the traditional associations of natural darkness with horrors and occult powers. There is great precision in Harker's account of his journey concerning the alteration of light and darkness, which, as already mentioned, sets the tone for the whole novel. Thus, for example, he does not fail to notice that it is "on the dark side of twilight" (Stoker 1989: 3) that he reaches the last town on his journey to Dracula's castle and, quite expectedly, as he was sitting on the coach bound there, "the sun sank lower and lower behind us, the shadows of the evening began to creep round us" (7). Similarly, the castle is predictably in the dark when he reaches it: "I expected to see the glare of lamps through the blackness; but all was dark. The only light was the flickering rays of our own lamps" (9). When Jonathan first meets the Count, Dracula is holding "an antique silver lamp, in which the flame burned without chimney or globe of any kind, throwing long, quivering shadows as it flickered in the draught of the open door" (15). The rooms in the castle are lit by log fire (16) and the natural nocturnal light of the moon dwarves the artificial light of Jonathan's lamp (35). Of course, this emphasis on the archaism of lighting in Dracula's castle echoes the general impression of the Count's rootedness in some dark, mysterious past and his initial backwardness with regard to the modern age of technology and progress. Archaic light images in the initial scenes of the novel represent a primitive past which haunts the progressive present embodied here by the young English lawyer. They reinforce the associations evoked by such details as the traditionally remote setting in "one of the wildest and least known portions of Europe" (1) or English magazines that Dracula reads: "none of them were of very recent date" (19).

So far there is the familiar use of classic Gothic conventions of darkness, gloom, and, correspondingly, obsolete ways of lighting. Gradually, however, the Count not only invades the heart of the British Empire but he also begins to participate in the discourse of modern technologies. His ability to manage the power of light and darkness increases. Dracula's first encounter with technological progress happens precisely when he reaches the coast of England. His arrival in Britain is signalised by the impressive battle between the natural gloom of night and the contemporary inventions designed to conquer it. Mina Harker, witnessing the great storm and the shipwreck of the *Demeter*, mentions "the new searchlight [that] was ready for experiment, but had not yet been tried" (77). This is the lighting appliance which ultimately enables the discovery of the schooner, aboard which Dracula is sleeping in one of the coffins. There is a spectacular, somewhat cinematic scene when its rays follow the ship in the darkness "which seemed intensified just beyond the focus of the searchlight" (79). The new searchlight tracking the ship in the darkness anticipates the Crew of Light haunting Dracula in London's labyrinth and, yet again, metaphorically represents the ostensibly simple opposition of modernity and primitive past. At this point Dracula can still only master the natural forces of moonlight and the fog. But Whitby – a small secluded town which is-located not somewhere in the exotic continental countries, as is usual in the classic Gothic tales, but on English soil – is the focal site of both the novel's internal shift from Rural to Urban Gothic and of Dracula's growing younger, more sophisticated, and, correspondingly, more adept at handling modern technologies.

Even at this stage, Dracula's night is by no means dark. Indeed, in the economy of the text it is imperative that there is a lot of light even after the sun is set, otherwise, how could the characters observe all the scenes that they describe to the reader in their narratives? Jonathan, for example, would not be able to see three sisters in the castle without some sort of illumination and, certainly, it had to be natural and not artificial light for appropriate effect: "My lamp seemed to be of little effect in the brilliant moonlight" (35). Similarly, Mina could not have seen Lucy being bitten by Dracula in the form of a bird if it weren't for "bright moonlight, so bright that, though the front of our part of the Crescent was in shadow, everything could be well seen" (94). It is also important to bear in mind that, despite Van Helsing's somewhat contradictory assertions, the vampire's power is not limited to the nocturnal luminary – the moon and her light – but it extends into day-time as well. The Dutch professor himself mentions noon as the time when Dracula can change his form. And Dr Seward notices the increased violence of his zoophagous patient at the stroke of noon and muses whether "there is a malign influence of the sun at periods which affects certain natures – as at times the moon does others?" (117). Thus, both luminaries, the moon and (though, of course, to a lesser extent) the sun, seem to be on Dracula's side.

By the same token, if Dracula's night is not always dark, the day, which Van Helsing (along with the reader) supposes to be the time of safety and dominance of the Crew of Light, is not always bright. Another natural force under Dracula's command is the fog. Importantly, in 19th century Britain fog was more than just a natural phenomenon; it was inseparably associated in the cultural consciousness of the Englishmen with their capital. London's fog was famous; its fame curiously surviving even into modernity long after the city's air had cleared. Although Van Helsing mentions that "the smuts [smog] in London were not quite so bad as they used to be when he was a student there" (113) –

thus again emphasising the aspect of progress and, concomitantly, increased light – at the end of the century the fog was still an inalienable part of the cultural image of London. If gas and later electricity were at least at the outset believed to turn night into day, it was this notorious 'London particular' which turned day into night. The very same London tourist, who enthusiastically admired the metropolis' illumination and splendour at night, complained bitterly of the despondency of the city by day:

> To the enormous mass of soot-laden smoke exhaled by the monster city's thousands of chimneys is joined a thick fog, and the black cloud which envelops London admits only a wan daylight and casts a funereal pall over all things.
>
> In London one draws gloom with every breath; it is in the air; it enters at every pore. Ah there is nothing so lugubrious, so spasmodic as the look of the city on a day of fog, rain or bleak cold! (Tristan 1980: 7)

The cause and effect of this both natural and industrial cultural phenomenon is described by a modern critic in almost Gothic terms: "Half a million coal fires mingling with the city's vapour [...] produced this 'London particular'. [...] The closer to the heart of the city, the darker these shades would become until it was 'misty black' in the dead centre" (Ackroyd 2001: 432). As the gas used in gaslights was also primarily made from coal, there was a kind of vicious circle of gas as both dispeller and creator of darkness.

The fog reduced visibility and created the atmosphere of danger and unfamiliarity which was typical of the city. If, due to its uneven distribution in London, gas lighting contributed to its fragmentation, the fog permeated all its parts, independent of their economic and social position. Thus, in a symbolic sense, the fog could function in Victorian texts (both fictional and non-fictional) as a levelling element which blurred seemingly safe boundaries between the light and wealthy and dark and criminal districts of the city.[8] However, it would again be wrong to simply juxtapose gas as a fracturing and the fog as an interconnecting medium. The fog does not only pervade the whole city and erase the safety of boundaries; it can also, in some sense like the pools of gaslight in the streets, create divisions between people. In the London streets people are lonely and isolated when walking in white muddiness and, by the same token, Dracula can wrap himself into its murky vapour and thus hide from his pursuers by obscuring their vision. On the other hand, both the fog and artificial light at night annihilated those clear distinctions between night and day which the characters of

---

8 The first chapters of Charles Dickens' *Bleak House* (1853) are a famous example of this imagery of the fog as permeating borders, connecting seemingly disparate and isolated locations.

the novel are so obsessed with. Still, despite these intersections, the fog was perceived as a natural opponent of the artificial lighting and indeed street lighting in London was to a large extent expected to minimise its impact.

Both gaslight and the fog came to be inalienable from the cultural representation of London at the end of the Victorian period. After electricity had raised expectations of the urban dwellers in the late 19th century, gas lamps were perceived to be impotent against the fog's mighty presence. Their coexistence was not felt to be antagonistic anymore, but, quite on the contrary, they seemed to reinforce each other in the creation of particular impressionistic images of the metropolis. Their uncanny interplay created an alternative reality, which was easily perceived as Gothic. Modern critics emphasise the fact that "there is a definitive Gothic code of a foggy, gas-lit cobbled street, threatened by an unseen malevolent presence" (Warwick 2007: 36) and that "images of the gaslit, fog-enshrouded streets of Victorian London [...] have become iconic, if not clichéd, in the signification of Gothic fiction" (Ridenhour 2013: 7). This close intertwining between light and murkiness, transparency and obscurity, science and mystery is crucial for late-Victorian Gothic novels in general and for *Dracula* in particular.

In the foggy and gas-lit capital of England, Dracula seems to extend his powers. His influence is not restricted anymore to the primeval forces of nature. Within the text the villain, who is a relic of the old centuries, threatens modernity not so much by his own ignorance and violence, but by his intrusion and participation in the modern scientific discourse. If there were just a simple opposition and division between the past and the present, between archaism and modernity, the threat would seem much less poignant. Indeed, one cannot successfully fight with bow and arrows against a rifle or a gun. But Dracula, in the novel, does not just simply represent an obsolete menace of violent barbarism; the actual horror is that he can intrude the present by modernising himself. Van Helsing mentions his crucial ability to learn: "In some faculties of mind he has been, and is, only a child; but he is growing, and some things that were childish at the first are now of man's stature" (Stoker 1989: 302). His desire to do so is manifested in the very beginning of the novel; indeed, his hunger for information is the main aim in his inviting Jonathan Harker to stay at the castle. And so, after his arrival in London, Dracula ceases to be exclusively associated with natural elements or archaic means of lighting. But what might seem surprising at first, the threat that he poses to the stability of the metropolis is in many ways closely related to the different dangers which were perceived to lurk in the gas distribution of the city, that very system which had been applauded as one of the most significant achievements of modernity only a couple of decades before.

Gas city lighting had acquired sinister – Gothic – undertones even before the brilliance of electricity overshadowed its predecessor, proving that the ambivalence of both light and darkness was manifested not only on the textual level within the fictional works of Victorian writers. There was no uniformity in London street lighting as different companies supplied gas to different districts. The power and purity of gas differed accordingly. Because of the lack of a central authority responsible for the regulation of street lighting in the whole city, it is not surprising that London was divided into light and dark areas according to the economic status of each particular district. Poorer districts, such as the East End and the Docks, were accordingly poorly lit, whereas fashionable upper- and middle-class neighbourhoods were boasting regular and bright rows of street lamps (Ridenhour 2013: 43–69). Thus, a peculiar cartography was created according to the intensity of the illumination of different districts by night. Besides, even in the best-lit neighbourhoods darkness was not annihilated completely. Rather, gas created alternating spaces of light and darkness, it "created patches of light interspersed with pools of darkness" (Nead 2000: 83). Thus, not only did gaslight not conquer or disperse the surrounding darkness; on the contrary, it made the gloom more palpable, more intense. In the novel, Stoker frequently mentions this ambiguous interplay between light and darkness in gas-lit spaces as, for example, in the scene when Van Helsing and Dr Seward go to the cemetery to ascertain that Lucy is the "bloofer lady": "[i]t was then very dark, and the scattered lamps made the darkness greater when we were once outside their individual radius" (Stoker 1989: 196). The imagery of isolated feeble lights in the street only serves to create a scarier, more Gothic aura.

Apart from this ambiguous poetics of chiaroscuro in gas-lit spaces, gas itself as a light source had acquired very clearly perceptible connotations of danger. First of all, there was a great risk of explosion, not only in public spaces but also within the houses of those who could afford private gas lighting.[9] There was always a possibility of leakage and hence gas transmission could easily transform from the beneficial technology into a treacherous fiend. The distribution of gas through the mains was easy and quick: "[i]ts silence, invisibility and speed were precisely the qualities that made gas seem uncanny and gas mains dangerous" (Schivelbusch 1995: 37). This invisibility and an enormously powerful killing force are further reasons for gas being easily Gothicised in the 19th century cultural imagination. Like a vampire, it could swiftly cross both material frontiers of houses and, more metaphorically, penetrate into the bodies of their inhabitants. Also, gas-fittings had first to be installed, which was also a pri-

---

9 Note that this limitation to the economic and social strata of affluent, presumably upper-middle class citizens is echoed within the novel. Dracula himself is interested only in mastering the members of wealthier classes.

vate decision of the members of each individual household. Hence, gas, like a vampire, "may not enter anywhere at the first, unless there be someone of the household who bid him to come; though afterwards he can come as he please" (Stoker 1989: 240).

Because of the invisibility of gas and its murderous facility of penetration, gas lighting also fitted into the discourses of medical disease and the danger of infection, which were so characteristic of the urban discourse at the end of the century. Both the imagery of vampire threat in the late-Victorian novel and the issue of gas supply in contemporary discussions of everyday amenities partake of the rhetoric of disease, infection, and, ultimately, death. The Crew of Light must "sterilize" (298) the earth which the Count has imported from his castle, so that London's soil remains pure and, accordingly, immune against foreign intrusion. Mina Harker is made "unclean", her flesh is "polluted" (296) by Dracula and she would not touch her husband for fear of infecting him (284). Though the system of metropolitan gas supply was rarely brought into an explicit connection with sanitary issues, after the initial euphoria it came to be perceived as unsafe for public welfare. Like an infection, it could pollute air and kill unsuspecting people within their own houses. The poisonous and treacherous qualities of gas were close to those of infection: "there is nothing to indicate its presence; no noise at the opening of the stop-cock or valve – no disturbance in the transparency of the atmosphere" (qtd. in Schivelbusch 1995: 37). Both gas and Dracula can therefore easily intrude the deceptively safe bedrooms of wealthy Londoners and poison them in their beds. Interestingly, a contemporary journalist emphasises the fact that gas poisoning happens only at night while people are asleep (cf. 40). In daytime, its stench would warn the inhabitants of the house that there is a leak somewhere. So it is only under the cover of darkness that sleeping people are exposed to its deadly poison. Like Dracula, who infects the blood of his victims only after the sun has set, the killer gas attacks at night, when its victims are at their most vulnerable. The image of the arteries of the metropolis – gas tubes or mains – carrying the danger through the blood system of the city in the night is a curious intersection of urban, Gothic and medical discourses.

Although it is invisible, gas has an unpleasant smell,[10] a quality which had been perceived as disturbing from the very start (Schivelbusch 1995: 38 – 39). According to the miasma theory, which was widely believed in the 19th century, dis-

---

10 In the 19th century the gas used for lighting purposes was coal gas, which is different to the natural gas used today. Contrary to natural odourless gas, coal gas has a very unpleasant smell of rotten eggs when burnt due to the sulfuret of hydrogen, its most hazardous contaminant.

ease was transmitted by air and its presence was signalled by foul odours (which in turn were caused by bad sanitation). In this context the bad smell of gas ceases to be just one of its chemical properties and acquires medical connotations, indicating the danger of infection and contamination. It signals that the air has become deadly because of a leak somewhere. Dracula also exudes "a deathly, sickly odour" (Stoker 1989: 47) and his presence in his London lairs is betrayed by the bad smell. Jonathan Harker's description of the old chapel at Carfax – one of Dracula's dens – rings a bell to the readers familiar with the language of corruption and decay in the works of medical and sanitary reformers:

> We were prepared for some unpleasantness, for as we were opening the door a faint, malodorous air seemed to exhale through the gaps, but none of us ever expected such an odour as we encountered. [...] There was an earthy smell, as of some dry miasma, which came through the fouler air. But as to the odour itself, how shall I describe it? It was not alone that it was composed of all the ills of mortality and with the pungent, acrid smell of blood, but it seemed as though corruption had become itself corrupt. Faugh! it sickens me to think of it. Every breath exhaled by that monster seemed to have clung to the place and intensified its loathsomeness. (Stoker 1989: 250 – 251)

Importantly, the stench indicates not only physical but also moral decay. Expressions such as "all the ills of mortality" and "corruption becoming itself corrupt" can be easily interpreted both in the literal sense of decomposing physical matter and metaphorically as moral unsoundness (which in the cultural parlance of the time was almost always synonymous with aggressive sexuality).[11] To quote just one of the numerous descriptions of the Victorian London city slums, here are the lines from *London Labour and the London Poor* (1851) by Henry Mayhew, one of the most famous Victorian social researchers: "Nothing can be worse for the health than these places, without ventilation, cleanliness, or decency, and with forty people's breaths perhaps mingling together in one foul choking steam of stench" (Mayhew 1861: 409). The stench thus is not merely disagreeable for the high hygienic standards of a Victorian middle-class gentleman, it is above all a sign of seeping disease, caused by overpopulation, bad sanitation, and, importantly, sexual looseness, which in the novel is also associated with the Count. The image of "one foul choking steam of stench", which could be used in connection with either gas or vampire, symbolically expresses both bodily and moral corruption and consequent decay of body and soul.

It is also possible to suggest that in the mind of a late-Victorian Londoner, Jonathan's description of Dracula's dens would have an uncanny association with gasworks, the depositaries where gas was stored before it was distributed

---

11 For a general discussion cf. Nead (1988).

through the system of pipes. Linda Nead mentions that in the vicinity of gas manufacturing works and gasholder stations "the land seemed poisoned by pollutants and the stench of gas" (2000: 93). Besides, there was, as always with gas, the ever-present danger of explosion but because of the huge amount of gas stored in gasworks, this danger was multiplied by many times wherever these works were set up. The explosion of any of them would have meant a catastrophe of an enormous extent for the metropolis. Hence the map of the locations of London gas works becomes, like that of Dracula's lairs, the chart where sites of danger are distributed within the metropolitan area.

Apart from these manifold associative similarities between the vampire and gas, in the novel, quite simply, gaslight always seems to be in the Count's power and Dracula can manipulate it at will. It is either too feeble to produce enough light to illuminate the scene and make space transparent and thus safe: "gas flame was like a speck rather than a disc of light" (Stoker 1989: 311); or it is too slow to make Dracula visible: "the moonlight suddenly failed, as a great black cloud sailed across the sky; and when the gaslight sprung up under Quincey's match, we saw nothing but a faint vapour" (282); or it produces an eerie effect which not only does not dispel but, on the contrary, intensifies the Gothic atmosphere: "a small oil-lamp, [...] gave out, when lit in a corner of the tomb, gas which burned at fierce heat with a blue flame" (214),[12] the images of "fierce heat" and "blue flame" raising quite apocalyptic associations.

The pivotal scene in this context is that in which Dracula steps into Mina's room and forces her to drink his blood. The episode is rendered in the words of Mina herself who starts by describing the chiaroscuro familiar from the novels of the rural Gothic tradition: "All was dark and silent, the black shadows thrown by the moonlight seeming full of a silent mystery of their own" (257–258). Then, however, she turns from the scenery in the outdoors to the dangerous interpellation of light and darkness within the domestic space:

> The gas-light which I had left lit for Jonathan, but turned down, came only like a tiny red spark through the fog, which had evidently grown thicker and poured into the room. [...] The mist grew thicker and thicker, and I could see now how it came in, for I could see it like smoke – or with the white energy of boiling water – pouring in, not through the window, but through the joinings of the door. It got thicker and thicker, till it seemed as if it became concentrated into a sort of pillar of cloud in the room, through the top of which I could see the light of the gas shining like a red eye. [...] But the pillar was composed

---

12 A real oil lamp would not, of course, emit blue gas when lighted. It is possible that the device meant by Stoker was either a kerosene lamp or an Argand burner, which was originally an oil lamp, but which was successfully adapted for gas in the middle of the century (cf. Taylor 2000).

of both the day and the night guiding, for the fire was in the red eye, which at the thought got a new fascination for me; till, as I looked, the fire divided, and seemed to shine on me through the fog like two red eyes. (Stoker 1989: 258–259)

In this scene Dracula employs in his service both the natural obscurity of the fog and the artificial light of treacherous gas, whose flame here acquires quite diabolic undertones. Gaslight turns into Dracula's eyes and thus becomes, in an unexpected twist, the eye of darkness, the concentration of evil.[13] Importantly, Dracula invades Mina's room not from the outside, but from within the very house – the smoke pours in 'not through the window, but through the joinings of the door.' This image of a pestilent cloud creeping through an ever so small aperture in the room would conjure up in the late-Victorian reader's imagination the everpresent danger of gas poisoning and thus it puts him in an uneasy proximity with the horror, which at first glance seems to be completely fictional.

Incidentally, Mina remarks that "the pillar was composed of both the day and the night guiding" (258), thus again drawing attention to the fact that it would be wrong to fix Dracula only within the realm of night and darkness. The day guiding, which the heroine associates with the fire of gas, loses its positive connotations. It is not the beacon of progress and rationality anymore, but, on the contrary, an accomplice of the nocturnal nightmare. In this episode gas lighting not only fails to dispel the nightly fears of the terrified (female) tenant, but, as a matter of fact, enhances the uncanny effect of the vampire intruding into the middle-class domestic space, which ceases to be the safe haven glorified by the ideology of separate spheres.

Against this power of Dracula over gas Van Helsing and his crew employ the modern force of electricity. As I mentioned at the beginning, in the discussions of technological improvements at the end of the century, electricity was favourably compared to the gaslight, which by that time seemed to be old-fashioned and feeble. Electric light, on the other hand, was seen as the epitome of progress in technology. The task of making the metropolitan space completely transparent, which gaslight had ultimately failed to fulfil, was now trusted to the electric illumination. As Anthony Vidler suggests, it was precisely this absolute transparency of space that was expected to "eradicate the domain of myth, suspicion, tyranny, and above all the irrational" (1996: 168). Hence, electric light can be regarded as an obvious opponent of the Gothic villain. In accordance with this

---

13 This imagery of the gaslight shining as a red eye in the clouds of fog seems to shape the way we imagine Gothic London at night up to the present day. Modern critics still juxtapose gas and fog in London streets in very similar terms: "street-lamps seemed like points of flame in the swirling miasma" (Ackroyd 2001: 433).

pattern, Van Helsing counts electric light among his aids against both "spiritual" and "mundane" enemies (Stoker 1989: 249).

The concrete aid, however, which the Professor is talking about, is rather an anachronistic element in the novel. Van Helsing has in his possession what may be called a prototype of an electric torch: "these so small electric lamps, which you can fasten to your breast" (ibid.). These electric lamps seem to be the last word in lighting appliances, making portable lanterns and other lamps look cumbrous and dim in comparison. Worn on the breast, they are, obviously, much more convenient and safe than gas lamps as they both leave the hands of Van Helsing and his friends free to break into one of Dracula's dens, and they emit less heat and smoke so that the air in a closed space is not further polluted. But unlike other modern inventions mentioned in the novel, this technological gadget is an anachronism. The first electric flashlight was invented in 1896, only one year before the publication of Stoker's novel. It was only in the year of publication that the creator of the electric flashlight, David Misell, obtained several patents for his brainchild in the US. Also, the first portable electric light was by no means 'small' and had to be carried by hand as it was actually a relatively long tube with a lens at one end (cf. Schneider 2014). Under no circumstances could it be fixed on the breast in such a way that it could illuminate something in front of its bearer. No wonder that back in Transylvania "[t]he men were scared every time we turned our electric lamp on them, and then fell on their knees and prayed" (Stoker 1989: 358). People in the London of that time would have doubtlessly been similarly astonished to see this sort of appliance in the hands of Van Helsing and his friends.

Yet again, it would be wrong to ascribe to this sort of neoteric device the unambiguous power which electricity was expected to possess when employed to illuminate the city streets. Van Helsing himself brings this apparently ultra-modern technology in an explicit connection with archaism and superstition: "Let me tell you, my friend, that there are things done to-day in electrical science which would have been deemed unholy by the very men who discovered electricity – who would themselves not so long before been burned as wizards" (191). Electricity is labelled 'unholy', the scientists, those drivers of progress, become 'wizards'. Although a technological novelty such as this is supposed, in the logic of the novel, to combat the dark forces of superstition, the effect the electric light really creates is far from dispelling that darkness: "The light from the tiny lamps fell in all sorts of odd forms, as the rays crossed each other, or the opacity of our bodies threw great shadows. I could not for my life get away from the feeling that there was someone else amongst us" (250). Curiously, in the effect it produces, the electric flashlight does not really differ from a relatively old-fashioned gas lamp. The lamps are so tiny that, far from panoptically controlling the space, their chaotic light enhances the uncanny effect of the scene. Like London gas-light, it creates odd forms and shadows and Jonathan Harker feels the presence of the Gothic Other in the darkness intensified by it. Similarly, after the friends intrude into the chapel and see the swarming rats, electric light does not, as might have been expected, dispel the horror of the place but, quite on the contrary, it participates in the discourse of mystery and terror: "the lamplight, shining on their moving dark bodies and glittering, baleful eyes, made the place look like a bank of earth set with fireflies" (252). Again, the simple dichotomy of 'progressive' and 'obsolete' does not work out in the text. The power of electricity turns out to be much smaller than that of the sacred wafer, which indeed sterilises the English soil and makes it immune against Dracula's infection. The invincibility of science and technology, so faithfully believed in by Van Helsing and his friends, proves to be a myth.

It has been pointed out that despite both Stoker's and Van Helsing's admiration of the technological achievements of their "scientific, sceptical, matter-of-fact nineteenth century" (238), the Crew of Light are not averse to using such miraculous weapons as crucifixes and sacred wafers in their battle against the vampire (cf. Jann 1989: 275). The lighting appliances used by the Crew of Light are also manifold, and they are not restricted to those technological wonders of gas and electricity. They also quite readily employ archaic means of lighting. Apart from availing themselves of the then non-existent flashlights, they illuminate the scene by means of such obsolete lighting appliances as a "dark lantern" (Stoker 1989: 208), "two wax candles" (213) and an "oil-lamp" (214). Importantly, it is such primitive means of lighting that serve to intensify sexual undertones in the famously suggestive scenes in Lucy's tomb.[14] One of the most obvious episodes when candles become phallic symbols in the hands of Van Helsing and his friends is his night visit to Lucy's tomb with Dr Seward: "holding his candle so that he could read the coffin plates, and so holding it that the sperm dropped in white patches which congealed as they touched the metal, [Van Helsing] made assurance of Lucy's coffin" (197). Sperm in this context means spermaceti, a wax which is found in the head of the sperm whale. Both words do have the same etymology[15] but, of course, the image of sperm dropping in white patches cannot but evoke some very obvious associations in the readers. In this novel rich with sexual symbolism, the ultimate power of sexuality is associated with Dracula and his animalistic vitality. Candles and their archaic light serve to displace sex-

---

14 Cf. Christopher Craft's reading of the scene in tomb when Lucy's body is penetrated by stake in "'Kiss me with those Red Lips': Gender and Inversion in Bram Stoker's *Dracula*" (1984:107 – 133).

15 They derive from Greek *sperma* or 'seed'.

ual desire. Van Helsing, who is supposed to counteract the dangerous influence of fierce sexuality embodied by Dracula, metaphorically betrays in this scene his own sexual hunger.

The image of late-Victorian London at night was shaped by the confrontation of both gas and electric light and natural darkness. These issues are also central in the Urban Gothic genre. In Dracula the imagery of light and darkness does not only create visual effects. Both natural and artificial means of lighting in the novel represent on the symbolical level that pattern of opposition between the present and the past, which is supposed to be crucial for the Gothic mode. In Stoker's novel, Dracula as well as the Crew of Light use as their weapons both modern and obsolete means of lighting, hence both antagonists participate in discourses of enlightened modernity and superstitious past. The battle between Van Helsing and Dracula cannot be simply interpreted as modernity and science trying to repress the ignorant and violent past. The traditional duality of science and archaism, progress and barbarism is misleading. Dracula is not only a "child of the night" (18), rather he is a truly polyvalent creature, who can both illuminate and obscure and who oscillates between the apparently antagonistic realms of light and reason, and darkness and archaism.

Works Cited

"The New Electric Light" (1879). The monologues.co.uk Music Hall Lyrics Collection, n.d. <http://monologues.co.uk/musichall/Songs-N/New-Electric-Light.htm> [accessed 02 April 2015].
Ackroyd, Peter. 2000. *London: The Biography*. London: Vintage Books.
Auerbach, Nina. 1995. *Our Vampires, Ourselves*. Chicago: University of Chicago Press.
Bethell, John. 1843–1844. "On the Atmospheric Bude-light". *Transactions of the Society, Instituted at London, for the Encouragement of Arts, Manufactures, and Commerce.* Vol. 54: 198–200. <http://www.jstor.org/stable/41326947?seq=1#page_scan_tab_con tents> [accessed 24 May 2015].
Byron, Glennis. 2007. "Bram Stoker's Gothic and the Resources of Science". *Critical Survey* 19.2: 48–62.
Craft, Christopher. 1984. "'Kiss me with those Red Lips': Gender and Inversion in Bram Stoker's *Dracula*". *Representations* 8: 107–33.
Jann, Rosemary. 1989. "Saved by Science? The Mixed Messages of Stoker's *Dracula*". *Texas Studies in Literature and Language* 31.2: 273–287.
Mayhew, Henry. 1861. *London Labour and the London Poor* (1851). London: Griffin, Bohn, & Co.
Nead, Lynda. 1988. *Myths of Sexuality: Representations of Women in Victorian Britain*. Oxford: Basil Blackwell.
Nead, Lynda. 2000. *Victorian Babylon: People, Streets and Images in Nineteenth-Century London*. New Haven, CT: Yale University Press.

Page, Leanne. 2011. "Phonograph, Shorthand, Typewriter: High Performance Technologies in Bram Stoker's Dracula". *Victorian Network* 3.2: 95–113.

Punter, David. 2007. "Bram Stoker's Dracula: Tradition, Technology, Modernity". In: John S. Bak (ed.). *Post/modern Dracula: From Victorian Themes to Postmodern Praxis.* Newcastle: Cambridge Scholars. 31–41.

Ridenhour, Jamieson. 2013. *In Darkest London: The Gothic Cityscape in Victorian Literature.* Plymouth, MA: Scarecrow Press.

Rumbelow, Donald. 1975. *The Complete Jack the Ripper.* Boston, MA: New York Graphic Society.

Schivelbusch, Wolfgang. 1995. *Disenchanted Night: The Industrialization of Light in the Nineteenth Century.* Berkeley, CA: University of California Press.

Schneider, Stuart. 2014. *Flashlight Museum*, April 2014. <http://www.wordcraft.net/flashlight.html> [accessed 02 April 2015].

Sedgwick, Eve Kosofsky. 1986. *The Coherence of Gothic Conventions.* New York, NY: Methuen.

Senf, Carol A. 2000. "*Dracula* and *The Lair of the White Worm*: Bram Stoker's Commentary on Victorian Science". *Gothic Studies* 2.2: 218–31.

Spencer, Kathleen L. 1992. "Purity and Danger: *Dracula*, the Urban Gothic, and the Late Victorian Degeneracy Crisis". *ELH* 59.1: 197–225.

Stoker, Bram. 1998. *Dracula* (1897). Ed. Maud Ellmann. Oxford: Oxford University Press.

Taylor, Jonathan. "Lighting in the Victorian Home". *The Building Conservation Directory*, 2000. <http://www.buildingconservation.com/articles/lighting/lighting.htm> [accessed 02 April 2015].

Tristan, Flora. 1980. *London Journal 1840.* Trans. Dennis Palmer and Giselle Pincetl. London: George Prior Publishers.

Vidler, Anthony. 1996. *The Architectural Uncanny: Essays in the Modern Unhomely.* Cambridge, MA: MIT Press.

Warwick, Alexandra. 2007. "Victorian Gothic". In: Catherine Spooner and Emma McEvoy (eds.). *The Routledge Companion to Gothic.* London: Routledge. 29–37.

Jarmila Mildorf
"Light of Life": Gender, Place, and Knowledge in H. G. Wells' *Ann Veronica*

H. G. Wells' novel *Ann Veronica*, which caused a scandal on its first publication in 1909,[1] tells the story of 21-year-old Ann Veronica Stanley, who runs away from her family because she feels oppressed by the rigid moral rules and boredom of her secluded suburban and upper middle-class home. The novel shows how Ann Veronica explores different paths towards alleged freedom in the city of London, her struggles and adventures before she finally settles down as the second wife of Capes, her biology instructor at the Central Imperial College of London. Ann Veronica's discontent at the beginning of the novel is captured in free indirect discourse and finds expression in the following image:

> All the world about her seemed to be – how can one put it? – in wrappers, like a house when people leave it in the summer. The blinds were all drawn, the sunlight kept out, one could not tell what colours these grey swathings hid. She wanted to know. And there was no intimation whatever that the blinds would ever go up or the windows or doors be opened, or the chandeliers, that seemed to promise such a blaze of fire, unveiled and furnished and lit. Dim souls flitted about her, not only speaking but it would seem even thinking in undertones.... (Wells 1993: 5)

The house and, for that matter, a house that has been shut up for the summer, is an apt symbol not only for the domestic sphere, to which women were confined in Victorian family ideology, but also for the potential oppressiveness of this sphere. Windows, which allow women a view outside into the world while at the same time keeping them in their rightful place, can also become a means of shutting women off from the world (cf. Gilbert and Gubar 2000: 202, 278, 292), especially if the blinds are drawn as in the quotation above. What Ann Veronica longs for is light: foremost broad daylight, but also the excitingly glamorous light of "the chandeliers, that seemed to promise such a blaze of fire". Kirsten Hertel, who primarily discusses Wells' novel from the vantage point of its juxtaposition of suburban and city centre spaces, sees in the image of the "light" a metaphor for life (1997: 352–353). Indeed, Ann Veronica herself uses

---

1 Macmillan refused to publish the book on moral grounds, and part of the uproar can probably be attributed to the fact that Ann Veronica was partially modelled on Amber Reeves, a young woman with whom Wells (just like the character Capes in the novel) had an extramarital affair (cf. Coren 1993: 84–86).

this metaphor in a letter to one of her suitors, Mr Manning, to explain to him why she could not possibly marry him, namely because a life like the one she had had at home would make her feel as if she had been "shut in from the light of life, and, as they say in botany, etiolated" (Wells 1993: 77). The scientific term "etiolated" refers to the phenomenon that some plants lose their green colour when shut off from sunlight and begin to grow longer and leaner because they search for light. The light metaphor thus not necessarily relates to life or 'being alive' alone, I argue, but also to a search for knowledge. What Ann Veronica misses is not so much having a life, but having a life that is fulfilled and that affords her knowledge and experience, e.g. in sexual matters.[2] This nexus between images of light and darkness, knowledge and the protagonist's formative experiences, which are also closely linked to certain places, will be at the centre of this paper.

When using images of light and darkness in connection with the protagonist's search for life experience, Wells draws on a metaphorical association which has had currency at least since the Enlightenment: light is or stands for knowledge. As Elisabeth Bronfen contends in her book *Tiefer als der Tag gedacht*, in which she offers a cultural history of images and imaginaries of the night from ancient cosmologies to the present day, night and day as well as darkness and light are ultimately interdependent (Bronfen 2008: 27).[3] All cosmogonies start out from the idea that the world has developed out of some unstructured, impenetrable darkness and that the subsequent rhythmical alternation between day and night, darkness and light, death and renewal forms a counterpoint to the initial chaos in the dark (cf. 37). Against this background, Ann Veronica's "light of life" (Wells 1993: 77) metaphor can be said to touch on questions related to primordial existence and to the essence and ultimate meaning of life. In the Enlightenment period, notably in the philosophy of Descartes, Bronfen argues, light and darkness represented two diametrically opposed poles of knowledge to which human beings had no direct access. Only through thinking could humans ever hope to obtain a sense – though not a fully conscious grasp – of these two poles and thus gradually move towards the 'light' of reason (Bronfen 2008: 91). In this discourse, night and day as images or imaginaries are mapped

---

2 It is interesting to note that, in comparing herself to a plant shut off from light, Ann Veronica inadvertently also admits that she depends on some outside force (the sun) for her development rather than being able to develop independently from within. As we shall see, it is Capes who assumes this role of the 'sun', which ultimately renders the ending of the novel unsatisfactory (see below).

3 The English translation of Bronfen's book was published by Columbia University Press in 2013 under the title *Night Passages: Philosophy, Literature, and Film*.

onto human beings' souls (today one would probably say 'minds') and thus become interrelated facets of (conflicting) inner states. As I hope to show in this paper, Ann Veronica's inner states of 'light' and 'darkness' are often externalised and correlated with natural and artificial light, night and day, while external times of day and places not only form a backdrop for Ann Veronica's experiences but often symbolise more generally her life as a young woman in Edwardian London.

City Lights and Women's Freedom: Walking through London by Day and Night

When Ann Veronica arrives in London after she has run away from home, she is very enthusiastic about her future, and the way she perceives the city reflects her own elated disposition at that moment. Literary London can be said to fulfil the functions of atmospheric setting ("gestimmter Raum"), scene of action ("Aktionsraum") and visual field ("Anschauungsraum") (Haupt 2004: 70)[4] all at the same time. Ann Veronica walks about in the city, which thus becomes her new scene of action, and she observes places and people, taking them into her visual field. Light is used in this context to emphasise London as an atmospheric setting:

> The river, the big buildings on the north bank, Westminster, and St. Paul's, were rich and wonderful with the soft sunshine of London, the softest, the finest grained, the most penetrating and least emphatic sunshine in the world. The very carts and vans and cabs that Wellington Street poured out incessantly upon the bridge seemed ripe and good in her eyes. A traffic of copious barges slumbered over the face of the river – barges either altogether stagnant or dreaming along in the wake of fussy tugs, and above circled, urbanely voracious, the London seagulls. She had never been there at that hour, in that light, and it seemed to her as if she came to it all for the first time. And this great mellow place, this London, now was hers, to struggle with, to go where she pleased in, to overcome and live in. (Wells 1993: 70)

---

4 The term "gestimmter Raum" refers to the fact that places and spaces create a certain atmosphere, which is usually filtered through a character in fictional texts and thus depends on this character's current emotional disposition. "Aktionsraum" relates places to a character's actions: certain aspects of a place can, for example, enable a character to do something or thwart his/her actions. As "Anschauungsraum", places and spaces in fiction primarily function as a physical background or setting against or in which the characters' actions and movements take place. In this sense, places contribute significantly to a fictional work's world-making.

Especially the depiction of the sun infusing the city with a mellow light is an example of what John Ruskin termed "pathetic fallacy", i.e. the (mis)attribution of human emotions to inanimate objects or to plants and animals observed in nature (cf. Ruskin 1987: 362–368). After all, the sunshine cannot be "least emphatic" but it can be perceived as such by someone who is deeply contented. Furthermore, that the buildings on the north bank of the Thames appear to be 'rich and wonderful' and that even the various vehicles coming out of Wellington Street seem to Ann Veronica 'ripe and good' is barely an effect of the 'soft sunshine' alone but also of Ann Veronica's particularly tainted vision 'at that hour, in that light'. It is interesting that the light is specifically mentioned in this context. We will see later that its function is to contrast Ann Veronica's experience of the city at this moment with her experience of the same cityscape later in the day, when the gradual shift to night-time brings forth elements of danger. What is more, the sunlight's quality is presented in almost scientific terms when it is described as 'the finest grained' and 'the most penetrating'. These expressions allude to natural light's division into spectral colours and to the fact that it consists of waves which enter the eye or optical devices. In alluding to scientific terminology (see also the word 'etiolate' above), Wells follows a tradition of writing already observable in Victorian authors like George Eliot, for example (cf. Levine 1988). In this passage, such terminology may relate to Ann Veronica's scientific mind (after all, she takes up biology as her chosen subject of study) because she is the focaliser through whose eyes the entire scene is filtered. It may also underline the narrator's quasi-scientific observation of Ann Veronica as she undergoes the social 'experiment' of breaking free from the confines of her more or less predetermined social position and life path.

Moreover, light is here connected to a moment of initiation: Ann Veronica experiences London "as if she came to it all for the first time" (Wells 1993: 70). Later we are told "that for the first time in her life so far as London was concerned, she was not going anywhere in particular; for the first time in her life it seemed to her she was taking London in" (71). This combination of 'first experiences' and 'light' recurs later in the novel when Ann Veronica's physical desire is awakened and when she is initiated into sexuality (see below). We shall see that, when drawing on this nexus, Wells also resorts to scientific discourse. It is here that Wells is at his most original in his presentation of Ann Veronica, even if, as I indicated, the reference to scientific discourse was by no means innovative anymore at the time when Wells' novel was published.

While London in the day-time appears to Ann Veronica splendid and affords her a new sense of freedom, the same cityscape is suddenly filled with both morally and physically dangerous people such as prostitutes and lecherous men as soon as the sun goes down. We have to remember that Wells' novel is set at a time when walking abroad unchaperoned during the night was still unaccepta- ble and morally repudiated as deviant behaviour for a woman.[5] London thus shifts in all three of Haupt's aspects (atmospheric setting, scene of action, visual field) under the influence of the changing time from day to night, sunshine to darkness: instead of freedom, Ann Veronica increasingly feels oppressed; she experiences the restrictions curtailing her moves and actions; and darkness seemingly "swallows up" (74) her surroundings. Ann Veronica is, for example, shocked when it dawns on her that a woman she sees in the street, "who at the first glance seemed altogether beautiful and fine", must be a prostitute. The recognition of this fact is once again expressed in words associated with darkness and light:

> Then as she drew nearer paint showed upon her face, and a harsh purpose behind the quiet expression of her open countenance, and a sort of unreality in her splendour betrayed itself for which Ann Veronica could not recall the right word – a word, half understood, that lurked and hid in her mind, the word 'meretricious'. [...]
>
> It was a second reminder that against her claim to go free and untrammelled there was a case to be made, that after all it was true that a girl does not go alone in the world un- challenged, nor ever has gone freely alone in the world, that evil walks abroad and dangers, and petty insults more irritating than dangers, lurk. (Wells 1993: 73)

On second sight, the woman's 'splendour', her bright and glamorous appear- ance, turns out to be unreal and 'meretricious', i.e. outward appearance and in- trinsic value or the visible and the invisible clash here. It is also noteworthy that the verb "lurk" is used twice in this excerpt: first, to denote that Ann Veronica's 'knowledge' of something as morally deviant as prostitution is hidden away in her mind and needs to be brought to her consciousness; and second, that danger secretly awaits unprotected women in cityscapes, especially in darkness, as the common collocation of 'lurk' with 'danger' and 'darkness' suggests.[6] Darkness thus becomes significant in two ways, referring to real, physical danger in city-

---

5 As Deborah Epstein Nord (1995: 4) puts it, women in big cities were marked by "their ab- sence, their dubious legitimacy, their status as spectacle, and the eroticization of their presence on the streets". This precarious position in turn made it impossible for women to become observ- ers and to "exercise the privilege of the gaze" (Nord 1995: 4). In this context, it is the more in- teresting that Wells' novel is focalized through Ann Veronica and thus implicitly endows her with an observer position, albeit perhaps an unintentional one.

6 Dictionaries such as the *OED*, the *DCE*, or the *ALD*, for example, typically present under the lemma 'lurk' sample sentences that also contain the words 'dark' or 'darkness'.

scapes on the one hand[7] and symbolising Ann Veronica's naivety concerning all things sexual and immoral on the other.

When Ann Veronica is eventually even pursued by an unknown man, the transition from day to night underlines Ann Veronica's changed attitude towards London, which is also connected to her loss of control and direction:

> The afternoon had passed now into twilight. The shops were lighting up into gigantic lanterns of colour, the street lamps were glowing into existence, and she had lost her way. She had lost her sense of direction, and was among unfamiliar streets. She went on from street to street, and all the glory of London had departed. Against the sinister, the threatening, monstrous inhumanity of the limitless city, there was nothing now but this supreme, ugly fact of a pursuit – the pursuit of the undesired, persistent male. (Wells 1993: 74)

Ironically, the city's artificial lighting (lanterns and street lamps), rather than offering relief and guidance, only illuminate the fact that Ann Veronica "had lost her way". As we are told, she "walked through gaunt and ill-cleaned streets, through the sordid *under side of life*, perplexed and troubled, ashamed of her previous obtuseness" (78; my emphasis), and she cannot avert a "sense of being exposed and indefensible in a huge *dingy* world that abounded in sinister possibilities" (79–80; my emphasis).[8] Another irony or reversal consists in the fact that it is the city's night-life, its dark underside, that 'brings to light', i.e. to Ann Veronica's awareness, her vulnerability not only as a woman walking London's city streets by herself but also as a woman who wishes to live independently. Metaphorically speaking, one can say that night and darkness here engender light or knowledge and thus bring about a moment of recognition.

The dark or rather ill-lit cityscape also forms the backdrop to another adventure Ann Veronica has in the course of her explorations of possibilities to gain independence. When she walks through "lamp-lit obscurity and slimy streets" on a "dark and foggy" morning (162) to join the suffragette movement she is im-

---

7 Cities become dangerous places especially during the night. Statistics show that the hour of day is the greatest decisive factor in determining types of crime (Felson and Poulsen 2003), and that violent crimes committed by adults peak at night-time (OJJDP 2010). These facts alone will influence people's experiences of cityscapes, depending on whether a city is travelled through by day or by night. It is not difficult to imagine how much more time of day must have influenced people's perceptions of a city when the nocturnal cityscape was laden with moral implications: "The literary construct of the metropolis as a dark, powerful, and seductive labyrinth held a powerful sway over the social imagination of educated readers" in the late Victorian age, as Judith R. Walkowitz (1992: 17) points out.

8 This is in contrast to later, modernist novels, e.g., by Dorothy Richardson, where the lighting up of dark city streets through electric lanterns is also associated with greater freedom for women because it allowed them to walk about the city experiencing a less acute sense of danger.

mediately recruited for a nightly raid on the House of Commons. Ann Veronica is asked to come to an appointed place near Westminster, and on arriving there she discovers that it is "a yard in an obscure street" (166), where the "light was poor" (167). This "oblique ruddy lighting" distorts the women gathered in this place and makes "queer bars and patches of shadow upon their clothes" (167).[9] When the narrator describes how eventually a man herds these suffragettes into vans, "leaving the women in darkness" (168), it seems plausible to assume a symbolic implication that relates the suffragettes' cause and actions to blindness and ignorance. This reading is further strengthened through the subsequent, satirical presentation of the raid, which takes on "the forms of wild burlesque" (166), as the narrator already points out before depicting the whole event in detail. The usage of images of darkness and night in connection with Ann Veronica's explorations of freedom contrasts with the presentation of Ann Veronica's awakening to physical desire, which foregrounds the prominence of light and day imagery.

Light, Perception, and Sexual Awakening

At college, Ann Veronica falls in love with her tutor, Capes. Interestingly, her sexual awakening is carefully choreographed as an experience that combines images of light and perception. Its description also resembles the depiction of her initially positive experience of London since the sunlight plays a crucial role. The following passage describes how Ann Veronica becomes aware of Capes' physical attractiveness and, by implication, of her own physical desire for him. All this happens while Ann Veronica and Capes are working on microtome sections, looking at them under a microscope. This instrument, which enables its users to see better or more clearly through the combination of artificially intensified light and magnification, assumes a symbolic dimension as Ann Veronica's scrutinising of Capes' body parallels a microscopic analysis:

> She had been working upon a ribbon of microtome sections of the developing salamander, and he came to see what she had made of them. She stood up and he sat down at the microscope, and for a time he was busy scrutinizing one section after another. She looked down at him and saw that the sunlight was gleaming from his cheeks, and that all over

---

9 The 'queer bars' can be said to anticipate the fact that these women are in fact going to end up behind bars, i.e. in prison. The image may thus implicitly point to a contrast between the suffragettes' (illicit) activities, which take place at night, and patriarchal law, which – some may argue – has the light of reason on its side.

his cheeks was a fine golden down of delicate hairs. And at the sight something leapt within her. Something changed for her.

She became aware of his presence as she had never been aware of any human being in her life before. She became aware of the modelling of his ear, of the muscles of his neck and the textures of the hair that came off his brow, the soft minute curve of eyelid that she could just see beyond his brow; she perceived all these familiar objects as though they were acutely beautiful things. They were, she realized, acutely beautiful things. Her senses followed the shoulders under his coat, down to where his flexible, sensitive-looking hand rested lightly upon the table. She felt him as something solid and strong and trustworthy beyond measure. The perception of him flooded her being.

He got up. 'Here's something rather good,' he said, and with a start and an effort she took his place at the microscope, while he stood beside her and almost leaning over her. (Wells 1993: 130)

The extended use of verbs of perception coupled with expressions of realisation or growing awareness in this excerpt already emphasises the significance of seeing, both physically (seeing through one's eyes) and, on a metaphorical level, emotionally (seeing love). Sunlight plays an important role here as it brings to light the beauty inherent in the beloved person, a beauty that is also captured in a bright colour usually associated with light: Capes' cheeks show a '*golden* down of delicate hairs' (my emphasis). Just as the microscope with its artificial light magnifies for Capes a biological sample, the sun enables Ann Veronica to see more clearly the details of Capes' physical features and thus incites in her a sense of (be)longing. 'The perception of him flooded her being', we are told, much in the way that water can flood an area or, indeed, sunshine can flood a room. The point of this metaphor is to suggest the all-pervasiveness of the emotions aroused. Moreover, by presenting Ann Veronica's physical attraction to Capes in parallel to the beauties observable through the microscope in natural things, the novel implicitly posits desire as something natural and beautiful. Finally, the metaphor also suggests that an object of desire – if seen through loving eyes – becomes magnified just like a research object in microscopic analysis.

The link between sexuality, nature, light, and freedom is foregrounded even more strongly later in the novel when Capes and Ann Veronica elope together and travel to Switzerland. They already cross the Channel "in sunshine and a breeze that just ruffled the sea to glittering scales of silver" (234), and to Ann Veronica the experience of a foreign country resembles the discovery of a new world:

Except for one memorable school excursion to Paris, Ann Veronica had never yet been outside England. So that it seemed to her the whole world had changed – the very light of it had changed. Instead of English villas and cottages there were châlets and Italian-built houses shining white; there were lakes of emerald and sapphire and clustering castles, and such sweeps of hill and mountain, such shining uplands of snow, as she had never seen before. Everything was fresh and bright [...]. (Wells 1993: 235)

The dinginess of English houses and English weather is exchanged for the brightness of the Alps in summertime, which also affords the two lovers unprecedented freedom and moments of intimacy:

Later they loitered along a winding path above the inn, and made love to one another. Their journey had made them indolent, the afternoon was warm, and it seemed impossible to breathe a sweeter air. The flowers and turf, a wild strawberry, a rare butterfly, and suchlike little intimate things had become more interesting than mountains. Their flitting hands were always touching. (Wells 1993: 239)

However, while this beautiful setting in the daytime offers room and opportunities for sensual experiences (the 'love-making' alluded to here most likely refers merely to courtship), the rightful time of day for sexual intimacy remains the night, as is indicated in the following description:

They lay side by side in a shallow nest of turf and mosses among boulders and stunted bushes on a high rock, and watched the day sky deepen to evening between the vast precipices overhead and looked over the tree tops down the widening gorge. (Wells 1993: 240)

The "nest of turf and mosses" with its implicit reference to procreation and family foundation already sets the scene for Capes' and Ann Veronica's sexual union, which is eventually only hinted at when the novel describes how Capes

bent down and rested his hand on her shoulder for a moment, with his heart beating and his nerves a-quiver. Then as she lay very still, with her hands clenched and her black hair tumbled about her face, he came still closer and softly kissed the nape of her neck .... (Wells 1993: 243)

The scene (and indeed the chapter) ends in this romantic tableau of two lovers coming closer physically, and the remainder – merely indicated by four dots – is left for the reader to imagine. Just as the night veils the sexual act, the narrative strategy of leaving things unspoken covers up what around the turn of the century was still difficult to express more openly in fiction. And yet, Capes' heartbeat and nervous quivering as well as Ann Veronica's loosened hair and clenched hands already give away the true nature of the characters' ensuing union.

The usage of the night in connection with Ann Veronica's gaining of experience in sexual matters is both traditional and innovative. On the one hand, the night has had a long tradition in offering lovers a heterotopic counterpoint to, and means of escape from, the control of fathers and parents, as Bronfen (2008: 177) points out. The night hides what is disallowed in broad daylight. Furthermore, the ancient personification of the night as a mother who brings forth daylight[10] implicitly anticipates Ann Veronica's future role as mother and wife and alludes to primordial notions of womanhood and sexuality. At the same time, if considered together with *Ann Veronica*'s theme of the heroine's search for knowledge and experience, the night again assumes a paradoxical function: it ultimately empowers Ann Veronica to 'see' more clearly and to learn for herself what sexuality is all about and how to find an outlet for her physical desire in her intimate relationship with Capes.

The Dimness of Life: Compromise and Disillusionment

Ann Veronica's enthusiasm for Capes and for their relationship corresponds to the sublime setting of the Alps, which is also linked with the idea of absolute freedom. It is therefore not surprising that the lovers' return to a rather conventional form of cohabitation, marriage, also makes Ann Veronica sad in the end.[11] Wells' novel ends with a domestic scene: Ann Veronica, who is by now married to Capes and expects her first child, receives her father and aunt for dinner and they are reconciled. However, the imagery of light and darkness, coupled with the domestic setting that Ann Veronica sought to escape from at the beginning of the novel, suggests an ambivalent, rather than a happy, ending. The dining-room, which is "lit by skilfully shaded electric lights" (Wells 1993: 250), the curtained doorways and the "pretty little hall" (252) convey a sense of enclosure and

---

10 Cf. the myth of Nyx in Hesiod (Bronfen 2008: 37–44).

11 There has been some controversy about how to evaluate the ending of Wells' novel. Feminist scholars have taken issue with the seemingly positive ending, in which Victorian ideals of marriage and motherhood are confirmed. Some have seen in this ending a reflection of Wells' own wishful thinking. Interestingly, some of Wells' own contemporary reviewers partially objected to the novel's ending because it seemed to condone and affirm an essentially illegitimate and immoral relationship. For a discussion of these arguments, cf. John Allett, who himself regards "the conclusion of the novel as unresolved" (1993: 72) and, because of its ambivalence, ascribes to it a more feminist stance than Wells is commonly credited with. Dillon Johnstone reviews Wells' own autobiographical comments about his "libertine novels" (1972: 355) and shows how the author uses mitigating strategies to deflate the scandalous reception of *Ann Veronica*, for example. See also Buitenhuis' claim that "Wells knew [...] that he had dodged the issue in finding such a safe haven for Ann Veronica and Capes after they had dared to flout the conventions of the time" (1984: 90–91).

pettiness not only in the couple's apartment in London but also in Ann Veronica's new life more generally. It certainly forms a stark contrast to the description of the brightness and vast expansiveness of the Swiss Alps in the preceding chapter. Interestingly, Ann Veronica herself, in a moment of distress (she begins to cry), makes this comparison when she exclaims:

> 'Do you remember the mountains? Do you remember how we loved one another? How intensely we loved one another! Do you remember the light on things and the glory of things? [...] Even when we are old, when we are rich as we may be, we won't forget the time when we cared nothing for anything but the joy of one another, when we risked everything for one another, when all the wrappings and coverings seemed to have fallen from life and left it light and fire. Stark and stark! Do you remember it all?' (Wells 1993: 257)

Ann Veronica's speech is agitated as can be seen in the numerous questions and exclamations. This emotionality suggests that she is upset about the fact that her life apparently has returned to being "in wrappers" (5), as she put it at the beginning of the novel. Instead of the 'light and fire' that Switzerland had temporarily offered her, Ann Veronica now finds herself in a closed domestic setting. The "light of life" (77) she had sought and seemingly found has been dimmed down again: metaphorically speaking, the artificial light of the dining room does not suffice to 'illuminate' her life as the brilliant, and natural, sunshine did. Even though Ann Veronica in the end urges Capes never to forget the unique freedom they once participated in – the "light on things and the glory of things" (257) – the reader becomes wary that this memory might fade away just as the light as a symbol of life has already lost its lustre.

As I mentioned above, Wells' novel has been discussed controversially. It is perhaps impossible to determine once and for all whether the novel reaffirms the status quo of women at the time by assigning to Ann Veronica a rather conventional role in the end, or whether Wells offers us a more critical view of the institution of marriage by showing us his protagonist's discontent and mixed feelings. Josette Ducamp (1989: 87) argues that the novel's historical significance lies not so much in the presentation of a woman transgressing social and moral boundaries but in the fact that Wells offers a psychoanalytical interpretation of love and women's sexuality by using symbolic imagery and metaphors. Ducamp discusses, for example, Wells' use of the seasons to point towards Ann Veronica's anxiety about death in life (cf. 1989: 80); her choice of a corsair's bride's costume for a fancy dress ball, which exemplifies Ann Veronica's rebellion against the sexual constrictions imposed by society (cf. 81–83); or the image of dancing, which liberates the body (cf. 84). On one occasion, Ducamp also alludes to the "light of life" metaphor (ibid.) when she quotes Capes, who, in view of the beauty of the Swiss Alps says: "Here we are, [...] shining through each other like light through a stained-glass window. With this air in our blood, this sunlight soaking us ...." (Wells 1993: 246). Ducamp interprets this image as an expression of the characters' almost spiritual discovery of their mutual passion and as a symbol of how they have surpassed a society that is dead and that has 'killed' passion (cf. 1989: 84). However, it is quite surprising that, despite her emphasis on Ann Veronica's sexual emancipation, Ducamp generally fails to take note of the recurrent images of day and night, light and darkness, and of the ways in which these images support the delineation of Ann Veronica's development.

Ann Veronica's move from inexperienced girl to mature woman also follows a spatial pattern: first, she leaves her initial familial and domestic sphere to explore various possibilities of liberation in the city of London; she then experiences real freedom and is initiated into sexuality in the sublime mountainous area of Switzerland only to return yet again to domesticity, as epitomised in the London apartment in which she lives as Capes' wife. Wells' presentation of London illustrates the gendered experience of cityscapes (cf. Watson 2002), especially in a Victorian moral climate. More interestingly, however, the spatial movement is flanked by images of day and night, light and darkness. These images generally support the various places' functions as scenes of action, visual fields, and atmospheric settings. Often, the quality of the light reflects Ann Veronica's own mood, and her perception of places changes with the changed time of day, for example. Moreover, light and darkness come to stand in for life itself, as is suggested by Ann Veronica's own "light of life" metaphor, which is used in several variations throughout the novel. Ann Veronica longs for 'light', and her escape from the 'wrappered life' she so detests culminates in the glorious sunshine of the Swiss Alps, which also becomes a symbol for self-fulfilment and for the discovery of (sexual) love. In the end, however, Ann Veronica experiences a kind of anti-climax when she finds herself in the conventional role of wife and future mother – the very 'wrappered life' she sought to escape. The domestic setting and its potential oppressiveness is further underlined by the image of the "shaded electric lights" (Wells 1993: 250) in the home, which cannot compete with the brilliance of natural light and the life it stands for.

In the context of Ann Veronica's sexual awakening, the symbolism momentarily reverts to the night and thus to more ancient, mythological dimensions, as I pointed out. After all, the night is related to intimacy and fertility and thus draws on a primordial imaginary framework: the night as mother of all. On a critical note, one could argue that, while Wells first makes use of the intersection of time of day, city experience, and gender to seemingly allow the reader an insight into female subjectivity, his investment of especially the night with ultimately clichéd imagery and symbolism undermines this endeavour. To link female sexuality with motherhood on one level seems to reinforce contemporary cultural expectations and more conservative discourses surrounding womanhood. At the same time, the fact that Wells devotes so much space to describing a young woman's exploration of her own sexuality and to endow her with such audacity makes the novel stand out. Here I agree with Ducamp, who also sees the novel's significance in its presentation of female sexual desire. In this regard, the connection between images of light and darkness and Ann Veronica's search for knowledge and experience – again by no means a new nexus – occasionally even makes the novel quite innovative, especially where Wells combines descriptions of moments of initiation or recognition with scientific imagery, e. g., etiolated plants, the spectral division of natural light, or microscopic analysis. Another aspect which renders Wells' presentation of the Enlightenment formula that light equals knowledge more interesting is the fact that it is often the night or darkness that triggers a moment of recognition or that allows Ann Veronica to perceive something more clearly. For example, it is the experience of London in twilight that brings to Ann Veronica's awareness her own gendered position and the immoral side and danger of the previously idealised cityscape. Likewise, her real sexual awakening can only take place under the protective cover of the mountainous night sky. To repeat a metaphor I used above, night can be said to engender daylight, or darkness knowledge.

Works Cited

Allett, John. 1993. "The Ambivalent Feminism of Ann Veronica". *Studies in the Humanities* 20.1: 63–75

Bronfen, Elisabeth. 2008. *Tiefer als der Tag gedacht: Eine Kulturgeschichte der Nacht*. München: Carl Hanser.

Buitenhuis, Peter. 1984. "After the Slam of *A Doll's House* Door: Reverberations in the Work of James, Hardy, Ford and Wells". *Mosaic* 17.1: 83–96.

Coren, Michael. 1993. *The Invisible Man: The Life and Liberties of H. G. Wells*. Toronto: McArthur & Company.

Ducamp, Josette. 1989. "La signification historique de *Ann Veronica*". *Cahiers Victoriens et Edouardiens* 30: 79–92.

Nord, Deborah Epstein. 1995. *Walking the Victorian Streets: Women, Representation, and the City*. Ithaca, NY: Cornel University Press.

Felson, Marcus and Erika Poulsen. 2003. "Simple Indicators of Crime by Time of Day". *International Journal of Forecasting* 19: 595–601.

Gilbert, Sandra M. and Susan Gubar. 2000. *The Mad Woman in the Attic: The Woman Writer and the Nineteenth-Century Literary Imagination*. 2nd ed. New Haven, CT: Yale University Press.

Haupt, Birgit. 2004. "Zur Analyse des Raums." In: Peter Wenzel (ed.). *Einführung in die Erzähltextanalyse: Kategorien, Modelle, Probleme.* Trier: WVT. 69–88.

Hertel, Kirsten. 1997. *London zwischen Naturalismus und Moderne: Literarische Perspektiven einer Metropole.* Heidelberg: Winter.

Johnstone, Dillon. 1972. "The Recreation of Self in Wells's 'Experiment in Autobiography'". *Criticism* 14.4: 345–360.

Levine, George. 1988. *Darwin and the Novelists: Patterns of Science in Victorian Fiction.* Cambridge, MA: Harvard University Press.

OJJDP. Office of Juvenile Justice and Delinquency Prevention. 2010. *Statistical Briefing Book.* 21 December 2010. <http://www.ojjdp.gov/ojstatbb/offenders/qa03401.asp?qa Date=2008> [accessed 20 April 2015].

Ruskin, John. 1987. *Modern Painters* (1856). Ed. David Barrie. New York: Alfred A. Knopf.

Walkowitz, Judith R. 1992. *City of Dreadful Delight: Narratives of Sexual Danger in Late-Victorian London.* Chicago, IL: University of Chicago Press.

Watson, Sophie. 2002. "City A/Genders" (1999). In: Gary Bridge and Sophie Watson. *The Blackwell City Reader.* Malden, MA: Blackwell. 290–296.

Wells, H. G. 1993. *Ann Veronica* (1909). London: Everyman.

Richard Leahy

The Literary Realisation of Electric Light in the Early 20th Century: Artificial Illumination in H. G. Wells and E. M. Forster

Perceptions of electric light in the late 19th and early 20th century witnessed a rapid turnaround of popular opinion on the light source; following its widespread adoption from the 1880s, it was at first met with derision, before perceptions shifted around the fin-de-siècle period, and it eventually developed into the light source that would come to define the 20th century. It evolved from something that was perceived as a 'symbol' of the modern – it was a fantastical presence in the literature of Jules Verne many years before its realisation, for example – to something that solidified a sense of modern life. Electricity, Alex Goody writes, "transformed Victorian culture", and suggests that

> it was electric light that epitomized this transforming power. [...] The coming of electric light is a transformation of culture at a fundamental level; it marks the coming of what Marshall McLuhan, in *Understanding Media,* calls 'the electric age'. (Goody 2011: 7)

However, electric light did not just act as a symbol but also as a catalyst of the late 19th-century emergence of the truly modern world of capitalism and mass-society. McLuhan claims that this early emergence of the electric age had a distinct cultural and psychological impact on the way people thought about modernity: "electric light is pure information [...] a medium without a message," further suggesting that its light "has no content, and in this purity it ushers in a modern world where instant communication connects us in a web of interaction" (McLuhan 2001: 8). McLuhan's analysis of the early electric age suggests a continuation of the burgeoning qualities and perceptions of the processes initiated by the use of gaslight – the invention of a networked system of light took the power of lighting away from the individual; people no longer felt as intimate a connection with the light they 'inhabited' as they did with fire or candlelight. There was a decided difference between perceptions of electric light and gaslight due to the qualities of electricity's light and power. Electricity's light is instant, it is triggered by merely flicking a switch, and therefore it does not contain any sense of personal attachment as the flame does due to the process of lighting it: "You come home, turn on the switch, and without fire, without a match, the whole house lights up" (de Parville 1883: 355). McLuhan's analysis of electric light as a 'medium without a message' can be explained based on the quality of the light itself: it affects its surroundings differently to a flame-light, the shadows are bolder in electric light, vision is more absolute. Unlike gaslight or candle-light, there is less of a sense of romance or poetry to electric light; electric light exposes reality, rather than effecting it as flame-lights do.

Changing Perceptions of Electric Light

McLuhan's suggestion of electric light as pure 'information' corroborates with many lighting historians' accounts of the nature of electric light. It was perceived as harsh, impersonal, and stark. Its whiteness was at the same time praised for its purity and criticised for its blinding power. Upon trials of electric lighting systems in the City of London, it was remarked that using electric light amongst the winding streets and alleys tended "to make the task of lighting with a medium giving intense and sharply-defined shadows one of considerable difficulty" (qtd. in Otter 2008: 244). Wolfgang Schivelbusch states that "[e]lectric light called for completely different treatment, not so much because it was brighter, but mainly because it was incandescent light, which possessed a hard, disembodied, abstract quality" (1995: 177). There was an odd, paradoxical sense of both interconnectedness and isolation to electric light. Unlike any of the artificial light sources that preceded it, illumination was made white, as opposed to a yellow orange, a symbol of man's ultimate control over nature as it now shaped lightning rather than tamed fire.

During the 1880s, electric light struggled to establish any sense of illuminatory dominance in towns and cities. London's Victoria Embankment lit the northern side of the Thames with electric light starting in 1878; however, six years later in 1884, the arc lamps were replaced by the gaslights that had preceded them. It was too expensive to run such an isolated group of electric Jablochkoff candles, and the light of the arc lamps were too bright, so they were repurposed again into lamps that ran off the well-established gas networks of London. It was an issue that hindered the growth of electric light in Britain until the creation of the National Grid in 1926, which connected the fragmented electric networks that emerged across the country in the late 19th century. Alongside the more technologically-minded criticisms of the lights, and the economic problems surrounding their installation, there was also opposition to the quality of their light. Chris Otter summarises these perceptual shifts as he notes that "new perceptual habits had to be slowly learned: instantaneous revolution in colour perception is, perhaps, physiologically impossible since such perception is always relative and never absolute" (2008: 185). Gaslight and electric light became two forces intent on the same goal, yet with intensely different attributes and qualities; people had to learn to understand these contrasts, the phenomenon of abundant light was still barely a generation old and many, especially in cities, had to acclimatise to it. Years earlier, gas had been criticised for many of the same reasons as electric light was now, while in the face of this new light, gas was being praised.

Early reactions to widespread electric light are made explicit in Robert Louis Stevenson's 1881 essay "A Plea for Gas Lamps", which argues against the use of electricity on London's streets. Stevenson's essay encapsulates Otter's notion of clashing perceptual habits that formed in the wake of the rapid changes to artificial light in the 19th century. He extols the virtues of the lamplighter, the last link between humanity and light that was to be eradicated once systems of electric light made their jobs obsolete:

> God bless the lamplighter! [...] God bless him, indeed! For the term of his twilight diligence is near at hand; and for not much longer shall we watch him speeding up the street and, at measured intervals, knocking another luminous hole into the dusk. (Stevenson 1907: 253)

Stevenson's respect for these stewards of light suggests the further loss of any psychological human connection with artificial illumination in the wake of impersonal electric lighting systems. He also touches on this notion as he discusses the psychological importance of understanding the process of lighting, and the actual light of, the gas lamps:

> Now, like all heroic tasks, his labours draw towards apotheosis, and in the light of victory himself shall disappear. For another advance has been effected. Our tame stars are to come out in future, not one by one, but all in a body and at once. A sedate electrician somewhere in a back office touches a spring – and behold! From one end to another of the city, from east to west, from the Alexandra to the Crystal Palace, there is light! *Fiat Lux*, says the sedate electrician. (Stevenson 1907: 253; emphasis in the original)

Stevenson's concerns are reminiscent of the contrast drawn by Gaston Bachelard between the intensely personal poetics and reveries of the flame-light and the electric light of the 20th century: "We have entered into an age of administered light. Our only role is to flip a switch. We are no more than the mechanical subject of a mechanical gesture" (2012: 64). Each major development in 19th century lighting further detached the individual from the agency involved in the processes and qualities of artificial light; Schivelbusch even suggests that many still chose to illuminate their homes by candlelight in the late 19th century, claiming that through this act they "symbolically distanced themselves from a centralised supply" (1995: 162).

Stevenson criticises the quality of electric light, as he writes of the lights of Paris: "a new sort of urban star now shines out nightly, horrible, unearthly, obnoxious to the human eye; a lamp for a nightmare!" (1907: 254). Electric light is seen to be unnatural. Stevenson goes even so far as to state that "[s]uch a light as this should shine only on murders and public crime, or along the corridors of lunatic asylums, a horror to heighten horror" (ibid.). He also reflects on humanity's relationship with the flame as he extols: "Mankind, you would have thought, might have remained content with what Prometheus stole for them and not gone fishing the profound heaven with kites and domesticate the wildfire of the storm" (255). Stevenson directly acknowledges the apocryphal tale of Benjamin Franklin's experiment with the kite, the key, and the lightning as he laments humanity's need to domesticate the violent natural force of electricity. The comparison that Stevenson draws between Prometheus' fire and the taming of electricity helps to indicate the inherently different qualities of electric and flame lighting. The impersonal starkness of the electric light's rays, compared to the softer tones of a flame light, heightens the feeling of distance between the individual and the light. However, even Stevenson could not avoid acknowledging the light as a symbol of encroaching modernity, as he described it as "star-rise by electricity" and as the "spectacle of the future" (ibid.). Electric light's pervasive nature as mass illuminator also emphasised the increasing lack of individuality in the face of an impersonal network of illumination, and the entrance into a highly connected and networked modern age. Stevenson's vision of electric light as a 'horror to heighten horror' exemplifies electric light's capability to create a starker sense of reality in comparison to other artificial light sources – it emphasised the surfaces of its environment more than gaslight ever did, which was more likely to imbue its surroundings with a distinct yellow hue than create the harsh image of electric reality.

Chris Otter documents a number of contemporary opinions of electric light that both corroborate and contrast with Stevenson's essay. He quotes from the records of a meeting of the Association of Municipal and Sanitary Engineers and Surveyors in 1882: "There is something irritating in the electric light, and the effect, if it were universally applied must be [...] to have some disastrous effect on the nerves" (Angell qtd. in Otter 2008: 181). Otter notes how

[t]he flight from yellowness, then, was not universally lauded. Most people were accustomed to seeing yellow. This is how normal light appeared: *ochreous, cosy, peppery.* The whiteness of electric illumination was often an unpleasant shock, registered chromatically as bluish. (Otter 2008: 185; my emphasis)

Similarly, the late 19th-century actress Ellen Terry contrasted the "thick softness" of gaslight with the "naked trashiness" of electricity (2008: 185). However, as electric light grew more widespread it was praised for its ease of use, and for its consistency and dispersal of light. Around the turn of the century, as electric lighting technology improved, attitudes began to shift from disgust at the quality of its light, to a form of acceptance of the illumination as a necessity, and a symbol of the future.

Mass Society and the Acceptance of Electric Light

Electric light was a symbol of modernity in the fin-de-siècle period, and reflected the parallel growth of monopolies and capitalism at that time. Wolfgang Schivelbusch makes an important point on the developing acceptance of electric light in this cultural climate:

> We can now say that in addition to electricity's cleanliness, odourlessness and harmlessness, there was another factor that made it easier for people to accept a central energy source.
>
> The nineteenth century definition of a lamp *before* electrification was as individualistic as the mentality of enterprise capitalism. The new definition was as 'collective' as [manager of General Electric] Steinmetz's opinion that the large enterprise guaranteed individual development. (Schivelbusch 1995: 76; emphasis in the original)

What Schivelbusch suggests is a mirroring of the perceptions of networked artificial light in the changing attitude towards the collective capitalist enterprise, a shift which characterised the movement into the modern period at the start of the 20th century. Gaslight, as Schivelbusch also points out, was met with disdain at first due to the invasive nature of its networked technology. Yet now, instead of perceiving the possible encroachment of a regulated network into their lives, the public attitude shifted towards the reassuring notion of being part of a collected whole. Collective capitalism began to be envisioned as something that should be encouraged in order to benefit both businesses and individual entrepreneurs. There was a shift in perceptions of the idea of the 'mass', from something to be avoided (as evidenced by individuals' ongoing reliance on, and relationships with, candles in the face of networked gaslight and electric light) to something that provided a satisfying feeling of connectivity.

The world was in a state of rapid transition during the early years of the 20th century, not only in terms of its lighting. Schivelbusch remarks that "between

1880 and 1920 electricity began to permeate modern, urban life" (73), further adding that the period of electrification also witnessed changes in the economic structure of capitalism: "The transformation of free competition into corporate monopoly capitalism confirmed in economic terms what electrification had anticipated technically: the end of individual enterprise and an autonomous energy supply" (74). The rapid electrification of light in the last few decades of the 19th century mirrored the growth of corporate capitalism; just as the individual responsibility involved in illuminating a space was taken out of a person's hands by gas and electric networks, economic power, too, was focused within big banks and corporations. Wealth, power, and light were now concentrated in larger corporate entities, rather than in a myriad individuals. Light was now a commodity, especially when considering Karl Marx's definition of the term as something "outside us, a thing that by its properties satisfies human wants of some sort or another" (Marx 2004: 665). Electric light, unlike candle- or firelight, and to a lesser extent gaslight, was a form of illumination that was 'outside us', a commodity that was beyond the control of an individual. Jane Brox states that in the later years of the 19th century, extending into the early 20th century, electric companies, still often called 'light companies', "were private corporations, and since access to electricity was not yet considered the right of every citizen, they felt no obligation to deliver power to individual homes" (2012: 163). Corporations had the capability to control the perceptions of the people, both in terms of the light that illuminated them, and how they understood those lights. They could light the streets, a social space where a large number of people could experience the illumination, yet there was still a distinct lack of homes that were lit by these companies – largely because the companies did not see this as being beneficial to their profit.

Yet as Schivelbusch points out, attitudes towards this corporately driven society were generally more accepting. This was due to the networking of light, power, and money being encouraged to be seen by the individual as providing a sense of inclusion within the 'collective' (cf. Schivelbusch 1995: 76). James Naremore and Patrick Brantlinger identify the confusion that surrounded the idea of the 'masses' as they outline the two blurred definitions that emerged in the late 19th century. Using the example of the German Social Democratic Party, they point out how the rise of Labour parties at the end of the period "sharpened the Marxist identification of the masses with the industrial proletariat preparing to shake off its chains", yet this was disturbed by another definition that was growing, that of the masses as the anonymous, apparently classless "'crowd', the indiscriminate urban conglomeration" (Naremore and Brantlinger 1991: 5). However, they suggest that the factors that contributed to these meanings are "summed up in the phrase 'consumer society', characterized by a sharpening separation between the spheres of production and consumption from about 1870 forward" (ibid.). The idea of the social 'mass' was something that gained more currency in the late 19th century than it ever had before; there was a reflection of the growth of consumer culture in both the evolving idea of the interconnected 'masses' of society and the networks of light and power that pervaded it. The de-individualisation of light, as lighting autonomy was taken from the hands of the individual and placed under the governance of gas and electric companies, mirrored the shift of economy from cottage-industry to much larger corporations. There was, as Schivelbusch documents, "a new faith in technical, scientific and politico-economic planning that emerged around this time" (1995: 75). The lamp, a single source of light, was no longer understood to be complete; instead of the individual source, people began to appreciate the value of being part of an interconnected network.

H. G. Wells' and E. M. Forster's Electrically Lit Dystopias

H. G. Wells' stories deal with the concepts of utopia (and dystopia), degeneration, science, and technology, his texts often intertwining these themes to provide criticism of the uncertain changes and transitions the world was going through at the threshold of the 20th century. Justin E. A. Busch asserts that Wells was "bound by the best science of his day" as he aimed to convey the message that "humanity is subject to the same laws of decay and dissolution as the rest of the universe" (2009: 1–2). Busch's vision of Wells' writing is corroborated by Wells' own interpretation of the Niagara Falls Power Station in 1906:

> The dynamos and turbines of the Niagara Falls Power Company for example, impressed me far more profoundly than the Cave of the Winds; are indeed, to my mind, greater and more beautiful than that accidental eddying of air beside a downpour. They are will made visible, thought translated into easy and commanding things. They are clean, noiseless, and starkly powerful. All the chatter and tumult of the early age of machinery is past and gone here; there is no smoke, no coal grit, no dirt at all. The wheel-pit [...] has an almost cloistered quiet about its softly humming turbines. The dazzling clean switch board, with its little handles and levers, is the seat of empire over more power than the strength of a million, disciplined, unquestioning men. (Wells 1906: 1019)

Wells' account of this monument to electric power unarguably resonates with awe, yet his amazement is tinged with a sense of disbelief that grows into a kind of uncanny concern with the power it holds. It is both natural, in terms of the source of its power, and unnatural at the same time. He sees the structure as being 'will made visible', a symbol of mankind's technological progress and harnessing of nature. To Wells, the turbines and dynamos are 'thought translated into easy and commanding things' – there is a sense of mindlessness to these dynamos, as human thought is infused into these machines which will never stop, the verb 'commanding' suggesting a further sense of imperial subservience to the turbines and the power they generate. Wells' most obvious moment of uncertainty regarding the powerful new technology occurs as he describes the 'dazzling clean switchboard' as 'the seat of empire', further suggesting that the turbines hold more power than 'a million, disciplined, unquestioning men'. He describes the power station as an imperial force, recognising that such power placed under the control of one dazzling switchboard is both awe-inspiring and terrifying at the same time. During this period, Wells' political thinking was distinctly socialist, adding an element of political criticism to his view of electric power as imperialist. Matthew Taunton summarises Wells' socialist reasoning in the following questions: "[...] how could politics and society be made to catch up with the advances of science and technology? How could social and political institutions become more scientific—which for Wells always meant more efficient and ordered?" (2009). In the turbines and dynamos of Niagara Falls, Wells saw the potential of an organised, networked system; a reflection of the advances of science and technology in an imperial, not a socialist sense.

Wells' understanding of electric power may be seen earlier in *The Sleeper Awakes*. Originally published as *When the Sleeper Wakes* in 1899, but revised and republished under the new title in 1910, the novella postulates the role of electric light in a supposedly utopian future, as well as providing an insight into Wells' trouble to truly envision a society that followed his socialist ideals. The story focuses on an insomniac named Graham, who falls into a trance-like sleep on the Cornish coast of England in the late 19th century only to awake 203 years into the future as owner and master of all of Earth following inflated interest on his accounts and a number of financial bequests.

Awakening to two centuries' worth of technological, architectural, and social development, Graham's first impression of the new, future London is one of

> overwhelming architecture. The place into which he looked was an aisle of Titanic buildings, curving spaciously in either direction. Overhead mighty cantilevers sprang together across the huge width of the place, and a tracery of translucent material shut out the sky. Gigantic globes of cool white light shamed the pale sunbeams that filtered down through the girders and wires. (Wells 2005a: 42)

In this future world, technology and industry have continued on the trajectory set by the rapid industrialisation of the 19th century. Electric lighting develops into a technology that unites night and day. The electric whiteness 'shames' the sun, meaning that even during the day electric light holds sway over this ultra-modern London; day and night have been placed under the same governable order. When taken through the city upon his awakening, Graham ponders this idea: "he had observed no windows at all. Had there been windows? There were windows on the street indeed, but were they for light? Or was the whole city lit day and night for everyone, so there was no night there?" (55). The light is psychologically oppressive, the lack of windows suggesting a distinct lack of liminality or transition. The whole city is constantly lit 'for everyone', the lighting system suggests the state of extreme totalitarianism that now dominates London. It makes everyone the same and places everyone under the observation of the central power that governs the city. Wells later directly addresses the socialist character of his new London as he writes about how Graham "thought of Bellamy, the hero of whose Socialistic Utopia had so oddly anticipated this actual experience" (59). Wells refers here to Edward Bellamy's *Looking Backward: 2000 – 1887,* an 1888 novel that attempts to predict the effects of technological and commercial growth on America, a place which was also electrically lit. Bellamy notes in the novel: "Electricity, of course, takes the place of all fires and lighting" (1996: 57). However, Wells' image of 22nd-century London is by his own admission far from Bellamy's socialistic ideal: "But here was no utopia, no socialistic state" (Wells 2005a: 59).

As rebels liberate Graham from his apartment, they fight against their subjection through their own use of light:

> Then abruptly they were in darkness. The innumerable cornice lights had been extinguished. Graham saw the aperture of the ventilator with ghostly snow whirling above it and dark figures moving hastily. Three knelt on the van. Some dim thing – a ladder – was being lowered through the opening, and a hand appeared holding a fitful yellow light. (Wells 2005a: 68)

By defeating the light, the rebels freeing Graham gain a sense of autonomy they do not have in the face of the electric glare. They use a 'fitful yellow light' to rescue him, which we may presume is a flame-based light due to its colouring and behaviour. This reinforces the idea that the individual flame light signifies notions of independence and agency. By extinguishing the electric globes and returning to flame light, the rescuers cultivate the independence and agency that is unattainable by them under the constant gaze of the electric light.

Electric light speaks for power in *The Sleeper Awakes*, as its infrastructure does to Wells seven years later at Niagara Falls. Those who control the light control the power; the authoritarian government attempts to control the riotous city by causing the people to be "thrown into confusion by the extinction of the lights" (86). Light is power: the rebels extinguish it – thereby neutralising its power – in order to rescue Graham, and later the 'Council' switches it off to cause confusion among the rebels. Further adding to the flame's connotations as a light of freedom and autonomy, Wells describes how "[h]ere and there" in the government-enforced darkness "torches flared, creating brief hysterical shadows" (107). The flame is a symbol of ultimate catalytic change; within its light there are connotations that cannot possibly be drawn from the static starkness of electric light. The shadows the flame casts are themselves 'fitful', 'brief', and 'hysterical', thus further suggesting a sense of movement and liminality that is impossible within the authoritarian gaze of electric light.

When the lights are turned off in an attempt to disorientate the people rising against the Council, it is possible to see how removing this framework for social behaviour fragments the people of a city so assimilated within a network: Graham "felt a curious sensation – throbbing – very fast! He stopped again. The guards before him marched on; those about him stopped as he did. He saw anxiety and fear in their faces. The throbbing had something to do with the lights" (83). As the electric lights begin to throb in the darkness, Graham *feels* the pulse of the darkening lights. By awakening into a society that has been forced into interconnectedness, a totalitarian state symbolised by the electric light, Graham has himself become assimilated into the network. He himself throbs with the beat of the lights. Wells describes the globes of electric light in an organic way, making them the living heart of the city: "Each huge globe of blinding whiteness was as it were clutched, compressed in a systole by a transitory diastole, and again a systole like a tightening grip, darkness, light, darkness, in rapid alternation" (84). The terms 'systole' and 'diastole' link the organic function of the cardiac system to the illumination, which ensures a constant flow of work, productivity, and subservience to a greater system, acting as both a symbol of the connection and as a literal aid to the systematic whole.

After the city is captured, the Council defeated, and Graham instated as 'Master', London is relit: "The re-illumination of the city came with startling abruptness. Suddenly he stood blinking, all about him men halted dazzled, and the world was incandescent" (107). The city re-emerges in a false dawn, the rise of light is not gradual but instant; this acts as a reminder that even though the malevolent Council has been ousted, their systems and structures are still in place, as later evidenced by Ostrog's attempt to take control of London and continue the legacy of the totalitarian regime. The systems, both social and technological, that have developed in this 19th-century vision of the future, are the true enemies of the text. Technological connectivity and networks are seen as eradicators of what may be deemed natural and of any idea of the individual self. Wells makes this explicit, stating: "After telephone, kinematograph and phonograph had replaced newspaper, book, schoolmaster and letter, to live outside the range of the electric cables was to live an isolated savage" (127). Electricity is presented as the technology of a modern utopia, but its connectivity encouraged society to grow into a faceless mass. To remain an isolated individual and shun the worth of electricity was to be a 'savage'. Furthermore, Graham considers the changes since his own Victorian era as inevitable:

> He perceived at once how necessarily the state of affairs had developed from the Victorian City. The fundamental reason for the modern city had ever been the economy of co-operation. [...] Those promises had by this time attained their complete fulfilment. The locked and barred household had passed away. (Wells 2005a: 178)

Wells describes a system of living that had developed from the growing capitalist tendencies of the Victorian period into a society where an individual's only role in life was to contribute to this network of production and consumption. In this future London, society has evolved into a more interconnected and social space. Everything is shared, and individuality is destroyed in an example of capitalist totalitarianism. Wells presents us with an extreme form of his contemporary reality, where the completely modern vision of electric lights illuminating cities was an indicator of the colonisation of industry and capitalism over everyday life, and massively suggestive of an individual's need for inclusion within a network.

In E. M. Forster's "The Machine Stops", a 1909 short story, electric light illuminates a dystopian society in a similar, yet subtly different way to Wells' *The Sleeper Awakes*. The light, confined to an interconnected underground network of individual dormitories is different to the penetrative surveillance of Wells' novel. The illumination is less aggressive in its control over its subjects, but still sinister in its spread and connectedness; the way Forster describes his characters' response to light suggests that they are pacified by the illusion of choice and control that their electric lights provide them with. Forster writes about how the governing body of 'the Machine', The Committee, attempts to "defeat the sun" (2011: 17). This last effort at conquering the natural order of day and night meant that

> [i]t was the last time that men were compacted by thinking of a power outside the world. The sun had conquered, yet it was the end of his spiritual dominion. Dawn, midday, twilight, the zodiacal path, touched neither men's lives, nor their hearts, and science retreated into the ground, to concentrate herself upon problems that she was certain of solving. (Forster 2011: 17)

The idea of defeating the sun is an inherently 19th-century one, bound together with the development of artificial light in the period; Luckiesh writes that

[w]ithout artificial light, mankind would be comparatively inactive about one half its life-time. [...] The working-periods in many cases may be arranged in the interests of economy, which often means continuous operations. The sun need not be considered when these operations are confined to interiors or localised outdoors. (Luckiesh 1920: 8)

By defeating the sun, humanity extends waking and working hours, yet also loses the most natural rhythm of life. The Committee of Forster's story replaces the balance of night and day with individuals' ability to control their own light within their personal living spaces, turning a natural order into something artificially manipulable – it reinvents the symbiotic gulf of light and dark as a synthetic copy, something that provides a sense of decision and choice to the inhabitants of the Machine.

Forster describes the loneliness Vashti feels after her son Kuno abandons their video phone call, and how the instantaneousness of the light she generates, and the control she has over it reinvigorates her: "For a moment Vashti felt lonely. Then she generated light, and the sight of her room, flooded with radiance and studded with electric buttons, revived her" (Forster 2011: 6). By having control over her own lights, Vashti is comforted by her ability to illuminate herself and her surroundings. Yet this is only an illusion of choice, she does not 'generate' the light, it is generated for her by the Machine itself and put into practise by the electric buttons that litter her apartment. This illusion plays on the differing psychological processes of switching on an electric light. The instantaneous starkness of electric light suggests a rapid transition from one state to another, reinforcing Vashti's instant revival at the switch from dark to light. It sublimates the lack of natural order of the cycles of day and night into something designed to suggest control within a regulated network. Forster repeatedly uses the phrase "she made the room dark and slept; she awoke and made the room light" (9, 44), which suggests the monotony and artificiality of the false sense of autonomy Vashti experiences; her experiences are devalued, and her life falsified by the hyper-real copy of the day-to-night cycle. It is Bachelard's 'administered light'; Vashti is "no more than the mechanical subject of a mechanical gesture" (Bachelard 2012: 64). She is only permitted control to reproduce a distorted substitute for the natural cycle of night and day.

Kuno, her son, begins to see the Machine differently to his mother; he sees it for what it is: a controlling, authoritarian force. He asserts that "[e]verything is light, artificial light; darkness is the exception" (Forster 2011: 26). He sees darkness as liberating, something outside the authoritarian technocracy of the Machine. It is telling that Forster's final words as the story ends, the two characters buried in the rubble of the collapsed Machine, speak of them looking up into an "untainted sky" (56). They find liberation in the natural order of day, yet they are still buried within the technology of their world; the two seem incompatible. Electric light, in this instance, creates subservience and passivity; it provides an illusion of control as it satisfies the Machine's population's desire for light, and a semblance of autonomy and agency, without relinquishing the reliance on the Machine it has cultivated in its citizens. However, within Forster's more realist fiction, we can see a subtly different attitude towards electric light, and a growing acceptance of its illumination.

Electric Light From 1900 to 1914: Growth and a New Literary Realism

In the early years of the 20th century, electric light was perceived both in a way that reinforced images of it as authoritarian and faceless in its dissolution of the individual, and also as a light of the inevitably modern. In industrial countries, smaller networks of cities and towns became more interconnected after a long period of "flimsy and impermanent" (Otter 2008: 214) electric infrastructures; experiments with alternating current were arguably the most important improvements that led to electric light's widespread use. However, it is important to remember that electricity was still limited to densely populated urban areas – it was only introduced in many more rural areas decades later. City dwellers had "grown accustomed to electric light" (Brox 2012: 155) in public and, thanks to new innovations in different types of currents, in homes and interior spaces too. According to Brox, in cities with highly developed electric networks, "any open flame, however bright, had become easy to disparage and at best carried a hint of nostalgia" (159). Electric light was a beacon of the modern age the western world was entering at the start of the 20th century, as direct contrasts between electric light and its predecessors tinged the flame-based lights with associations of the past.

Matthew Luckiesh suggests that the most radical improvement in electric lighting technology occurred in this period. In 1906, the filaments of electric light bulbs were first 'treated' in the heat of an atmosphere of hydrocarbons which meant that the filaments could burn brighter and longer and were more reliable (1920: 131). In 1907, electric incandescent light bulbs provided illumination at the average candle-power of 18.0, yet by 1914, this figure had more than doubled to 38.2 candle-power. Electric light was constantly improving and evolving during the pre-World War I years. Cities and homes were growing brighter all the time; it is hard to comprehend that less than 100 years prior to this growth of electric illumination, people were still allowing medieval attitudes towards the order of day and night to dictate their lives. Electric light became more consistent in the early 20th century; newly developed networks ensured its light was brilliant and easy to use, and perhaps most revolutionary, it was instant. Chris Otter describes how electric light switches "made illumination tame and easy" (2008: 231). Electric light's instantaneous nature had eradicated the processes involved in illuminating one's self or home; in the switching on of electric light, we may understand how the personal act of lighting became removed from the actions of lighting that had been associated with other light sources – the tending to the fire, the lighting of candles or gas. Artificial light was easier to control now, yet it meant that an individual held less of an intimate connection with it. *Electrician* magazine described it as an "infant" that had "fought its way onward, and soon arrived at lusty manhood" (qtd. in Otter 2008: 244). George Ponderevo, in H. G. Wells' 1909 semi-autobiographical novel *Tono Bungay*, speaks of how thirty years previously, in school, he learnt "[of] the electric light as an expensive, impracticable toy, the telephone as a curiosity, electric traction as a practical absurdity" (Wells 2005b: 85). Wells' narrator is in disbelief at how quickly technology had improved by the early years of the 20th century; the first example he notes is of electric light, which had moved beyond being an expensive toy, and towards more widespread public appreciation.

Within E. M. Forster's realist fiction, we can see a divergence of the beliefs that characterised electric light in "The Machine Stops", and a reflection of the adoption of the illumination into everyday modern life. Forster's 1907 bildungsroman *The Longest Journey* establishes electric light through the acknowledgment of the reality of its effects and qualities. In its first scene, we meet Rickie Elliot and his Cambridge college friends as they discuss existential quantum mechanics by the light of a match and the fireplace. Yet this philosophical reverie is broken by Agnes Pembroke, a woman who will later become Rickie's wife, as she enters the room and interrupts their discussion: "She turned on the electric light. The philosophers were revealed with unpleasing suddenness" (Forster 2006: 6). The instantaneousness of the electric light reveals the philosophers for what they are – dreaming college students – and breaks the philosophical reveries encouraged by the flames.

Agnes herself both embodies the qualities of electric light, and is symbolised by it. Forster presents her as the charge that changes Rickie's life. Rob Doll suggests that "Rickie's diseased imagination, which had invested Agnes with reality, has now led him to a false vision of love" (Doll 2002). Rickie's life is changed by his feelings for the woman: he abandons his writing career and begins teaching at Sawston School but eventually their relationship falls into "emptiness and sterility" (Doll 2002). During a conversation between Ansell and his friend Widdrington in the British Library, Widdrington remarks on Agnes: "Well, I am inclined to compare her to an electric light. Click! She's on. Click! She's off. No waste. No flicker" (Forster 2006: 179). Agnes' symbolic relationship with electric light makes her more real, and suggests her as the light that casts a sense of solidity on her relationship with Rickie. There is no sense of ambiguity as there is in the opening passages of the book where the Cambridge boys, lit by the light of match and hearth, discuss the reality of a cow's existence. Agnes' own nature and reality is likened to the sharp duality of electric light; her stoniness of character insinuated through the inflexibility of the light source – always on or off, nothing in between the two states, and without any waste or imagination.

As Otter writes,

> [s]witches allowed one to control one's light: they also potentially enabled the control over the light of others or the formation of technologically mediated hierarchies of perceptual control. Illumination technology could, thus, reify social relations. (Otter 2008: 232)

Although Otter is discussing the social reification that takes place in institutes such as prisons, Agnes' first action of turning the electric light on and illuminating the philosophising scholars suggests her dominance over the realities and perceptions of Rickie. The novel is concerned with pronouncing 'reality', and the choices we face in life, in determining our own idea of it. Electric light symbolises those choices through its absoluteness, as well as Agnes' role in limiting Rickie's imagination and creativity; it is either on or off, real or not. Upon the death of Gerald, Agnes' first husband, Rickie muses: "Who wants visions in a world of Agnes and Gerald?", immediately after which Forster describes how "he turned on the electric light and pulled open the table-drawer", taking out a short story that he now deems "nonsense" (2006: 60). Electric light acts as a symbol of the realities of life, and the absoluteness of Rickie's decisions. There is no need for 'visions' in a world lit by electric light; within its glare everything is relentlessly real – creativity and imagination are shattered by its starkness.

A similar sense of the solid realities of electric light may be read in Forster's *Howards End*. Electric light's glare in this story often highlights the reality of the characters' situations. For instance, the electric lights in various homes indicate the shallowness of middle to upper class desires to constantly move up the social ladder. The Schlegels gaze over at the Wickham Mansion where the Wilcoxes live, and desire a place like that for their own, yet their Aunt Juley points out: "Turn the electric light on and it's almost the same room. One evening they may forget to draw their blinds down, and you'll see them; and the next, you yours, and they'll see you" (Forster 2000: 51). Electric light exposes, Aunt Juley pointing out here that when caught in the glare of the light, the Schlegels' and the Wilcoxes' lives are not that different. This electric light exposes the reality of the Schlegels' desire to establish themselves more firmly within society, and draws a sharp contrast between their desires and Leonard Bast's reality. Bast's home, a place "known to house-agents as a semi-basement, and to other men as a cellar" (Forster 2000: 41) is also lit with electric light. It is described as

> an amorous and not unpleasant little hole when the curtains were drawn and the lights turned on, and the gas stove unlit. But it struck that shallow makeshift note that is so often heard in the modern dwelling-place. It had been too easily gained, and could be relinquished too easily. (Forster 2000: 41)

Electric light now finds itself lighting many different types of homes, Leonard Bast's cellar dwelling a much different type of home to the Schlegels' apartment. The electric light that dominated everything in "The Machine Stops", brings people together in a different way in this realist text. Through presenting Bast's home as a not unpleasant little hole lit by electricity, we get an idea of the 'makeshift note' of the 'modern dwelling-place'. Bast's home, the Schlegels' apartment, and the Wilcoxes' Wickham Mansion are all presented as stepping stones to something else; there is no sense of home to them as there is, for example, to Howards End itself.

Forster views the rural home as "England's hope", describing Hilton, where Howards End is situated, as being

> ruled, not by a London office, but by the movements of the crops and the sun. [...] [T]hey kept to the life of daylight. They are England's hope. Clumsily they carry forward the torch of the sun, until such time as the nation sees fit to take it up. (Forster 2000: 276)

Electric light, as it does in *The Longest Journey,* cultivates thoughts of the modern realities of life; Forster sees a much more 'noble' and old-fashioned natural life in the understandable order of day and night. Everything is starkly obvious in electric light, whereas there is a sense of mysticism and romance in other light sources. Consider, for example, the depiction of Mrs Wilcox, as Forster describes how "[t]he light of the fire, the light from the window, and the light of a candle-lamp, which threw a quivering halo round her hands, combined to create a strange atmosphere of dissolution" (2000: 58). Mrs Wilcox exists in a strange confluence of lights, a mystic figure who suggests the romance and mysticism of history – a sharp contrast to Agnes' electric harshness in *The Longest Journey.*

The image of the ever-evolving London bears the brunt of Forster's criticism of the new England in *Howards End.* For example, Margaret describes how she "hates this continual flux of London. It is an epitome of us at our worst – eternal formlessness; all the qualities, good, bad and different, streaming away, streaming for ever" (156). Furthermore, Forster depicts night-time in the city in a way that blurs the perceptual differences of the various artificial light sources:

> London was beginning to illuminate herself against the night. Electric lights sizzled and jagged in the main thoroughfares, gas lamps in the side streets glimmered a canary gold or green. The sky was a crimson battlefield of spring, but London was not afraid. (Forster 2000: 104)

Alongside being confusing in its perceptual patterns, London visualises the 'battlefield' of old and new in the form of its lights, which clash so clearly in the night-time. Old London, and old values, are nostalgically defined by the green and gold gaslights, and the new, modern city and its associations are symbolised by the sharply threatening sizzling and jagged electric lights; yet there is a sense of acceptance of this type of light now, suggested by Forster claiming that London was 'not afraid' of these changes.

In these early years of the 20th century, as electric lighting grew more prominent, its literary use grew to be more symbiotic within the language and poetics of the text. Progressing from the image of Wells' detached, monolithic electric lights, more at home within Science Fiction than reality, electric illumination became something within which a sense of humanity could be found in the literature of the early 20th century. Agnes Pembroke's electric stoniness, and the binding nature of electric light in the Schlegel, Wilcox, and Bast homes suggest that electric light became more intimately involved with identifiable individuals; it connected them as opposed to making them part of a faceless mass. Instead of anonymising these characters within a network, this early 20th century use of electric light emphasises how they are individuals within a collective – a subtly different notion to the networked authoritarianism of Wells' early depictions of electric light. As was the case with the changing attitudes towards corporate capitalism and connected cultures, people began to understand electric light for its value within a network; knocking out one lamp would not trip them all. There was a sense of solidarity to the interconnected light source, which fit in well with the altered image of collectivism. The public felt connected to the instantaneousness of electric light, and were astounded at the possibility of instant light as technologies improved. The increasing adoption of electric light in the cities and towns of this period, and the improvement in its technology and delivery, humanised its literary presence in the early years of the 20th century. Perceptions of electric light evolved quickly in the last decades of the 19th century; the technology was changing and improving almost constantly, and while some associations did linger (see "The Machine Stops", and electric light's ability to expose in Forster's realist texts), it was treated in a much more personal way in the early 20th century than it had been before. It helped with individual characterisation rather than creating a sense of mass alienation. Electric light's acceptance, and subsequent realisation in literary fiction, was due to a combination of a gradual perceptual acceptance of the new type of white light and an improvement in the delivery and accessibility of technology. This is reflected in its literary use, as it develops from something that lit early scientific romances in a positive, exploratory way, to a technology that defined an emerging technological claustrophobia around the turn of the century, before becoming gradually accepted, and something that did not simply act as a symbol of the 'other', but as something which could speak symbolically for a sense of humanity.

Works Cited

Bachelard, Gaston. 2012. *The Flame of a Candle*. Trans. Joni Caldwell. Dallas, TX: The Dallas Institute of Publications.

Brox, Jane. 2012. *Brilliant: The Evolution of Artificial Light*. London: Souvenir Press.

Busch, Justin E. A. 2009. *The Utopian Vision of H. G. Wells*. Jefferson, NC: McFarland and Company.

de Parville, Henri. 1883. *L'Electricité et ses applications*. Paris: Librairie de l'Académie de médecine.

Doll, Rob. 2002. "E. M. Forster's *The Longest Journey:* An Interpretation". <http://www.emforster.info/pages/lj.html> [accessed 27 May 2015].

Forster, E. M. 2000. *Howards End*. London: Penguin Books.

Forster, E. M. 2006. *The Longest Journey*. London: Penguin Books.

Forster, E. M. 2011. *The Machine Stops*. London: Penguin Books.

Goody, Alex. 2011. *Technology, Literature and Culture*. Cambridge: Polity Press.

Luckiesh, M. 1920. *Artificial Light: Its Influence on Civilisation*. New York, NY: The Century Company.

Marx, Karl. 2004. "Capital". In: Julie Rivkin and Michael Ryan (eds.). *Literary Theory: An Anthology*. Malden, MA: Blackwell Publishing.

McLuhan, Marshall. 2001. *Understanding Media*. New York, NY: Routledge.

Naremore, James and Patrick Brantlinger (eds.). 1991. "Introduction: Six Artistic Cultures". *Modernity and Mass Culture*. Bloomington, IN: Indiana University Press.

Otter, Chris. 2008. *The Victorian Eye: A Political History of Light and Vision in Britain, 1800–1910*. Chicago, IL: University of Chicago Press.

Schivelbusch, Wolfgang. 1995. *Disenchanted Night: The Industrialisation of Light in the Nineteenth Century*. Berkeley, CA: University of California Press.

Stevenson, Robert Louis. 1907. "A Plea for Gas Lamps". *Virginibus Puerisque*. Boston, MA: Small, Maynard & Co.

Stoker, Bram. 1996. *The Jewel of Seven Stars*. Gloucestershire: Alan Sutton Publishing.

Taunton, Matthew. 2009. "H G Wells's Politics". <http://www.bl.uk/romantics-and-victorians/articles/h-g-wells-politics> [accessed 27 May 2015].

Wells, H. G. 2011. "The Diamond Maker". In: *H. G. Wells: The Complete Short Story Omnibus*. London: Gollancz.

Wells, H. G. 1906. "The Future in America: A Search of Its Realities—The End of Niagara". *Harper's Weekly* 50. July 21: 1019.

Wells, H. G. 2005a. *The Sleeper Awakes*. London: Penguin.

Wells, H. G. 2005b. *Tono Bungay*. London: Penguin Books.

Laura E. Ludtke
Public and Private Light in Virginia Woolf's *Night and Day*

In "Street Haunting: A London Adventure", Virginia Woolf reflects that an evening of "rambling the streets of London" is the "greatest pleasure" (2009b: 187).[1] Though her representations of characters walking the city streets in novels like *Mrs Dalloway* (1925) and *Jacob's Room* (1922) might be more familiar, Woolf's essay is significant because it solidifies the association of what she calls 'street haunting' with one's sensual, emotional, and intellectual experience of the city. Part encomium to the city at night, part meditation on the relationship between consumerism, women's urban autonomy, and the city's illumination, "Street Haunting" belongs to a longer literary tradition of depicting walking the streets of London by night.[2] For, though the pleasure Woolf describes radiates from the 19th-century tradition of the *flâneur*, first articulated by Edgar Allan Poe in his short story "The Man of the Crowd" (1840) and prominently theorised by essayist Charles Baudelaire in *The Painter of Modern Life* (1863), literary representations of nocturnal perambulations date to the Middle Ages and relate to ideas of transgression in both the liminal and criminal sense (Beaumont 2015: 5–15). Woolf's 'street haunting' is transgressive because she feels the need for an "excuse" or to use a "pretext" to justify her deeper desire for "rambling the streets of London" (Woolf 2009b: 177); her urban experiences are mitigated by a sense that "[o]ne must, one always must, do something or other; it is not allowed one simply to enjoy oneself" (185).

Despite the similarities in the way she explores the sensual delights of the city by night, characterising her pleasure as a desire to be anonymous in a crowd and to be delighted by the stimulation of urban culture, implicit in the above sentiment is that her experience will always be less autonomous than that of the *flâneur*, whose gender is male by default. And, though the existence of the *flâneuse* – the female equivalent of the *flâneur* – is a critically contested concept, Woolf's description of 'street haunting' proposes an alternative mode of experiencing and representing the city to that offered by the *flâneur*, a mode that is aware of and engages with the Baudelairian figure but is neither

---

1 Woolf's essay was first published in the *Yale Review*, NS 17 (Oct. 1927). The version quoted here is from *Selected Essays*, ed. David Bradshaw (2009).
2 For a recent and extensive discussion of such representations, see Beaumont (2015).

derivative of nor equivalent to it.[3] Other scholars have argued convincingly for treating the term *flâneur* as both an ideologically and historically contingent term, for an understanding of the 'urban observer' that extends into the early 20th century and thus includes more female experiences, and for understanding the *flâneuse* as more than just a female *flâneur*.[4] And, while I am indebted to these findings, I am here more interested in the connections Woolf draws in the essay between her experience of, and imaginative engagement with, London and its unique lightscape. For Woolf, the city's sensual delights are predicated on its illuminary conditions:

> How beautiful a street is in winter! It is at once revealed and obscured. Here vaguely one can trace symmetrical straight avenues of doors and windows; here under the lamps are floating islands of pale light through which pass quickly bright men and women, who, for all their poverty and shabbiness, wear a certain look of unreality, an air of triumph, as if they had given life the slip, so that life, deceived of her prey, blunders on without them. But, after all, we are only gliding smoothly on the surface. The eye is not a miner, not a diver, not a seeker after buried treasure. It floats us smoothly down a stream, resting, pausing, the brain sleeps perhaps as it looks.
>
> How beautiful a London street is then, with its islands of light, and its long groves of darkness [...]. (Woolf 2009b: 178)

This passage is significant for a number of reasons, not in the least as it offers a critical apparatus for approaching the relationship between urban observer and visual phenomenon.

Firstly, it demonstrates how essential light is to Woolf's ideal urban observer, as she aligns the eye with illumination so that illumination subtends vision. In the chiaroscuro of the 'islands of light and long groves of darkness', the eye 'floats' from island to island, taking in a series of seemingly disconnected images. In this way light also indirectly subtends narration, though the eye cannot "compose [images] in such a way as to bring out their more obscure angles and relationships" (179) and make a unified or coherent whole out of their fragments. Light may elide the experiences of the urban observer but it does not necessarily connect them.

---

3 A number of excellent articles have approached the topic from different perspectives, notably Janet Wolff's "The Invisible Flâneuse: Women and the Literature of Modernity" (1985), Griselda Pollock's *Vision and Difference: Feminism, Femininity and Histories of Art* (2012), and Elizabeth Wilson's "The Invisible Flâneur" (1992). More recently, in *Streetwalking the Metropolis*, Deborah Parsons has demythologised the *flâneur* (2000).

4 See Lynda Nead's *Victorian Babylon* (2000) and Parsons' *Streetwalking* (2000).

Secondly, in this passage, Woolf engages with three experiences Parsons identifies in her re-reading of Baudelaire as significant to the modern city: "ephemerality, transience, and the chance encounter" (Parsons 2000: 21). Woolf treats beauty as something that is 'at once revealed and obscured'; figures 'pass quickly' through 'floating island[s] of pale light', and one can only 'vaguely [...] trace' the shapes of the sensory world. Because of the way the eye moves, images seem impermanent, though in this passage, as in the mind, they are superimposed, rendering one's experience of light in the city like a palimpsest.

Thirdly, this passage – taken in the context of the essay as a whole – suggests that, for Woolf, urban observing can be a dissociative process, as the observer is separated both from the subjects of her gaze – the 'bright men and women' who 'wear a certain look of unreality' – and from herself, reduced only to her 'eye', her 'brain'.[5] This is a process informed by the street's illuminary conditions. Yet, 'street haunting' can also be a way of writing the self across the city, as in her urban reverie, facilitated by her use of free indirect discourse and memory, Woolf becomes others in her narrative imagination, and to encounter past selves (2009b: 186–187). The city, then, is the ultimate locus of the interpenetration of past and present, temporal boundaries which are delimited by the larger chiaroscuro of night/day.

Finally, though Woolf privileges the visual in this passage, 'street haunting' is not only a visual experience essential to her imaginative engagement with the city but supplementary to the movements of her 'floating', 'gliding' eye. Thus, if walking the city by night is a bodily experience, walking is a way of knowing.[6] On 31 May 1928, Woolf observed in her diary that "London, itself perpetually attracts, stimulates, gives me a play & a story & a poem, without any trouble, save that of moving my legs through the streets" (Woolf 1983: 186). Discussing Woolf's notebooks, Hermione Lee remarks that

---

5 Both Parsons and Lee also comment on this passage, respectively noting that it "epitomizes the perspective of the woman amidst the crowds, empathizing to the point of identification with strangers glimpsed in passing in the city" (Parsons 2000: 27) and in it Woolf "becomes 'an enormous eye' which can leave 'I' behind, leave the 'tether' or a 'single mind' and 'the straight lines of personality', and deviate into the 'bodies and minds of others'" (Lee 1996: 413). Parsons also draws on the work of Georg Simmel, for whom, in *The Philosophy of Money*, the "artistic gaze [...] needs this detachment in order to find formalized beauty in the city, which 'becomes aesthetic only as a result of increasing distance, abstraction and sublimation'" (Parsons 2000: 30).
6 I am here indebted to the observation that Carolyn Marvin makes in *When Old Technologies Were New* that the "body is the most familiar of all communicative modes, as well as the sensible center of human experience" (1988: 109). See also Beaumont (2015: 11); Parsons (2000: 41); and Nead (2000: 7).

[s]he [i. e. Woolf] *wanted* boundaries to overlap: it was a form of cross-fertilisation. Above all, she wanted reading and writing to infiltrate each other. In [her essay] 'How Should One Read a Book?', both reading and writing are compared to walking through city streets." (Lee 1996: 413; emphasis in the original)

"Street Haunting" revisits and formalises ideas Woolf first articulated in *Night and Day* (1919), where she explores the relationship between the urban observer and London's distinctive lightscape.[7] *Night and Day* is often regarded as Woolf's most traditional and least experimental work, in part due to how Woolf herself later conceived it (1978: 231). Despite its status as work-in-practice, the novel is important not only because of the way it prefigures the experimentation of her later novels but also, in its own right, because of Woolf's privileging the experience of the female observer and her representation of the city's light. Provisionally entitled *Dreams and Realities*, the novel traces the lives, aspirations, and relationships of four intertwined characters: Katharine Hilbery, the daughter of a respected bourgeois family; Ralph Denham, a solicitor from a large family in Highgate; William Rodney, a poet and a bureaucrat with a good name and an overbearing concern with appearing the gentleman; and Mary Datchet, a suffragist from a rural parsonage now living and working in London. Though each one is driven by their own dreams and realities, their nocturnal and diurnal perambulations are at the heart of their relationships with one another and of the narrative itself. Together, Katharine, Ralph, William, and Mary represent the possibilities available to individuals in a society on the cusp of great social change, in the ways in which they adopt or eschew the traditions and mores that typify their parents' generation.

This was a liminal moment Woolf herself experienced – the seven years after the death of her mother, Julia Stephen, in 1895 until the death of her father, Leslie Stephen, in 1904 in which she lived at 22 Hyde Park Gate. Reflecting on this experience in "A Sketch of the Past", written in the last two years of her life, she remarks that "[t]wo different ages confronted each other in the drawing room at Hyde Park Gate. The Victorian age and the Edwardian age" (1989: 160). In her mind, her father and her two half-brothers, George and Gerald Duckworth, "were living say in 1910" and she and her sister, Vanessa, "were living in 1860" (161). Describing her childhood home as "the cage" (128), it is clear where Woolf stood on the society to which she was expected to belong and why she felt it was so important to revisit this period in fiction.

7 Woolf's second novel was first published in 1919 by Duckworth. All quotations are from the 2009 Oxford World Classics edition, edited by Suzanne Rait.

Beginning by considering the impact of light on women's interactions with the urban, this chapter will explore the implications of a female scopic authority and possibilities of female subjectivity as they are manifest in the relation of gender and the city in the novel. It will then offer a (re)conceptualisation of public and private space that emerges during the Great War, when Woolf begins writing her novel, in terms of two important consequences of the increased illumination: surveillance and the 'chance encounter'. The generational conflict between the Victorian/Edwardian ideologies Woolf depicts takes places across the private, domestic spaces and the city's publicly illuminated spaces in the novel. It is a conflict that Woolf dramatises alongside the younger generation's struggle for autonomy against authority and traditional gender roles in the late 19th and early 20th centuries.

In *Night and Day*, Woolf weaves a complex web of night/day, dark/light, dream/reality, solitude/community, illusion/perception, the clandestine/surveillance, obscurity/observation, autonomy/authority, and public/private. From the opening sequence, describing Katharine's inner process on that early October evening, as her stray thoughts "leapt over the little barrier of day which interposed between Monday morning and this rather subdued moment, and played with the things one does voluntarily and normally in daylight" (2009a : 3), Woolf pays close attention to the relationship of light with social conventions. In daylight, Katharine and the others escape into daydreams and dream worlds, keep their innermost selves secret from one another, and feel the most isolated in the crowded streets of the city. At night, the characters become more self-aware and self-reflective, feel part of a compelling intellectual community, and come to realise that the complexities revealed by these artificial lights correspond more accurately to the reality to which they ascribe than to what is seen in the "cold light of day" (413). This is because, as Elisabeth Bronfen contends, Woolf's texts "perfect a refusal to ban the night from the concerns of the day, even as they resist the temptation to remain in the night so as to refuse the responsibility posed by the day" (2013: 26). By challenging the traditional associations of night and darkness with dream, solitude, illusion, the clandestine, obscurity, autonomy, and the private and of day and (natural) light with reality, community, perception, surveillance, observation, authority, and the public, she invites her readers to question what is 'normal' during daylight hours and what is 'normal' after dark.[8] In the novel, not only is light a way of making sense of urban experience,

---

[8] According to Bronfen, this is a challenge inherent to the Enlightenment project itself, as "the night – with all the fears, promises, desires, and fantasies it evokes – always contains elements of the day that precedes and succeeds it" (2013: 15).

but it also becomes a metaphor for the experience of modernity in the city. However, just as light encourages the autonomy of the female urban observer, it also facilitates a superintendence over those whose alternative experiences of, and interactions in, the city can be seen as transgressive or subversive to the accepted mores. Yet, by aligning her narrative with a female scopic authority, Woolf makes representing alternative modes of experiencing and representing the city to those offered by the *flâneur* not only possible but plausible.

Light, Gender, and the City

Until the end of the Edwardian period, the dominant representations of women in the city had been as objects of the male gaze – whether as subversive, transgressive, or exceptional – and were based on perceptions of the urban woman's lack of respectability and lower social status. Though it was not acceptable for women of certain social positions to be unaccompanied in the city, especially at night, working class and impoverished women could not afford such scruples.[9] Both Woolf's predecessors – female authors, artists, and urban observers such as Amy Levy, Berthe Morisot, Edith Wharton, Kate Chopin, and Olive Schreiner – as well as the New Women types represented in fiction – Ethel Henderson in H. G. Wells' *Love and Mr Lewisham* (1899), and Marian Yule in George Gissing's *New Grub Street* (1891), to name a few – are often considered exceptions to the virtual nonexistence of a "female urban expression" (Parsons 2000: 4–5) or cited as proof of the impossibility of the *flâneuse* in a world were women lacked the "freedom to walk and gaze in public spaces" (6). This is not to say that women did not have urban experiences, rather that such experiences were rarely recorded by men and, even more rarely, by women themselves. Where Woolf is concerned, she offers not only the possibility of a female urban observer, but two possible models, contrasting the experiences of Katharine and Mary. While her use of free indirect discourse may not be as established and finessed as it is in her later novels, especially in *Mrs Dalloway*, she uses it to move between multiple perspectives. Woolf's use of this narrative technique "acknowledges the variety, fragmentation, and sense of being situated that are inherent within subjectivity" (Snaith 1996: 138), as well as the multiplicity of the female urban experience. She does not portray the city "as a monolithic, fixed realm, but as the meeting of the empirical fact and private interpretation and re-

---

9 For more on this, see Leonore Davidoff, *The Best Social Circles: Society, Etiquette and the Season* (1973).

sponse" and, in giving a "voice to many", as the "narrator is continually surrendering the story to the various characters" (Snaith 1996: 146), she establishes an experience of the city as diverse as her characters. For, with no fixed perspective, no single voice or experience has more authority than the others, allowing the female urban experience to flourish, to be discordant.

Katharine and Mary represent different ways in which women of diverse circumstances interact with, and relate to, the city. Whereas Katharine, aged twenty-seven, lives with her parents in a very affluent part of Chelsea, Mary, who is a few years younger than Katharine, works for a suffragist organisation in their office in Russell Square and has lived in London semi-independently for six months. While Mary is autonomous in terms of how she spends her time, where she lives, and with whom she associates, she is nevertheless financially dependent on her father, a country cleric. At this time, very few middle-class women earned money from their work, which was primarily voluntary. Woolf, for instance, gave classes at Morley College in 1905, but was not paid for her work (cf. Whitworth 2009: 11–12). While both women are relatively young and technically spinsters, Mary's experience of the city is more indicative of the New Woman's relationship with the city than that of Katharine. The Hilbery's liberal values afford Katharine a certain degree of autonomy, though their social prominence and literary pedigree mean she is nevertheless obliged to participate in the "tea-parties of elderly distinguished people" (Woolf 2009a: 3) hosted by her mother and to pay social calls to family friends. Mary, lacking these social and class connections, has no such obligations and, as a result, has greater autonomy in the city and in her daily life. This contrast is particularly evident in the reasons for which both Mary and Katharine walk about the city; for the former it is part of the pattern of her workday, while for the latter it is a form of leisure, of escape.

Katharine's primary occupation, helping her mother prepare her grandfather's biography, does not permit her interactions with the city. Mary's at-homes – informal social occasions where friends and acquaintances meet up to participate in passionate political and intellectual debate and to give papers, as William does – offer Katharine a greater opportunity to engage with those outside her class and neighbourhood than her 'employment' or family life permit.[10] As such, Mary is arguably a bigger influence in expanding Katharine's world than any of the novel's male characters. These interactions also tend to occur

---

10 These at-homes are reminiscent of those hosted by Thoby Stephen shortly after he, Virginia, and Vanessa moved to 46 Gordon Square in 1904 (Lee 1996: 208–215; Whitworth 2009: 10–11). It was from this group of young men – many of whom Thoby and his brother Adrian had met while at Cambridge – and women that the Bloomsbury Group later coalesced.

at night, though some of Katharine's solitary forays into the city involve running errands, but many are just to wander. These forays elicit experiences she has difficulty expressing. For, though walking the city streets provides an escape from the confines of her domestic life as well as a location for autonomous thinking, the streets also coincide with a desire she cannot quite articulate. In one such instance, while walking with Ralph after taking tea with Mary, Katharine shuts out her confused thoughts about Ralph and Mary "from all share in the crowded street, with its pendant necklace of lamps, its lighted windows, and its throng of men and women, which exhilarated her to such an extent that she very nearly forgot her companion" (Woolf 2009a: 97). Not only does this passage produce the first of the novel's two most significant illuminary metaphors – 'the pendant necklace of lamps' – but it also demonstrates the way in which the urban environment can serve as an extinction of the self, and the sensual experience of the streets as a distraction from present concerns. For Woolf, night is an essential condition of such an experience – a sentiment she more fully articulates in "Street Haunting", wherein at night "the champagne brightness of the air and the sociability of the streets are grateful" and the "evening hour, too, gives us the irresponsibility which darkness and lamplight bestow" (2009b: 177).[11] In another instance, following an afternoon of paying social calls with her mother, when Katharine decides to wander from Bond Street to Temple rather than to visit William, the indecision and emotional crisis prompted by her wanderings bring her to visit Mary, whom she both admires and envies for "living alone and having [her] own things" (2009a: 291). The city strengthens connections between the two women and the anonymity of the street allows her the solitude necessary to process existential questions, while the association of private space with private thoughts is inverted.

Mary, on the other hand, conceives of her experience of the city in a manner more similar to what Woolf describes in "Street Haunting". She has a greater imaginative engagement with the city and, unlike Katharine, finds the anonymity offered by the crowd to be unifying rather than dissociative. For, in the city, "she liked to think herself one of the workers [...] [;] she liked to pretend that she was

---

11 In *Night Passages*, Elisabeth Bronfen explores the importance of the night to Woolf, arguing that the author is "equally concerned with counting life in nights as much as days" because she "thinks of the day in relationship to and in terms of the night" (2013: 404). As the culmination of her study on the relationship of night to the Enlightenment project, which attempted to extinguish the night and its clandestine associations, Bronfen proposes that Woolf's "nocturnal scenes" offer the ultimate revision of the Enlightenment project, as they "ultimately always lead back into a day" (404).

indistinguishable from the rest" (76). Mary is, of course, not 'indistinguishable', as her inner processes are distinct from those she imagines herself among. Rather, her observations and reflections upon these urban experiences make her exceptional.

What is more, Mary's imaginative engagement with the city produces not only the second of the novel's most significant illuminary metaphors but also addresses a number of tropes associated with urban modernity: the city versus the country, the relationship between London and Empire, and the influence of technology on daily life. Working with wool in her rooms near the Strand while waiting for her guests to arrive for her Wednesday at-home, she conjures up images of

> [...] the various stages in her own life which made her present position seem the culmination of successive miracles. She thought of her clerical father in his country parsonage, and of her mother's death, and of her own determination to obtain education, and of her college life, which had merged, not so very long ago, in the wonderful maze of London, which still seemed to her, in spite of her constitutional level-headedness, like a vast electric light, casting radiance upon the myriads of men and women who crowded round it. And here she was at the very center of it all, that center which was constantly in the minds of people in remote Canadian forests and on the plains of India, when their thoughts turned to England. (Woolf 2009a: 46)

Framing her progress as the move from somewhat rustic beginnings to the 'wonderful maze' of civilisation, Woolf perpetuates the association of modernity and civilisation with the city – an association Raymond Williams identified in *The Country and the City* (1973) as having been constructed by writers and artists over time. The city is a place we have come to equate with "the idea of an achieved centre: of learning, communication, light" (1); an association that also intensifies over time. Williams uses the example of Richard Le Gallienne's poem, "A Ballad of London" (1895) to explain that the poem's depiction of gas lighting represented "an obvious image for the impressive civilization of the capital" (1973: 228), for, in the late 19th century, this "version of a glittering and dominant metropolitan culture had enough reality to support a traditional idea of the city, as a centre of light and learning, but now on an unprecedented scale" (229). In *Night and Day*, the metaphor of the city as 'a vast electric light' updates the metonymic association of civilisation with the city's lights for the Edwardian imagination.

And yet while it is evident from this passage that Woolf contributes to the portrayal of London as having an unparalleled importance and of the modern urban experience as being the most desirable experience, this metaphor is not without its problems. For the 'vast electric light' is the product of a single, intense source of illumination. Its purpose is to cast a general, yet overwhelming beam (i.e. the collection of many rays) or light, thereby illuminating the whole city, perhaps even the Empire, at once. The concept behind it makes a case for the undesirability of over-illumination. As the editor of the *Electrician*, a popular technical journal, wrote, "to light a whole city with a huge electrical sun is a great scientific achievement; but it is not the sort of light that any body wants" (qtd. in Otter 2008: 9). Taken as a metaphor for narration, it further betrays the undesirability of total narrative omniscience, especially when compared with the Katharine's 'pendant necklace of lamps' or 'the islands of light and long groves of darkness' from "Street Haunting", which more accurately portray Woolf's preference for free indirect discourse. Indeed, throughout the novel, Woolf depicts a rich illuminary lightscape which complements perceptual processes, for, though shadows can only fall when light is cast, too much light extinguishes particularity, nuances, and variegation produced by the interplay of light and dark. Should everything be illuminated at once or equally, in narration as in life, the sensual delight of such a chiaroscuro would be lost. As a representation of artificial light in the novel, however, the image of the 'vast electric light' is at odds with Woolf's careful depiction of a rich, diverse lightscape. For though the light "cast[s] radiance upon the myriads of men and women who crowded round it", the crowds are attracted to the light, to the city like moths and the light, like London itself, extends its influence like rays beyond the city, to the ends of the Empire. Ultimately, however, the 'vast electric light' is confined to Mary's imaginative engagement with the city; she is brought back to the present moment by the "nine mellow strokes [...] from the great clock at Westminster itself" (2009a: 46). Yet for both women, though they use different illuminary metaphors to articulate their engagement with the city, light remains an important and perceptive way of comprehending the city.

With these metaphors in mind, the comparison Woolf invites by contrasting Mary's and Katharine's urban experiences is important because of the way it promotes a plurality of female experiences in the city, privileging their female scopic authority. Though both women are friends, each, at times, appears resentful of the autonomy or advantages they perceive the other to possess and each desires the happiness for which they feel they must compete. This false competition is indicative of the limited scope for female autonomy and for the fulfilment of female desire during the Edwardian period – a limitation which contributes to the prevention of the widespread emancipation of the female experience, urban or otherwise – as well as a tendency to categorise non-transgressive, non-subversive female urban experiences as exceptional. And yet, by privileging alternative, female urban experiences, in which women interact with London in new and sometimes transgressive ways, Woolf is writing modern London – and its distinct lightscape – into being.

Life Under the Lamp Post: Surveillance and the Chance Encounter

In *Night and Day*, Woolf explores the boundaries between self and other as well as those between public and private space. She is acutely aware of the differences between light and darkness, the light of day and the light of night, and how public and private space(s) are conceived. Indeed, she captures a moment when the division between what is conceived as public and what is conceived as private is shifting in terms of generational conflict, gender roles, and an increasing sense of individual autonomy. This moment coincides with an increase in illumination in public spaces, due to the adoption and increased regulation of gas and electric street lighting throughout the city[12] and, while this increased illumination made the streets safer, it also heightened the visibility of transgressive behaviour, creating a conflict between safety and privacy or intimacy. And, at the same time, the fact that "wartime controls had increased the efficiency of the supply industry" (Bowers 1982: 161) was challenging the principle of the competitive supply of electricity by corporations and local authorities to autonomous consumers, as electricity was gradually being considered a public utility. Yet, while this shift was welcomed by domestic, commercial, and industrial consumers, "regulation of electrical distribution [...] provided a more contentious topic" for the corporations themselves, as "their priority was the preservation of the value of their existing investments, confining public control of the generation and co-ordination of bulk electrical supply" (Gillespie 1989: 114). Of course, the autonomy of consumers was preserved in the way in which they consumed electricity and had their houses fit with electricity. But, taken together, these changes signal both a conflict of progressive and conservative values, and a clash between the politics of individualism and localisation on the one hand

---

12 While the first electric street lights were introduced in London in 1878, due to the city's bureaucratic and administrative idiosyncrasies as well as to technological setbacks and the cost associated with replacing an established, functional lighting system with a less cost-effective one, gas was the predominant form of street lighting until after the Great War. According to Stephen Inwood, in 1911, only 32,000 of London's "121,000 public gas and electric lamps" were electric (2005: 292). Of the nearly 90,000 gas lamps, most "were now much brighter and more economical than before" (292) (cf. Bowers 1982: 108, 112, 158; Gillespie 1989: 114; Inwood 2005: 285, 291–292; and Otter 2008: 250–251).

and collectivism and centralisation on the other. In *Night and Day*, these conflicts manifest as Woolf's association of artificial light with themes of watching, looking, observing, overseeing, and surveillance. As Bronfen explains, such an association of knowledge with power and, consequently, control is an extension of the Enlightenment project to make that which is knowable controllable (2013: 65). The concerns for propriety of the older generation coincide with a certain prurient interest in the relationships that are being negotiated amongst the younger generation, between Katharine and Ralph, William and Cassandra, as well as between Katharine's cousin Cyril and the mother of his two children. As part of this, the double bind of visibility is that artificial illumination increases such connections and creates a possibility for the "chance encounter" (2000: 21), described by Parsons as being essential to the experience of the modern city.

In *La Flamme d'une chandelle*, Gaston Bachelard asserts that "tout ce qui brille voit", or 'everything that casts a light sees', positing a reciprocal relationship between light and surveillance (1961: 48). Light, often in the concentrated form of the lantern but also in the pools of light cast from a succession of street lamps or the dazzling light emitted from shop windows at night, permits individuals to see as well as be seen. Darkness carries with it the threat of that which cannot be seen and may conceal nefarious or transgressive individuals in the shadows created by the increased street lighting. This is because, as Foucault figures it, night resists order, control, and reason (cf. Bronfen 2013: 66). Darkness also gives the impression that whatever transpires at night, regardless of actuality or circumstances, is criminal or immoral. The increased illumination in streets and other public spaces, however, carries its own social consequences for those who are seen at night. Light neither translates into an increased clarity of understanding of what is observed, often at a distance, nor accompanies an immediate reconsideration of acceptable nocturnal behaviour. In *Night and Day*, this disjunction is particularly evident in the conflicting attitudes regarding visibility, propriety, privacy, and comprehensibility.

After leaving a social gathering at Mary's flat, Katharine and William walk along the Embankment – a recurrent location in literary representations of nocturnal London in the late 19th and early 20th centuries. Alone together, they are visible in a public space. The moonlight invokes the trope of illicit love while increasing visibility and, in theory, safety. Their public aloneness makes William uncomfortable, as he is in love with her, and is, for this reason, more concerned about appearances. Concerned they are contravening the standards of conduct which he believes in, he misreads Katharine's eagerness to return home as her being conscious of her reputation (cf. Woolf 2009a: 66). In turn, she derides his outmoded concern for her reputation, and though William's concerns are made to appear thus for comedic and thematic effect, they are not without merit, as what others have observed later threatens his relationship with Katharine's cousin Cassandra and as well as Katharine's relationship with Ralph. And, while Katharine may not have understood the possible consequences of being seen with William on the Embankment at the time, her family's reaction to the discovery that her cousin Cyril is cohabiting with the mother of his children presages their reaction to her decision to end her engagement with William and enter into a relationship of sorts with Ralph. Their reaction also galvanises her ideas about relationships and the importance of her autonomy.

As the family's ostensible patriarch, Katharine's father should be responsible for addressing the situation which he considers a matter of Cyril "behaving in a very foolish manner" (109). When Katharine wonders whether her father should force Cyril to get married, though he replies that "it's none of our affair" (110), what he means is that it should be none of 'his' affair. For, by having his daughter report it to her mother on his behalf, he simply transfers his responsibility, relying on his wife's meddlesome nature and her obligation to interfere and protect the family name. While Woolf's portrayal of Mrs Hilbery and her sister-in-law, Mrs Milvain, in the subsequent scenes is an unflattering caricature of the meddlesome, middle-aged upper-middle-class woman, it nevertheless reveals the burden placed on women to maintain the reputation of their families. Katharine's indecision about "what she thought of Cyril's misbehaviour" (113) turns to disillusionment when she learns her aunt has been spying on Cyril and his "wife" (122), and when she hears her aunt and mother conspiring against her cousin, his lover, and their children as though they were not autonomous beings: "How they talked and moralised and made up stories to suit their own versions of the becoming, and secretly praised their own devotion and tact!" (125). Throughout the novel, Katharine's aunts act as proxies for her parents, not only as receptors for gossip but as active agents of surveillance. Later in the novel, Mrs Milvain pays another call to the house on Cheyne Walk to dutifully report and confirm what others have seen the two almost-couples doing:

> People are saying that William goes everywhere with you and Cassandra, and that he is always paying her attentions. [...] At the Zoo they were seen alone together. [...] They say his manner is very marked—he is quite different when she is there. (Woolf 2009a: 428)

Mrs Milvain essentially admits she has "been spying upon [them, ...] following [them] about London, overhearing what people are saying" (432). Mrs Milvain's confrontation of her niece culminates when Katharine rejects her advice about "married love" (430) and asks her aunt to leave, declaring: "We don't understand each other" (429). This lack of understanding recurs with William ("You've never understood each other", Cassandra explains [436]), with her father, who admits that he is "completely in the dark" (488) about Cassandra's relationship with William, with her mother ("we're different" [509]) and with herself, as "gaining upon [her] clearness or sight against her will, and to her dislike, was a flood of confusion, of relief, of certainty, of humility, of desire [...]" (476). This series of misunderstandings demonstrates the importance of comprehension and the prominence of surveillance in the novel. Indeed, many instances of not only observation but surveillance are made possible by street lighting – as I will discuss below – so that the reader becomes complicit with the surveilling gaze of the undetected observer. And, while Woolf is not explicit that Mrs Milvain and her proxies conduct their surveillance with the aid of artificial light, nor are they encouraged by improved illuminary conditions, she has established that consequences of improved visibility and the disjunctive attitudes towards what behaviour is acceptable in public at night.

The conflict between visibility and privacy culminates when her father discovers she has broken her engagement to William Rodney – "you've very strange ideas of the proper way to behave .... People have drawn certain conclusions [...]" – and, when she refuses to disclose the nature of her relationship with Ralph Denham, he prohibits the latter from entering the family home (500). Mr Hilbery cannot stand not-knowing, seeing only in a half-light, so to speak, something which Katharine and Ralph themselves proclaim nearly impossible to express in words. This is, however, precisely the point of Woolf's fiction here: to write around the ineffable and experiences of it. Yet, the position from which Mr Hilbery and his sister are operating rests on the assumption that light should equal knowledge or comprehension and that complete comprehension is not only desirable but achievable. Woolf's free indirect discourse, supplemented by the city's fragmentary illuminary conditions, disrupts these assumptions, as social propriety – the polite manifestation of control – gives way to individual autonomy. This effect is particularly apparent in Woolf's description of Katharine's visits to Lincoln's Inn Fields in search of Ralph, a passage which recalls the passage in "Street Haunting" in which she develops the relationship between urban observer and visual phenomenon:

> The blend of daylight and lamplight made her an invisible spectator, just as it gave the people who passed her a semi-transparent quality, and left the faces pale ivory ovals in which the eyes alone were dark. They tended the enormous rush of the current – the great flow, the deep stream, the unquenchable tide. She stood unobserved and absorbed, glorying openly in the rapture that had run subterraneously all day. (Woolf 2009a: 463–463)

Not quite reduced to an eye/I, Katharine's perceptions are interpenetrated with those of the crowd; her autonomy as urban observer takes the form of 'glorying' in the experience.

What is often cast as a generational conflict is, in fact, also an ideological one, as is evident from the way in which Mrs Hilbery approaches Katharine's decision to break her engagement with William. For, the certainty of Mrs Hilbery's romantic ideals deflates the misinformed speculations of her sister-in-law as well as her daughter's equivocations. In her attempt to convince Katharine that marriage is the only way forward, Mrs Hilbery uses terms her daughter can understand – the language of light – to articulate the certainty she felt in the moment when she saw the play of light on the water's surface during her honeymoon on an ocean steamer (cf. 508–509). Yet, the language of light is not universal, as the lights that confirm her mother's certainty, for Katherine, come to represent the "fragmentary nature of their relationship" (498): "'we see each other only now and then–' / 'Like lights in a storm'" (447). For Katharine, her mother's dream, recalled from the not-so-distant past, is just an "ancient fairy tale" (508), one of the many she has heard while working with her mother on her late grandfather's biography: her mother "knew [she] was in love; but we're different" (509). The 'dream' recalls Woolf's analogy for Mrs Hilbery's "spells of inspiration" being akin to "will-o'-the wisp" (508; 37). However, as inherited familial mythology, the 'fairy tale' helps Katharine approach that "enchanted region" (534) described at the close of the novel. This 'enchanted region' is a place where daydream and reality can interpenetrate to create a new reality: "Moments, fragments, a second vision, and then the flying waters, the winds dissipating and dissolving; then, too, the recollection from chaos, the return of security, the earth firm, superb and brilliant in the sun" (534).

Another way of reading Katherine's attempts to resolve this conflict is as an example of Hegel's nocturnal thinking[13] – a concept Bronfen explores with great acuity, but does not connect with Woolf's *Night and Day* (cf. 2013: 67). Nocturnal thinking is, as Bronfen explains, essential to the development of the individual subject's "mind/spirit", in that night not only "contain[s] the potential fulfilment of the mental spirit", but also allows the individual to "know itself in its self-differentiated absoluteness" (ibid.). It is also central to the Enlightenment counter-narrative in that nocturnal thinking reveals the involvement of night in day. Indeed, "the play of dichotomies engendered by this reversion to the night should be thought of as a productive oscillation, comparable to the ordinary experience

---

13 Nocturnal thinking, while not a term used by Bronfen or Hegel, is a useful term I have adopted here for heuristic purposes.

of the alternation between night and day" (75). More simply put, for Bronfen, the process of nocturnal thinking is necessary for any self-revelation. And, while nocturnal thinking presupposes a return to day through the night, it is signifi-cant that Woolf's novel ends, quite firmly, in the night, with Katherine and Ralph whishing each other "Good night" (Woolf 2009a: 535). This suggest that, while nocturnal thinking can be productive, the dichotomies it addresses cannot always be resolved. In the case of the 'rare and wonderful chance' Ralph's offer to friendship poses to Katherine, the constant interplay of light and shadow ul-timately renders such a relationship unknowable, uncontrollable. For, with Ka-therine standing "upon the threshold", the light from within the house "lay in soft golden grains upon the deep obscurity of the hushed and sleeping house-hold" (ibid.).

Returning to the conflict between visibility and privacy, while public street lighting is what permits Katharine and William, William and Cassandra, and Katharine and Ralph to be surveilled, as I've suggested above, the overhead glow cast by lights hung from lamp posts also allows them to surveil others. When Ralph follows William and Katharine from Mary's flat on the Strand to and along the Embankment, despite his distance, he can see them well enough in the lights from the street to recognise them, though "the effect of light and shadow, which seemed to increase their height, was to make them mysterious and significant" (63). His surveillance, while benign, is deliberate, not coinciden-tal, but the experience is uncanny, and what he sees lacks context, rendering any observations he might make inconclusive, and potentially erroneous. It also re-alises William's worries that a friend might see him and Katharine together, though the consequences he fears are not so much destructive as transformative, for they serve as a catalyst for Ralph's desire for Katharine.

In the developing language of public space, street lighting, especially the lamp post, is associated with the 'chance encounter', as it allows those who would otherwise be strangers in the night to recognise each other (and their com-mon purpose) upon a chance meeting. This is the case when, later that same night, Ralph encounters William "beneath a lamp-post" (68). After a brief con-versation on the street, "with his eye on the lamp-post" (68) and passing under a series of "monitory lamp-post[s]" (69), he returns with William to the latter's rooms. Yet, despite this familiarity, the cone of light created beneath the lamp post is a common meeting place to which Ralph and William return throughout the novel, as its light creates a sense of familiarity and the conditions of recognition in a way that both counters and accompanies the strangeness of the night. At the same time, there is a double standard by which William and Ralph's nocturnal encounters and interactions are treated, especially when com-pared to those of Mary or Katharine, for the two men can be alone, or rather alone together, without eliciting much suspicion. This suggests that, as yet, the 'chance encounter' is not an urban experience accessible to women, whether or not they possess the burgeoning autonomy of the urban observer.

For this reason, it is important to read the lamp post not merely as a place of encounter but also of realisation, since the concentration of light from its lamp focuses the narrative and isolates the individuals from that which lies beyond its light. It is not only the place in which Katharine becomes most certain of her love for Ralph, looking "at his face isolated in the little circle of light" (329), but also that where William realises that Ralph aspires to marry Katharine. In this latter instance, Woolf is most explicit about the lamp post's epiphanic potential.

> [William and Ralph] looked at each other, queerly, in the light of the lamp. Fools! They seemed to confess to each other the extreme depths of their folly. For the moment, under the lamp-post, they seemed to be aware of some common knowledge [...]. (Woolf 2009a: 420)

The two men, illuminated by light from above, are at their most visible, most vulnerable. They are made 'common' by the light, but they are also strangers ('Fools!') to each other and themselves for what they cannot know and are unable to express. And yet, this a moment in which what is overseen or experienced can only be approximated, for they only 'seem to confess' and they only 'seem to be aware of some common knowledge' – the interactions between the two men and their significance can only be presented as speculation. Even under the maximum illumination possible at night in street, a complete and total comprehension of the scene remains unattainable; this ineffability becomes a condition for experiences of and in the modern metropolis.

Conclusion

Building on work by contemporaries such as Dorothy Richardson, E. M. Forster, and Arnold Bennett, in *Night and Day* Woolf prefigures the exploration of non-traditional urban experiences in British fiction of the interwar periods by writers as diverse as Aldous Huxley, Jean Rhys, Elisabeth Bowen, and Woolf herself – after all, without Katharine Hilbery and Mary Datchet, there might be no Clarissa Dalloway. These fictions can be read in terms of the re-configuration of boundaries between public and private, between generations and genders, as well as between day and night, natural and artificial illumination. This is a re-configuration Woolf frames at the close of her novel, when Ralph and Katharine establish their precepts of 'friendship' – an action which gesturally eschews the illusory conceptions they have developed of each other during the day. In this moment, they risk divulging their innermost selves to each other because of the sincerity they insist this 'friendship' requires. Katharine frames the considerations of the novel most perceptively:

> Why, she reflected, should there be this perpetual disparity between thought and action, between the life of solitude and the life of society, this astonishing precipice on one side of which the soul was active and in broad daylight, on the other side of which it was contemplative and dark as night? Was it not possible to step from one to the other, erect, and without essential change? Was this not the chance he offered her—the rare and wonderful chance of friendship? (Woolf 2009a: 365)

For Woolf, the 'astonishing precipice' Katharine imagines to describe the conflicting realms of night and day, of dreams and realities, can only be bridged by her 'friendship' with Ralph. This solution is puzzling, as it suggests that, by succumbing to the heteronormative values such a relationship could represent (i. e. marriage), Katharine can resolve the confusion created by the 'perceptual disparity' she perceives. The 'wonderful chance' Ralph offers Katharine is the subversive possibility of a life together 'without essential change', in which Ralph supports rather than suppresses Katharine's existential, perceptual, and experiential autonomy. She is excited by the possibilities for creativity, collaboration, and companionship such a relationship can offer her. Yet she struggles with the fear of losing control of her own life, of losing particularity, of losing distinctness: of becoming lost in the unending parade of lights and sights and sounds in the great mass of the city that might be her relationship with Ralph Denham (cf. Woolf 2009a: 529). At the same time, however, the precepts the two lovers establish represent the possibility of a new way of experiencing the city, revising the status of its streets and public spaces as male-only places to include those of women such as Katharine and Mary who were increasingly defining the urban on their own terms – a change that was furthered by increased illumination in the city.

Works Cited

Bachelard, Gaston. 1961. *La Flamme d'une Chandelle*. Paris: Presses Universitaires de France.
Beaumont, Matthew. 2015. *Nightwalking: A Nocturnal History of London, Chaucer to Dickens*. Brooklyn, NY: Verso.
Bowers, Brian. 1982. *A History of Electric Light & Power*. Stevenage: P. Peregrinus.
Bronfen, Elisabeth. 2013. *Night Passages: Philosophy, Literature, and Film*. New York, NY: Columbia University Press.

Davidoff, Leonore. 1973. *The Best Circles: Society, Etiquette and the Season.* London: Croom Helm.

Forster, E. M. 1989. *Howards End.* Ed. Oliver Stallybrass. Harmondsworth: Penguin.

Gillespie, James. 1989. "Municipalism, Monopoly and Management: The Demise of 'Socialism in One County', 1918–1933". In: Andrew Saint (ed.). *Politics and the People of London: The London County Council 1889–1965.* London: The Hambledon Press. 103–125.

Humphreys, Anne. 2002. "Knowing the Victorian City: Writing and Representation." *Victorian Literature and Culture* 30.2: 601–612.

Inwood, Stephen. 2005. *City of Cities: The Birth of Modern London.* London: Macmillan.

Lee, Hermione. 1996. *Virginia Woolf.* London: Chatto & Windus.

Nead, Lynda. 2000. *Victorian Babylon : People, Streets and Images in Nineteenth-Century London.* New Haven, CT: Yale University Press.

Otter, Chris. 2008. *The Victorian Eye: A Political History of Light and Vision in Britain, 1800–1910.* Chicago; London: The University of Chicago Press.

Parsons, Deborah L. 2000. *Streetwalking the Metropolis : Women, the City, and Modernity.* Oxford: Oxford University Press.

Pollock, Griselda. 2012. *Vision and Difference: Feminism, Femininity and Histories of Art.* London: Routledge.

Whitworth, Michael H. *Virginia Woolf.* Oxford; New York: Oxford University Press, 2009.

Williams, Raymond. *The Country and the City.* London: Chatto & Windus, 1973.

Wilson, Elizabeth. 1992. "The Invisible Flâneur". *New Left Review* 191: 90–110.

Wolff, Janet. 1985. "The Invisible Flâneuse: Women and the Literature of Modernity". *Theory, Culture & Society* 2.3: 37–46.

Woolf, Virginia. 1983. *The Diary of Virginia Woolf.* Vol. 4: 1931–35. Ed. Anne Olivier Bell. London: Penguin.

Woolf, Virginia. 1989. "A Sketch of the Past." *Moments of Being.* Ed. Jeanne Schulkind. 2nd ed. London: Grafton Books. 72–178.

Woolf, Virginia. 2009a. *Night and Day* (1919). Ed. Suzanne Rait. Oxford: Oxford University Press.

Woolf, Virginia. 2009b. "Street Haunting: A London Adventure" (1927). *Selected Essays.* Ed. David Bradshaw. Oxford: Oxford University Press. 177–187.

Robert Gillett and Isabel Wagner

Serenading the Night in Benjamin Britten's Opus 31

As Kafka's Josef K. discovered to his cost, the 30th is the most uniquely signifi-cant of all round birthdays, marking as it almost inevitably does the incontrover-tible end of being young. The English composer Benjamin Britten turned 30 in 1943, the year in which the trajectory of the Second World War changed decisive-ly with the end of the battle of Stalingrad. He had lost both his parents but had committed to a relationship with the tenor Peter Pears that would last for the rest of his life (Carpenter 1992: 93, 55, 130). Inspired by the Crabbe poem that was to provide the libretto for his operatic masterpiece *Peter Grimes* (1945), he had left the United States, the country of refuge for fellow left-wing pacifist homosexuals like W. H. Auden and Christopher Isherwood where he had lived since 1939, and returned to England (Carpenter 1992: 155). His health, which had not been good since he caught pneumonia as a child, gave way again and a bout of measles left him in hospital. While slowly recovering in his beloved Suffolk, he wrote the last work of his twenties, which was first performed in London's famous Wigmore Hall one month before his 30th birthday and which neatly bears the Opus 31: the *Serenade for Tenor, Horn and Strings* (Carpenter 1992: 184).

Both as a composition and in the texts it sets, this is unequivocally a night piece. Etymologically, the musical serenade stems from the Italian word *sera* (evening), with accompanying overtones of *serenus* (cheerful) and *al sereno* (out-side). And it is not for nothing that one of the most famous of all musical sere-nades bears the popular subtitle "Eine kleine Nachtmusik". By the same token, the backbone of Britten's night music is provided by a small anthology of English poems, ranging from the 16th to the 19th centuries. The earliest of the texts set is a folk song, known as "A lyke-wake dirge" (Anon. 2013: 104–105), collected by John Aubrey in 1686, but clearly of much earlier vintage.[1] Carol Rumens, for ex-ample, dates it to the 14th century (2009). The other five lyrics represent the Eliz-abethan age (in the form of the hymn "Queen and Huntress Chaste and Fair" from Ben Jonson's satire *Cynthia's Revels* of 1600), the Restoration (in the form of the "Evening Quatrains" by Charles Cotton, who died in 1687), Romanticism (in the form of "The Sick Rose", from William Blake's *Songs of Experience* of 1794 and Keats' "To Sleep" of 1819) and early Victorianism (in the form of Ten-

---

1 John Aubrey, *Remains of Gentilisme & Judaisme* (1686–1887) in the Lansdowne MSS., No. 231, folio 114 recto and verso (qtd. in Sidgwick 2011).

nyson's lyric "The Splendour Falls" from *The Princess* of 1847). Together they constitute an abbreviated history of 'classical' (as opposed to what Britten might have regarded as 'contemporary') English poetry. They are not, however, presented in chronological order. On the contrary, they are arranged in such a way as to maximise the dramatic impact on the one hand and to sketch out a compelling narrative on the other. One notable effect of this procedure is to draw attention to the broad range of associations invoked in connection with the night. Our aim here is to explore that drama and that narrative with a view to explicating the various aspects of the theme which Britten chooses to emphasise and explore. And this in turn will enable us to show how Britten equivocates between the personal and the historical, the individual and the universal while laying out for us in almost paradigmatic fashion the emotional and philosophical possibilities of the topic.

One of the most succinct summaries of this aspect of the work is the following, by Edward Sackville-West:

> The subject is Night and its prestigia, the lengthening shadow, the distant haze at sunset, the Baroque panoply of the starry sky, the heavy angels of sleep, but also the cloak of evil – the worm in the heart of the rose, the sense of sin in the heart of man. The whole sequence forms an Elegy or Nocturnal (as Donne would have called it), resuming the thoughts and images suitable for evening; but the total effect is serious and profound, and the associations with any kind of serenade are therefore to seek. (Sackville-West 1944: 114)

Sackville-West, as it happens, was the work's dedicatee, and so his opinion is weighted not just with the authority of one of the foremost music critics of the time, but also with a strong and intimate personal connection with the piece and its composer. Indeed, in his biography of Britten, Neil Powell notes both Sackville-West's unrequited love for the author of the *Serenade*, and the not unrelated fact that without Sackville-West Britten may never have discovered the Cotton poem with which the work begins (Powell 2013: 223). In the light of this, Sackville-West's oddly worded reaction to the title of the piece becomes understandable; despite the dedication, this piece of amorous night-music was not meant for him. Yet it does not take any great perspicuity to recognise in the piece an unequivocal expression of affection for the two performers for whom it was written: the tenor Peter Pears and the horn-player Dennis Brain. With Pears the case is clear; he was after all Britten's partner, and the letters leave us in no doubt about how and why the piece was written for him (Mitchell et al. 1991: 1133–1134). With Brain, the situation appears more complex. The accounts of the meetings between Britten and Brain are restricted to purely musical enthusiasm and generalised personal praise; the encounters between Brain and Pears to an anecdote about a gastrectomy (Pettitt 1976: 133–134). The only evidence for

Brain's not having been heterosexual comes from the website where a self-confessed Brain groupie records her double disappointment at her idol's posthumous unavailability (Tao 2011). Yet the intimate interaction between the voice and the horn, together with references to love in the texts set and the way these are voiced by the solo instrument, make of the horn and hence of the horn-player an active participant in the amorous discourse. The effect is a paradoxical projection: in performance Pears and Brain have no choice but to give expression to the composer's feelings. And that in turn gives a particular piquancy to the play Britten is here making on a central association of night as a time reserved for musical expressions of love and devotion that are both eminently public and shrouded in secrecy.

Britten's personal approach to the theme of night and sleep is comparably ambiguous. In an interview Donald Mitchell asks Britten about the different semantics of the subject: "Night and Silence, these are two of the things I cherish most", Britten tells Mitchell (1984: 92). Britten then elaborates on his fascination with dreams and the enthralling effect they can have; dreaming about meeting Schubert in Vienna once blessed the whole following day, Britten recalls. On the other hand, he states "it can release many things which one thinks had better not be released; and one can have dreams which one cannot remember even, I find, in the morning, which do colour your next day very darkly" (ibid.). Whilst night time is the time of rest and peace, it is also related to nightmares, melancholy, and death.

Night and sleep, with both sets of connotations, are recurring topics in Benjamin Britten's whole œuvre, especially of the thirties, forties, and the early sixties. Essential night compositions are *A Charm of Lullabies* (1947), *Nocturne* (1958), *Midsummer Night's Dream* (1960), *Night-Piece (Notturno)* (1963) and *Nocturnal after John Dowland* (1963), to name but a few. The interconnectedness between these pieces, and between these pieces and the *Serenade*, has often been commented on. Stephen Oosting, for example, devotes a whole subchapter to the topic of "the night as a subject in Britten's music" (1985: 9 – 20). There he defies chronology to note the exceptional closeness of the relationship between the *Serenade* and the *Nocturne* of 1958 (18 – 20). Donald Mitchell likewise speaks of a "remarkable anticipation of the orchestral song-cycle Britten was to compose in 1958, the *Nocturne*, op.60" (1989: 22). The piece he is writing about, though, is not actually part of the *Serenade*. It is a setting of Tennyson's famous poem "Now Sleeps the Crimson Petal", a second lyric from Tennyson's *Princess*, which was originally composed for possible inclusion in the *Serenade*, but which does not form part of the finished work. Mitchell traces Britten's motivation for excluding this poem from the *Serenade* and in so doing discloses how elaborately Britten laid out the order and poetic content of his night anthology:

"The song, we must conclude, could not make sense in the scheme – the shape – of the *Serenade* as it was finally and perfectly ordered by the composer" (26).

Architecture

This perfection of shape is something John Penny has also commented on: "Benjamin Britten's *Serenade for tenor, horn and strings* (1943) [...], rather than having a running narrative thread, comprises a psychological journey which weaves different aspects of the night into a tightly unified whole" (2012: 69). This whole is constructed in the form of an arch, with the two middle movements constituting a clear centrepiece supported on either side by two pairs of movements which mimic the rising and falling action of classic form theory and which correspond with each other in subtle and persuasive ways. Thus the first movement, which comes to rest on 'rest', is answered by the last, which is dedicated to sleep and ends with closure in the form of a 'sealed casket'. The first, Cotton's "Evening Quatrains" is a public poem, in which the personality of the poet only comes through in the quirkiness of his observations. The last, Keats' "To Sleep" is an emphatically inward poem, in which the lyrical subject, while urgently seeking salvation, ultimately cuts himself off from the rest of humanity. The first poem thus presents the night as a matter of social ritual in which the business of penning in and shutting up is common and commonplace, presupposing shared preoccupations and shared dangers faced in a broadly comparable manner:

> The hedge is stripped, the clothes brought in,
> Nought's left without should be within,
> The bees are hiv'd, and hum their charm,
> Whilst every house does seem a swarm. (Cotton 2013: 103)[2]

The last poem presents night as a time of radical individuality, in which the subject is left absolutely alone with his memories, fears and, dreams:

> Then save me, or the passèd day will shine
> Upon my pillow, breeding many woes;
> Save me from curious conscience, that still lords
> Its strength for darkness, burrowing like a mole;

---

2 The universality of the action is underlined, of course, by the contrast of 'naught' and 'ev'ry', and the idea of commonplace closure reproduced, with suggestive imperfection, in the rhyming couplets.

Turn the key deftly in the oilèd wards,
And seal the hushèd casket of my soul. (Keats 2013: 106)[3]

The two are presented as both polar opposites and as intimately related, with the whole piece enacting the movement from one to the other and the ogival structure underlining the fact that the most private-seeming nightmare is almost always also rooted in the public and the social.

Musically the poems are linked by a number of parameters, most notably the key (both are related by a third with the tonality of the prologue and epilogue in F: they stand in D-flat major and D major, respectively) and the tempo markings (Lento the Cotton, to be played dolcissimo; Adagio and tranquillo the Keats): slowly and solemnly introducing and resolving the composition. Both are also connected by the importance of their descending melody lines, especially meaningful in the horn's last three bars of the first poem, which anticipates the beginning of the sixth poem with its downward sliding chord pattern in the violas: D, D flat, E flat, C (bars 1–3). The "rocking, lulling element" (Oosting 1985: 182) in the Cotton mirrors the lullaby qualities in the Keats. And finally they are allied by their specific harmonic and metric openness, as Oosting emphasises: "In the Pastoral, the metrical and rhythmic ambiguity are pressed into service to fit the blurring colors and images of the physical world at twilight. In this final song, it is the spirit or consciousness which is being blurred by the onset of sleep" (158).

The correspondences between the second and the penultimate poems, by Tennyson and Ben Jonson respectively, are similarly complex. Thus the horns of Elf-land, which in the former are associated with the imperative "[b]low, bugle, blow" (Tennyson 2013: 103) find an echo in fanfares addressed to the "Queen and huntress, chaste and fair" (Jonson 2013: 105). Unspecific ancient and legendary 'splendour' is answered by the 'state' of a celebrated Renaissance monarch apostrophised as timeless. Both refer to an effect of light uncannily reproduced in music – in the first the dying sun, in the second the rising moon. Pivotal for these light and shade effects are the melismatic arcs and the interplay between the horn and the tenor. Both settings are characterised by an instrumental prelude which sets the scene for the play of illumination and shadow. The light effect of the dying sun in the Tennyson is conveyed primarily by the strings and their quick flashes in the high registers (fortepiano, the cellos and basses

---

3 In this, the closing sestet of the sonnet, words pertaining to the first person recur no fewer than four times, while the process of falling asleep is seen as a defence against painful intruders, with the past participles 'oiled' and 'hushed' feeling almost like the bars that secure a locked door.

pizzicato) which imitate the coming and going of the last rays of sunshine. The light of the rising moon in the setting of the fifth poem is represented by the extremely long and dazzling coloraturas on 'excellently bright' which compete with the cascades of virtuosic melismas in the horn – the effect being, as Sackville-West puts it, that tenor and horn "weave round each other, making an embroidery of stars" (1944: 115). Both pieces are also deeply connected by their Baroque disposition which is used here to give expression to the solar and lunar activities.

Moreover, for all the differences in tempo, mood, and tone between them, it is striking that the two poems are both made up of six-line stanzas with a recurring refrain that makes possible feats of textual repetition and musical elaboration not encountered elsewhere in the Serenade. The first two stanzas read, respectively, as follows:

> The splendour falls on castle walls,
>   And snowy summits old in story:
>   The long light shakes across the lakes,
>   And the wild cataract leaps in glory.
> Blow, bugle, blow, set the wild echoes flying,
> Blow, bugle; answer, echoes, dying, dying, dying.
>
> O hark, O hear! how thin and clear,
>   And thinner, clearer, farther going!
>   O sweet and far from cliff and scar
>   The horns of Elfland faintly blowing!
> Blow, let us hear the purple glens replying:
> Blow, bugle; answer, echoes, dying, dying, dying. (Tennyson 2013: 103–104)

And

> Queen and huntress, chaste, and fair,
>   Now the sun is laid to sleep,
> Seated in thy silver chair,
>   State in wonted manner keep:
>   Hesperus entreats thy light,
>   Goddess excellently bright.
>
> Earth, let not thy envious shade
>   Dare itself to interpose;
> Cynthia's shining orb was made
>   Heaven to clear when day did close:
>   Bless us then with wishèd sight,
>   Goddess excellently bright. (Jonson 2013: 105)

In both, then, the notion of night is bound up with the conundrum of time and eternity, of time passing and time past, evanescence and history, melancholy and politics. And that conundrum is expressed on the one hand in the paradoxical figure of synaesthesia and on the other through the technique, shared by music and poetry, of repetition and variation. Thus Tennyson varies the traditional six-line stanza by removing the end-rhyme from the stanza's third line and replacing it with an internal rhyme in its first (whereby 'scar' is so close to 'clear' as to constitute almost a half-rhyme). Jonson, though he keeps the 'ababcc' rhyme scheme, uses assonance to create a similar effect in the proximity of 'Hesperus en-' and 'bless us then'. Tennyson, moreover, varies the standard iambic tetrameter by introducing the chaos of the 'wild cataract' and its extended glory and by allowing the music to take over completely in the refrain. Jonson for his part conveys something of the peremptoriness of his subject by summarily removing the first syllable from each line, leaving them all 'acephalic' or headless. His refrain then is suitably cowed and submissive to the brightness of the moon, whereas Tennyson's is instinct with all the drawn-out melancholy of sunset. Britten conveys this musically by playing with the structural proportions of the poems, thus playing with time. Oosting shows convincingly how Britten, both in the Jonson and the Tennyson, extends the refrain towards the end of the poem, shifting its emphasis, skewing proportions, creating a "bravura energy" and "jubilant intensification" (1985: 135), for instance by repeating the word 'goddess' five times in the last refrain of the Jonson instead of the three times it appears in the other refrains. In the Tennyson the reflections on time and evanescence are intensified by the numerous repetitions of the word 'dying' and by the ending, slowly fading away with a long, time stretching note in the horn during which the last beams of the sun die off for good – morendo. The particular stress on the phrase 'for ever and for ever' by way of triplets, accent marks, and the instruction con forza is another indication of the preoccupation with time. The most striking effect, however, is the fact that the refrain of the second poem is temporally entirely at liberty: senza misura. The cadenza suspends time with the aid of a trill in the strings that is kept going whilst the horn and tenor perform their duet.

At its heart, the Serenade juxtaposes its longest and its shortest poems, Blake's "The Sick Rose" and the anonymous "A lyke-wake dirge". Both, curiously, are in quatrains, though in the former the form is rather desultory and in the latter absolutely insistent. Compare:

> O Rose, thou art sick!
> The invisible worm
> That flies in the night,
> In the howling storm,

Has found out thy bed
Of crimson joy:
And his dark secret love
Does thy life destroy. (Blake 2013: 104)

With

This ae nighte, this ae nighte,
   – Every nighte and alle,
Fire and fleet and candle-lighte,
   And Christe receive thy saule.

When thou from hence away art past,
   – Every nighte and alle,
To Whinny-muir thou com'st at last;
   And Christe receive thy saule. (Anon. 2013: 104; emphases in the original)

The first contains a first, glancing reference to night as a time of turbulence conducive to sexually transmitted disease; the second lays every imaginable stress on a night which is singular and universal, a time of transition and moral reckoning. The music in both cases is extraordinary, leaving the listener in no doubt as to the importance Britten attached to these two texts. A variation on a common motif links the two poems into an indissoluble whole in which the themes of the other poems – the private and the public, time and eternity – are taken up and enriched with a whole range of altogether darker associations: with sin and terror, death and judgment, corruption and the dark night of the soul. It is noticeable too that these two poems introduce into the work for the first time the pronoun of intimate address, the 'thou', invoking the night as a time of urgent interpellation and self-communion. And they expand the synaesthesia of sight and sound to encompass implicit scent in the first and touch and taste in the second.

The two poems are connected by another instance of Britten's framing technique: whilst the ABA form of the Blake leads to a long instrumental beginning and end that frames the text of the poem, the dirge opens and closes with the unaccompanied tenor. In both cases, a claustrophobic atmosphere is achieved by a relentless recurrence of nightmare-like motifs. In the Blake it is the menacing and monotonous syncopes of the strings at the beginning and end of the setting that give expression to the realm of sin and darkness; in the dirge it is the ninefold repetition of the same six-bar melody of the tenor. The two settings are also closely linked because both draw on the genre of the lament and its concern with the themes of death, loss, and memory – not only through their titles but also the use of chromaticism and descending motives. The introduction of the

Blake showcases all twelve tones of the musical scale in the horn which moves across the chromatic scale in semitone steps: "In Blake's 'Elegy', the horn's falling semitone figure, which generates the twelve-note melody of the introduction, is an apt musical illustration of the blight in the rose, and is eventually played in the final bars using horn handstopping, a magical idea which lends the flattened third an additionally eerie timbre" (Woodward 1999: 264–265). The music is "sick", just as the rose is sick; the chromaticism appears as "the canker" (Evans 1979: 92) of the music. In the dirge the lamenting element is emphasised by the melody line which slowly descends the interval of an octave from g2 to g1 before repeating the motion over and over again. The melody of the dirge is ripe with semitone steps, the g – a flat – g being the characteristic feature of the head-motive. And the extraordinary rhythm of the piece marks it out as a variation on a funeral march.

Links and Echoes

Alongside the architectural structure of the piece, the *Serenade* is held together both thematically and musically by a whole series of other links and echoes, which also have a significant bearing on the treatment of the theme of night. Thus the long shadows of the first poem ("The shadows now so long do grow"; Cotton 2013: 102) correspond with the long light of the second ("The long light shakes across the lakes" Tennyson 2013: 103), introducing an element of chiaroscuro into the piece and forcefully reminding us of the empirical and emotional interdependence of night and daylight. This theme is taken up again in the penultimate poem of the piece, in which Diana, the Goddess of the moon, is addressed as "Thou that mak'st a day of night" (Jonson 2013: 105). The second poem introduces, in a strangely whimsical mode (with musical tonalities to match), themes that in the third are reiterated as bleak and unadulterated anguish: love and death, *eros* and *thanatos*.[4] This third poem, framed as it is by a purely instrumental accompaniment that is the exact equivalent of Blake's enclosing rose-bush, enacts and thematises a journey instinct with that demonic terror and horror which, in the fourth poem become subject to a Manichaean dialectic, and ultimately returns the subject to the comfort of his or her own domestic surroundings.[5] This dialectic and the attenuated respite it

---

4 Contrast Tennyson: "Oh love, they die in yon rich sky" (2013: 103) with Blake: "And his dark secret love /Does thy life destroy" (2013: 104).
5 Contrast Blake: "That flies in the night, / In the howling storm" with the Dirge: "Fire and fleet and candle-lighte" (Anon. 2013: 105).

brings with it are both made explicit in the fifth poem, where the moonlight is invoked as able both to banish the darkness and briefly to suspend mortal anguish: "Give unto the flying hart/ Space to breathe, how short soever" (Jonson 2013: 105). The same gesture of supplication, which in the fifth poem was addressed to the Goddess of the moon, recurs in the sixth poem, which uses the same word – 'hymn' – to describe its own entreaty to the healing power of sleep.[6] This power too is precarious, and, as in the fourth poem, pits 'charities' against woes which, as in the third poem, come in animistic form, in order to lead a 'soul' which picks up echoes from the second poem to final, not unambiguous rest, as had been promised in the first.

The main musical features holding together the *Serenade* are the lombardic rhythms and the modal scales. With modality Britten draws on a musical system that predates our major-minor tonality. Eugene Lickey detects the use of Mixolydian elements in the prologue and epilogue, of Lydian in the nocturne and Phrygian in the dirge (1969: 22–23). The effect is a dream-like, other-worldy, Elfland-ish sound, which magically conveys the unreal world of sleep and night. The lombardic rhythm is used throughout the *Serenade*, again creating cohesion. It is an iambic rhythm also labelled 'Scotch snap' that is characterised by a very short, stressed note immediately followed by a longer one (cf. ex. 1).

Ex. 1: Pastoral, bar 2.

This rhythmic pattern appears in the prologue and epilogue, and opens the pastoral and the nocturne with different note values; even the iambic opening of the elegy is reminiscent of it. The rhythm is often associated with melancholy and mourning, for this reason Eric Roseberry remarks on "Britten's attachment to the Scottish lament genre, with its funereal tread and 'snap' (iambic) rhythms" (1999: 299). The prominence of the lombardic pattern sets the tone of the *Serenade* and shows once more why Sackville-West thought it so far away from its purely entertaining predecessors.

---

6 Compare Jonson, "Hymn to Diana": "Hesperus entreats thy light" (2013: 105), with Keats: "O soothest Sleep! If so it please thee, close, / In midst of this thine hymn, my willing eyes" (2013: 106)

Pastoral: Night and War

As for the different aspects of night which inform the psychological journey of Britten's *Serenade*, these too are intimately bound up with the form and the instrumentation of the piece. Most obviously, the work begins with a prologue and ends with an epilogue, which is identical to the prologue except that the horn that voices it has been removed from the stage and sounds at a distance, as if from a different world. This in itself has the effect of dramatising night as a time of muted recollection. This kind of reminiscence can be both soothing and appalling, as Keats makes overdeterminedly explicit by unexpectedly picking up the sonnet's opening rhyme to express a glare which is the opposite of the original comforting darkness.[7] In the case of the opening and closing of the *Serenade*, the ambiguity is focused particularly on the associations of the horn. By the time the instrument fades from our hearing at the end of the piece, it has been associated with the bugle and hence with war; with the hunting horn and hence with the mindless persecution of creatures unable to defend themselves; and with the *tuba mirum* of the Last Judgment and of the Apocalypse. So its return signals both a distanciation and a reminder that undermines it, both peace and personal safety, and isolation and a bad conscience.

These are precisely prepared for, and indeed find oblique expression in, the 'Pastoral' that is the first poem set. The horn here also demonstrates its pastoral potential, after all it used to be the instrument of the shepherds summoning their herds, and this is in line with Peter Evans' argument that Britten often uses the instrument for "evocations, nostalgic or even ironic, of a natural order, whether sublime or inexorable" (1979: 91). The very notion of the pastoral suggests an Arcadian utopia distinguished first from the corrupt world of the court, then from the soulless overcrowding of the city, and finally from the reality of modern warfare. Moreover, as Paul Kildea points out, when applied to music it can have nationalist overtones: "Although this was by no means an exclusively English phenomenon, its adoption by those keen to forge an English identity in music in the face of German cultural domination made the two nearly synonymous" (1999: 39). Cotton's poem is considerably more realistic than many other examples of the genre, including those that gained currency as part of the poetry of the First World War. But by subsuming a selection of Cotton's verses under this designation, the returning prodigal Britten is both establishing his credentials as an

---

7 In "or the passèd day will shine / Upon my pillow, breeding many woes" (Keats 2013: 106), 'shine' picks up the rhyme of the first quatrain ('benign', 'divine'), while 'woes' picks up the rhyme of the second ('close', 'throws').

anti-belligerent patriot and allowing himself a doubly proleptic act of quiet but defiant mourning. For although the killing was still going on in 1943, marking the night-time out as a time of terrible devastation and loss of life as a result of air-raids, and although Britten's own *War Requiem* (1962) was still nearly twenty years in the future, the intertext of Wilfred Owen's "Anthem for Doomed Youth" (1917), which opens the *Requiem*, peoples Cotton's landscape with the ghosts of the future dead by adding an implied extra activity to those communally associated with the transition for day to night: "And each slow dusk a drawing-down of blinds" (Owen 1990: 76).

Innocence and Experience

In this context, it is significant that the feature of the evening which Britten focuses on in the Cotton is the casting of shadows. In particular, the transformation of the 'stripling' into a 'Polypheme' ("Whilst the small stripling following them / Appears a mighty Polypheme"; Cotton 2013: 102), introduces into the piece, almost as if by accident, two of the central figures of *Peter Grimes* and indeed of Britten's work generally: the boy and the clumsy outsider. The identity between the two, together with the way in which the music mocks the alleged monstrosity of the latter, says a great deal about the psychology of the paedophile who explained his fondness for adolescent boys, which he well knew could lead to social ostracism, by reference to his own self-identification as a thirteen-year-old (Bridcut 2007: 7–8). And the fact that this delicate issue, which was the open secret of Britten's life and work, is here expressed explicitly in terms of light and darkness, gives a rich new set of meanings to the theme of night in the cycle, which thus comes to symbolise both those aspects of a personality which need to be kept hidden and the threat posed by society itself to those who fall foul of its arbitrary strictures.

If this reading is right, then what fades with the fading echo and the fading light of the second poem of the sequence, i.e. Tennyson's, is indeed something like childhood innocence. Or rather: what that poem and Britten's setting of it enacts is the substitution of the rolling repercussions of love for the failing magic of Elfland. The allusions, both verbal and musical, to *A Midsummer Night's Dream* (~1594) are inescapable, and they make of the night both a time of error, confusion, and amorous entanglement and a time set apart from reality in which such entanglements are either resolved or inconsequential. Something of this is conveyed in the eerie other-worldliness of the music. And that in turn serves to remind us of how the frame of *The Princess*, the poem from which the lines are taken, situates love in a realm made distant both by the act of narration and by the forbidding premise of the amazon intellectual and the fantastic alternative reality she inhabits.

The terrors of the transition from innocence to experience are mesmerisingly captured in the shift from the attenuated sadness of the Tennyson to the suppressed violence of the Blake. There the "dark secret love" (Blake 2013: 104) of a worm, who is also Satan, who is also a man, proves to be fatal. The possible implications are as rich as they are sinister. But it is not hard to imagine how, even now, a closeted paedophile might have his life destroyed by his 'dark secret love'. Or how the worms of gossip and homophobia might corrupt the most innocent burgeoning affection. Or how the phallic demands of heteropatriarchy might take the bloom off legions of English roses. Or how the corrosive hypocrisy of an indicatively heteropatriarchal society might constitute a canker in the heart of all apparent loveliness.[8] Quite literally, though, the howling storm of sexual intercourse can bring with it the corrupting worm of venereal disease.[9] In all these cases, night ceases to be the occasion of more or less innocent dalliance, of serenades, and takes on the full panoply of indignant mourning, of elegy. It is also no longer symbolic or sentimental, but becomes terrifyingly concrete and political. What in the previous poem had been a nostalgia for a partly imagined past ("old in story", "glory", "dying"; Tennyson 2013: 103) is confronted here with the shocking contemporary reality of disease, social ills, political corruption, and human wickedness, "[t]he invisible worm / that flies in the night" (Blake 2013: 104). Or, as Oosting puts it: "Now Britten begins to explore the hidden side of night and the things which occur under the cover of night and in the secret recesses of the soul, [...] reveal[ing] a fascination if not a preoccupation with the problem of evil [...]" (1985: 90).

The turning point comes in the following poem, "A lyke-wake dirge", where it is expressed, paradoxically but explicitly, in terms of a dark night of the soul ("This ae nighte", "And Christe receive thy saule"; Anon. 2013: 104). The theological and psychological complexity of this piece is conveyed in the music by the combination of funeral march – *alla marcia grave; come un lamento* – and fugue for five voices, with its ever growing fearsome impact. One of the fugue's crucial motives is a triplet followed by a quintuplet. This single motive is later extended by the horn in a blood curdling cry, resounding four times (bars 33–36), giving it a particularly harrowing urgency. At the climax there is a vivid musical vision of

---

8 In this context, to suggest that the poem is 'merely' about original sin, as E. D. Hirsch does, begins to look rather like conflating the effect with the cause: Christian morality with its misogyny and its pathological dislike of sex is as much the worm as it is about the worm (1964: 235).
9 In this context, it is ironic that Paul Kildea should contend that Britten actually died as a result of the secondary symptoms of syphilis passed on by Pears (cf. 2013: 532–536).

judgment that necessarily imbues the night with all the overtones of the sleep that precedes the resurrection of the body. In that sense the horn works as a kind of metaphysical wake-up call, and there is something about its brazenness that is once again associated with light. Yet there is a vicariousness about the whole thing, a kind of ventriloquism, which is underlined by the poem's circularity and the fugue's recapitulation which ultimately returns us to the firelight with a renewed resolve to do good. This is because, behind the metaphysical scenery, there is a relatively simple message about the importance of good works and Christian charity. In that sense there is a persuasive analogy between the dark nights of others, in the sense of times of want and suffering, and personal purgatory. What has been done to alleviate the one will necessarily and automatically alleviate the other as well. And by opposing the empathy of this poem to the pharisaical condemnation that subtends the Blake, Britten not only struggles through to a position of ethical defiance, he is also able to attain in his setting of Ben Jonson's "Hymn to Diana" something like the guarded upbeat jauntiness of a late Tchaikovsky scherzo.

Interlude by Moonlight

The musical form Britten actually uses, though, is a baroque obbligato aria. This helps to underline the artificiality of the text, which was originally meant for a masque, and the move from thick psychology to disingenuous rhetoric. Of a piece with this transition is the over-determined prominence in this piece of a light that is the other of sunlight, radiated by the sister of Phoebus, whose "chair" (Cotton 2013: 102) recalls his "chariot" (Jonson 2013: 105), except that its icy immobility is the opposite of his fiery motion. The effect is to make of the piece something like the photographic negative of those around it. Diana's silver-cold chastity, for example, contrasts with the warm red, the "crimson joy" (104) of Blake's rose; her calm loveliness with the terrors of whinny-muir and the bridge of dread conjured by the dirge (Anon. 2013: 104). And the plea addressed to the Goddess for a brief cessation of hostilities ("Give unto the flying hart / Space to breathe"; Jonson 2013: 105), reminds us both of the horrors of war, and, via the familiar pun on the 'heart', of the turbulence of love. Moreover the possibility of an eclipse, which is raised in the interposing rhymes of the second stanza, paradoxically conjures a more absolute darkness than any we have so far experienced and associates it with the workings of envy:

> Earth, let not thy envious shade
> Dare itself to interpose;

Cynthia's shining orb was made
Heaven to clear when day did close:
[...] (Jonson 2013: 105)

Psychologically, then, we have reached a plateau or a place of suspension; and in terms of the night, we are reminded of many of its negative connotations through the knowingly brief conjuring of their opposites.

Retreat into Sleep

True relief, though, is to be found elsewhere, in the light-shy world of sleep. What is relentlessly praised in Keats' poem is a comforting, secluding, lethe-inducing darkness ("gloom-pleased", "embower'd from light", "[e]nshaded"; 2013: 106), while danger takes the form of a memory of light ("shine / [...] breeding many woes"; 2013: 106). Yet darkness alone is not enough to stifle conscience, which waits for the ebbing of the day's business to do its subterranean work ("burrowing like a mole"; Keats 2013: 106). In that sense, then, this final poem can be read as the obverse of the Blake. There the night was a time of nefarious activity, whereas here it is a time of refuge from the memory of such activity. And yet at the same time, as we have seen, the poem not only cancels previous associations with its final closure, it also brings them back to life, recalling aspects of each of the previous poems and consigning them, one by one, to the hushed casket.

Musically this idea of the night as a redemptive force is realised by a number of parameters, especially the way certain words are emphasised. As early as the second bar the adjective 'still' receives a special accent through the long duration of its note. In bar 5 the tenor falls an eleventh in order to paint the word 'gloom', only to come to rest on F major when the text indicates that the eyes have been shut. The word 'forgetfulness' in bar 7–8 is especially ornamented with a crescendo, stressing once more that sleep allows respite from everything: memory, the mind and logic, and particularly the worms and moles of this world. This is combined in bar 12–16 with a rocking gesture in the strings moving up and down with remarkable gentleness, pianissimo, followed by another text-painted melisma describing exactly this – 'lulling', stretched over two bars (in bar 17–19). Special focus is also put on 'save me', repeated four times, as opposed to twice in the original poem. In setting Keats' poem "To Sleep" in this manner, Britten draws on Elizabethan compositions invoking sleep as sweet oblivion, for example John Dowland's "Come heavy sleep" (1597) which inspired Britten's later op.70. David Matthews summarises the meaning of sleep for Britten as follows:

his world is a place of danger and often of terror, where innocence is readily corrupted. There can be temporary reassurance in beauty and in love, but sleep is the only sure place where security and trust may be regained. The image of sleep as a refuge is something that Britten returns to again and again in his music. (Matthews 2013: 3–4)

Conclusion

With the hypnotic D-major ending, then, the rollercoaster journey adumbrated in the poems of this piece reaches its end, with the music, in a sense, coming home to rest. As the epilogue reminds us, however, while the protagonist may have found some respite in sleep, this does not mean that the various spectres associated with night in this sequence have been exorcised. The war is still continuing, though Britten has succeeded in having himself classified as a conscientious objector. Homosexuality is still illegal, though Britten can rightly imagine a future for himself in a stable relationship with another man. Syphilis is still incurable, and even more intractable than syphilis is the sexual morality of the Christian Church, to which Britten is both very close and from which he is very far away. His personal demons, too, as he well knows, are merely in abeyance: his fragile health, the shadow of depression, the inescapable horrors of adulthood. By turning inwards and locking the door behind him, by retreating into the closet of sleep, the protagonist can to an extent abstract himself from the world. But the process that led him to that point resonates to the end with all the cultural connotations of the Western discourse of the night, with its myths, its symbols, its affective cathexes, and its brutal realities.

Thus the selection of texts touches on all the major nocturnal themes: light, darkness, shadow; sleep, dream, and nightmare; death, damnation, and redemption; rest and peace; moonlight and the uncanny. But the piece also includes sex and sexuality, especially dangerous and dissident sexuality; love and tenderness, albeit attenuated and indirect; and suspended, projected, and hypothetical violence. It exemplifies the anguish of night in a terrifying shamanic journey; and it synaesthetically conveys different intensities of light through vivid musical effects. It touches on some of the most archaic aspects of the human condition while alluding to the ongoing horrors of the present. But as we hope to have shown, it weaves them all into a personal journey, which is, literally and unforgettably, a journey to Hell and back.

Works Cited

Anon. 2013. "A lyke-wake dirge". In: Boris Ford (ed.) *Benjamin Britten's Poets. An Anthology of the Poems He Set to Music.* Manchester: Carcanet. 104–105.

Blake, William. 2013. "The Sick Rose 'Elegy'". In: Boris Ford (ed.) Benjamin Britten's Poets. An Anthology of the Poems He Set to Music. Manchester: Carcanet. 104.

Bridcut, John. 2007. *Britten's Children.* London: Faber and Faber.

Carpenter, Humphrey. 1992. *Benjamin Britten: A Biography.* London: Faber and Faber.

Cotton, Charles. 2013. "Evening Quatrains". In: Boris Ford (ed.). *Benjamin Britten's Poets. An Anthology of the Poems He Set to Music.* Manchester: Carcanet. 102–103.

Donald Mitchell, Philip Reed, Mervyn Cooke (eds.). 1991. *Letters from a Life: The Selected Letters and Diaries of Benjamin Britten 1913–1976.* 5 vols. London: Faber and Faber.

Evans, Peter. 1979. *The Music of Benjamin Britten.* London: Dent.

Hirsch, Eric Donald. 1964. *Innocence and Experience. An Introduction to Blake.* Chicago and London: University of Chicago Press.

Jonson, Ben. 2013. "Hymn to Diana". In: Boris Ford (ed.) Benjamin Britten's Poets. An Anthology of the Poems He Set to Music. Manchester: Carcanet. 105.

Keats, John. 2013. "To Sleep". In: Boris Ford (ed.). *Benjamin Britten's Poets. An Anthology of the Poems He Set to Music.* Manchester: Carcanet. 105–106.

Kildea, Paul. 1999. "Britten, Auden and Otherness". In: Mervyn Cooke (ed.). *The Cambridge Companion to Benjamin Britten.* Cambridge: Cambridge University Press. 36–53

Kildea, Paul. 2013. *Benjamin Britten. A Life in the Twentieth Century.* London, Allen Lane.

Lickey, Eugene Harold. 1969. *An Analysis of Benjamin Britten's Serenade, Op. 31.* Indiana University: Unpublished Master Dissertation.

Matthews, David. 2013. *Benjamin Britten.* London: Haus.

Mitchell, Donald. "'Now sleeps the crimson petal': Britten's other 'Serenade'". *Tempo* 169 (June 1989): 22–27.

Mitchell, Donald. 1984. "Mapreading: Benjamin Britten in conversation with Donald Mitchell". In: Christopher Palmer (ed.). *The Britten Companion.* London: Faber and Faber.

Oosting, Stephen. 1985. *Text-Music Relationships in Benjamin Britten's Serenade for Tenor, Horn and Strings.* University of Rochester: Unpublished PhD Dissertation.

Owen, Wilfred. 1990. "Anthem for Doomed Youth". In: Jon Stallworthy (ed.). *The Poems of Wilfred Owen.* London: Chatto & Windus. 76.

Penny, John. 2012. "The Brain of Britten: Notational aspects of the 'Serenade'". *The Horn Call* XLIII 1: 69–74.

Pettitt, Stephen. 1976. *Dennis Brain. A Biography.* London: Robert Hale.

Powell, Neil. 2013. *Britten. A Life for Music.* London: Hutchinson.

Roseberry, Eric. 1999. "Old Songs in New contexts: Britten as arranger". In: Mervyn Cooke (ed.). *The Cambridge Companion to Benjamin Britten.* Cambridge: Cambridge University Press. 292–244.

Rumens, Carol. "Poem of the Week: the Lyke Wake Dirge". *The Guardian*, 16 February 2009, <http://www.theguardian.com/books/booksblog/2009/feb/16/lyke-wake-dirge-poem-week> [accessed 7 December 2014].

Sackville-West, Edward. 1944. "Music: Some Aspects of the Contemporary Problem III". *Horizon* August 1944: 114–127.

Sidgwick, Frank. "The Lyke-Wake Dirge". <http://www.readbookonline.net/readOnLine/ 43748/-> [accessed 18 May 2015].

Tao. 2011. "Life with the French Horn". *OSHO News Online Magazine* 12 October. <http:// www.oshonews.com/2011/10/french-horn-tao/> [accessed 19 April 2015].

Tennyson, Alfred Lord. 2013. "Blow, Bugle, Blow 'Nocture'". In: Boris Ford (ed.) *Benjamin Britten's Poets. An Anthology of the Poems He Set to Music.* Manchester: Carcanet. 103–104.

Woodward, Ralph. 1999. "Music for voices". In: Mervyn Cooke (ed.). *The Cambridge Companion to Benjamin Britten.* Cambridge: Cambridge University Press. 260–276.

Lars Heiler

Darkness Visible: Night, Light, and Liminality in Arthur Conan Doyle's *The Hound of the Baskervilles* and Jed Rubenfeld's *The Death Instinct*

At first sight, Arthur Conan Doyle's gothic detective novel and Jed Rubenfeld's post-modern historical thriller have little in common. Set in the moors of Devonshire, the rural setting of Doyle's whodunit is more than a far cry from the 1920 bombing of New York's Wall Street which forms the starting point of Rubenfeld's novel.

Nevertheless, there are striking resemblances between the two works. Both novels engage in the detection of mysteries, without being straightforward detective novels. Both narratives display a sustained interest in psychological and anthropological issues about the nature of humanity and mankind's fundamental instincts and drives. Moreover, both texts subscribe to an 'enlightened' narrative pattern in which dark secrets are revealed, analysed, and explained in a movement towards narrative closure, while at the same time creating an uncanny openness which resists full containment.

Sources of light are of major importance in both novels: luminescent materials (phosphorus in *The Hound of the Baskervilles* and radium in *The Death Instinct*) as forms of artificial illumination are contrasted with more conventional – natural or man-made – forms of lighting, the former ones providing a source of horror, ambiguity, and deadliness which deconstructs received notions of the light/dark(ness) opposition.

In this essay, I will show how the representation of lighting and darkness in Doyle's and Rubenfeld's texts produces forms of liminality and potentiality, which are reflected in a number of spatial, psychological, cultural, scientific, and technological transitions; how, in other words, the dialectics of the Enlightenment is underpinned by the dialectics of illumination.

Arthur Conan Doyle, *The Hound of the Baskervilles*

There is hardly a genre which owes more to the opposition of night and day than detective fiction and its numerous offspring. Light and darkness provide a force field around which the art of detection revolves: 'dark' secrets and 'inscrutable' mysteries are 'brought to light' by the figure of the detective who investigates 'gloomy' locales, identifies 'shady' characters, and exposes their 'murky' motives. Arthur Conan Doyle's Sherlock Holmes seems to be a perfect illustration of this type, embodying Enlightenment values such as uncompromising rationality and cool logic in abundance, making him the scientific detective *par excellence*. Yet, even Conan Doyle's *fin-de-siècle* human detection machine is not a straightforward representative of light, but often associated with more nocturnal spheres.

That Holmes is not a deviation from the norm becomes evident when comparing him to the character who is supposed to represent the blueprint of the modern sleuth, Edgar Allan Poe's gentleman detective C. Auguste Dupin. In Poe's three 'tales of ratiocination', in which Dupin is the protagonist, he solves mysteries (rather than clear-cut crimes) through the powers of analysis and methodical rigour. Nevertheless, his portrayal as a bringer of analytical light is riddled with contradiction and complicated by a number of factors. On the one hand, "he is a recluse of obscure, nocturnal and bookish habits" (Kayman 2003: 45), qualities which align him with the night in its physical manifestation, but also with a strong inscrutability of character. On the other hand, Dupin is marked by a moral duplicity which is summarised by Peter Thoms as follows: "Just as Poe's stories seem to construct the detective as a figure of order, they also critique that figure, subverting the opposition between detective and criminal and challenging the investigator's innocent or objective viewpoint of the world" (2002: 133).

In this light, Sherlock Holmes merely perpetuates the duality between day and night that is a central feature of his predecessor Dupin, and this is perhaps most true of the novel in which Conan Doyle resurrected Holmes after his death in "The Final Problem": *The Hound of the Baskervilles*.[1]

Illumination and Spatial Divisions

The Hound of the Baskervilles is a remarkable novel for several reasons. First, it marks a deviation from the classic detective genre, paying tribute rather to "other *fin-de-siècle* Gothic tales and romances than [...] to the early Holmes stories" (2005: 69), as Nils Clausson observes. Srdjan Smajic draws a similar conclusion, stating that "the genre transgresses its own rules and it becomes difficult to tell whether *The Hound* is a detective story with supernatural touches or a ghost story in detective-fiction format" (2010: 3). Secondly, the novel makes Holmes

---

1 Although chronologically *The Hound of the Baskervilles* is set before "The Final Problem".

and Watson leave their natural habitat of London, sending them to Baskerville Hall near Dartmoor in Devon, a change of setting which accounts for most of the liminal aspects to which I have already alluded. Finally, the novel stands out because it famously excludes Holmes from its middle section, at least for his partner John Watson and for the reader. That Holmes travels to Devon on his own and becomes a secret sharer of the moor's mysteries, while at the same time he is removed from the novel's textual surface, endows him with an ambivalence that will be analysed below. First, I will focus on questions of light and spatial representation in the novel.

As Clausson suggests, Watson and Sir Henry Baskerville's "journey through space is also a journey through time" (2005: 72), transporting them from the safety and comfort of modern civilisation in London to the rural backwardness of the Devonshire moors. The landscape is perceived by the autodiegetic narrator Watson in ambivalent terms:

> Rolling pasture lands curved upwards on either side of us, and old gabled houses peeped from amid the thick green foliage, but behind the peaceful and sunlit countryside there rose ever, dark against the evening sky, the long, gloomy curve of the moor, broken by the jagged and sinister hills. (Doyle 2003: 56)

Watson's observation conflates the rhetorical conventions of the pastoral *locus amoenus* and the barren *locus desertus* in a very effective manner. The contrast he creates between the sunlit fields and the gloom of the moor implies a fissure in the landscape and its depiction which pervades the entire novel and adds to its unpredictable and inscrutable nature.

Interestingly, the novel does not establish a clear-cut distinction between the darkness of the solitary moor and the potential brightness of Baskerville Hall, the estate which marks Watson's and Sir Henry's destination. Watson's account of their arrival at the estate anticipates a continuation of the ambiguous play of light and darkness that also characterises the countryside:

> Through the gateway we passed into the avenue, where the wheels were again hushed amid the leaves, and the old trees shot their branches in a sombre tunnel over our heads. Baskerville shuddered as he looked up the long, dark drive to where the house glimmered like a ghost at the farther end. (Doyle 2003: 58)

Both nature and civilisation seem to be infused with the potential to produce scares, and in this particular example they collaborate in this enterprise. While the trees in the avenue create a "sombre tunnel", the house contributes a light which is not construed as a source of relief and hope, but as a "glimmer", which suggests unsteadiness, dimness, vagueness, and a spectral quality that is captured in the quote's conclusion.[2] Sir Henry's mood is so subdued in this scene that he surmises his uncle Sir Charles was killed there, only to learn from Dr Mortimer that the Yew Alley, which is the actual crime scene, "is on the other side" (58), opening up to the moor and providing a mirror image to the gloomy avenue at the front, both framing the access to and the exit from the house.

The unease which Watson and Sir Henry share when approaching the house is perpetuated in their evaluation of the building's interior, which is depicted as old-fashioned and gloomy, lit by fire-places and individual gas lamps which contribute little to illuminate the place, but rather make the 'darkness visible', as in the following example:

> But the dining room which opened out of the hall was a place of shadow and gloom. It was a long chamber with a step separating the dais where the family sat from the lower portion reserved for their dependents. Black beams shot across above our heads, with a smoke-darkened ceiling beyond them. With rows of flaring torches to light it up, and the colour and rude hilarity of an old-time banquet, it might have softened; but now, when two black-clothed gentlemen sat in the little circle of light thrown by a shaded lamp, one's voice became hushed and one's spirit subdued. (Doyle 2003: 60–61)

Strikingly, Watson's comment contrasts the unsuitability of modern lighting that merely provides a "little circle of light" with the medieval or early modern "rows of flaring torches" for which Baskerville Hall had originally been designed. Sir Henry's reaction to the "house of gloom" (81) – gloom being an attribute often employed in the novel in connection with the moor – reveals a staunchly optimistic belief in the power of electric lighting to exorcise the darkness of the past and to embrace the blessings of modernity:

> 'It's no wonder my uncle felt as if trouble were coming on him in such a place as this,' said he. 'It's enough to scare any man. I'll have a row of electric lamps up here inside of six months, and you won't know it again with a thousand-candle-power Swan and Edison right in front of the hall door.' (Doyle 2003: 58)

The electric lamps inside and the powerful light outside are supposed to fortify the man and the house alike, turning the house into a safe haven, a site of civilisation, and an illustration of its new owner's faith in technological progress.[3]

---

2 The wording of this passage inverts the conventional positive notion of the term glimmer as in the expression 'glimmer of hope'.
3 Cf. Otter, "At the beginning of the twentieth century, artificial light was routinely viewed as the supreme sign of 'modernity' or 'civilization'" (2008: 1).

Light and Detection

Prior to sending Watson on his mission in the Devonshire moors, Holmes goes out of his way to encourage Watson's powers of detection, and he does so by tapping into a conventional symbolic field which associates investigation and detection with light. Yet, the technological metaphor he chooses is rather surprising:

> I am bound to say that in all accounts which you have been so good as to give of my own small achievements you have habitually underrated your own abilities. It may be that you are not yourself luminous, but you are a conductor of light. (Doyle 2003: 6)

Luminosity, the ability to produce light oneself and 'shine', is equated here by Holmes with ingenuity, but also with the spirit of deduction and detection that he possesses in abundance, whereas Watson's talents are deemed derivative and of an indirect and passive quality in this well-intended, but ultimately backhanded compliment. Watson's attempts to elucidate the mysterious events at Baskerville Hall are not completely futile, but circumscribed by the limitations he habitually suffers from when investigating matters without the aid of Holmes. Consequently, Watson's account of his observations is dominated by metaphors evoking the groundlessness of the dark moor – "So there is one of our small mysteries cleared up. It is something to have touched bottom anywhere in this bog in which we are floundering" (88) – or involving impaired vision: "But the moor with its mysteries and its strange inhabitants remains as inscrutable as ever" (98).

Once Holmes re-enters the scene and takes centre-stage again, the reader expects the conventional development from darkness to light, from mystery to solution, from chaos to order that underlies the logic of previous Sherlock Holmes narratives and is echoed at the end of the novel when Holmes searches Stapleton's house, "[catching] up the lamp, and [leaving] no corner of the house unexplored" (151). Rather surprisingly, Holmes has to learn that searching an enclosed structure with a solid foundation and a clear design cannot be compared to getting an analytical grip on the vast and unfathomable moor. In the face of the moor's overwhelming darkness, 'light' ceases to be the currency in which the power and success of the detective can be accounted for. Watson's reaction to a question asked by Sir Henry betrays an understanding of this notion: "'Well, Watson, what do you think of this new light?' 'It seems to leave the darkness rather blacker than before'" (104). Nils Clausson aptly summarises the consequences of this modified struggle between night and light for the novel's genre affiliations:

> Set over against Holmes's putative powers of reason and science are the equally powerful forces of darkness symbolized by the moor, and particularly by the great Grimpen Mire. [...] The rhetorical intensity with which the moor is impressionistically evoked by Watson, along with the amount of description afforded it, threatens to overpower the ratiocinative detective plot. (Clausson 2005: 72)

Liminalities

As critics like Clausson and Smajic have shown, *The Hound of the Baskervilles* orchestrates a number of anxieties that are often found in *fin-de-siècle* Gothic narratives: the fear of degeneration, atavism, and the other. Many of these anxieties are structured around a character constellation which involves a scientist and a 'primitive' creature, be it an actual animal or a monstrous character like Robert Louis Stevenson's Edward Hyde. Conan Doyle's novel follows suit in its confrontation of the scientific detective Holmes and the eponymous hound. This constellation is further enriched by the two characters who are human but are depicted in terms of the Gothic villain and his quasi-animal instinctual nature, the escaped convict Selden and Stapleton, the naturalist. Selden is more overtly associated with primitivism and atavism and represents the criminal type as described in the criminological anthropology of the 19th century medical professor and criminologist Cesare Lombroso:

> Over the rocks, in the crevice of which the candle burned, there was thrust out an evil yellow face, a terrible animal face, all seamed and scored with vile passions. [...] The light beneath him was reflected in his small, cunning eyes, which peered fiercely to right and left through the darkness, like a crafty and savage animal who has heard the steps of the hunters. (Doyle 2003: 96)

Stapleton represents a less straightforward case of primitivism, because he unites the qualities of the rational scientist with the uncontrolled rage, brutality, and desire of the stereotypical criminal or – from a late-Victorian point-of-view – animal. It is this duality which makes him such an exceedingly dangerous opponent, as Holmes observes on several occasions. The detective stresses Stapleton's intelligence when he admits that he himself has been "checkmated in London" (52), acknowledging the latter's powers of logic and reason, and he insinuates his animal nature when he tells Watson "that never yet have we helped to hunt down a more dangerous man than he who is lying yonder" (155). The hunting metaphor aligns Stapleton with Selden in the above-mentioned quote, and it associates him with the hound, who is equally hunted down by the detective (after having hunted its own prey).

The novel expands its frame of atavistic reference and links both men with the prehistoric life that is tangible in the Dartmoor area through the remains of a large number of ancient stone huts. Selden is explicitly likened to the prehistoric men who in Watson's imagination are mere "savages" (96), while Holmes, studying Hugo Baskerville's portrait, considers the latter's descendant Stapleton an "interesting instance of a throwback" (138), i. e. a product of phylogenetic regression.

Surprisingly, Holmes and Watson's narrative efforts to delimit the boundaries between culture and nature, civilisation and savagery, man and (man-)animal, light and darkness, are undermined by the novel's overall strategy which places Holmes, the temporary cave-dweller, in the same symbolic field as Selden, Stapleton, and the hound. When Watson sees a male figure on the moor, not recognising him as Holmes, he equates him with "the spirit of that terrible place" (97) and inadvertently identifies the great detective with the richly textured sphere of the primitive and atavistic, even calling him a "man of darkness" (104) and further upsetting the neatly designed narrative patterns of the classic detective genre. As Clausson concludes: "Once this self-proclaimed man of science leaves London and travels to Dartmoor, he is consistently represented through the same Gothic tropes that Watson uses throughout his narrative" (2005: 76). But the deconstruction of Holmes as a figure of light is not limited to his association with darkness: Holmes' admonition to Sir Henry to "avoid the moor in those hours of darkness when the powers of evil are exalted" (Doyle 2003: 54) glosses over the fact that these powers – in the figure of the hound – illuminate the darkness from which they are supposed to arise. The hound, whose muzzle has been treated by Stapleton with a phosphorescent substance,[4] glows in the dark and, like its predecessor in an old family legend (24), becomes "luminous" (155) – a quality that, as I have shown above, Holmes claims for himself (6). The metaphorical distribution of light and darkness is therefore blurred from both ends of the spectrum. By associating the forces of evil with an uncanny, fiery glow which contaminates Sherlock Holmes' narrative self-fashioning as a figure of light and defender of civilisation, and by simultaneously 'darkening' Holmes and locating him in an atavistic context, the novel reconfigures its own genre principles and symbolical patterns. Holmes ceases to be a coloniser of the dark[5] and becomes one of its chief representatives.

---

4 Conan Doyle's employment of "phosphorus" as the substance used by Stapleton is scientifically untenable, because it is highly poisonous, as Christopher Frayling remarks in his edition of the novel (Doyle 2003: 193 – 194).
5 The idea of colonising the darkness is a central feature of Murray Melbin's historical study *Night as Frontier: Colonizing the World After Dark* (1987).

In the second part of this paper, I will investigate the deconstruction of the light/dark opposition in Jed Rubenfeld's postmodern thriller which provides a lucid meditation on the scientific and technological optimism at the beginning of the 20th century.

Jed Rubenfeld, *The Death Instinct*

Jed Rubenfeld's *The Death Instinct* is a sequel to his acclaimed novel *The Interpretation of Murder*, first published in 2006, which mingles the historical event of Sigmund Freud's visit to the United States in 1912 with a fictional crime narrative, involving the New York detective Jimmy Littlemore and the American medical doctor, psychoanalyst, and rich heir Stratham Younger. In their joint attempt to solve a murder case, Littlemore and Younger profit from Freud's knowledge about and interpretation of the human psyche, e. g. when they try to unravel the mysteries of traumatic experience. Freud's insights fuel the solution of the murder plot and are made accessible to the common reader as well.

The Death Instinct sets in eight years later and revives the old collaboration between the three men, albeit in modified form. Younger, who fought in Europe during World War I and is left traumatised, has lost his belief in the basic tenets of Freudian psychoanalysis, and his encounters with Freud in post-war Vienna are awkward and marked by the younger man's resistance and doubt. Moreover, there is no direct contact between Freud and Littlemore, it is Younger who serves as intermediary between the two men and the novel's multiple layers and strands. Thematically, *The Death Instinct* is significantly more complex than its predecessor. It begins with the bombing of Wall Street on September 16, 1920, a terrorist attack that was never solved, and links this event to a war crime committed in World War I, Freud's budding belief in a (self-)destructive drive (the eponymous death instinct), and the mania revolving around Marie and Pierre Curie's discovery of radium and its use in medicine, but also in beauty products, watch dials, and other technical applications (cf. Lavine 2013).

Light and darkness

The opposition between light and darkness permeates Rubenfeld's novel in even more literal and metaphorical variations than Conan Doyle's. On his return from the battlefields of Europe, Younger contrasts the atrocities committed there with the apparent lack of impact this has had on the US: "'Amazing,' said Younger, 'how nothing's changed here. Europe returned to the Dark Ages, but in America time went on holiday'" (Rubenfeld 2011: 16). He is disproved not only by Little-more's contention that "[e]verything's different. The whole city's on edge" (16), but also by the imminent bombing of Wall Street, which the novel constructs in terms of epistemological, moral, and even literal "darkness" due to the smoke that obscures the sky for many days (19, 276 *et passim*).

The light/night opposition also fosters political discourse, when it is em-ployed to characterise the black-and-white views that 'patriotic' American poli-ticians hold of international politics. This strategy can be observed in the ultra-conservative Senator Fall's assessment of the role of the post-revolutionary Soviet Union in the world:

> These communists don't just want Russia. They're mean, nasty sons of bitches – you mark my words – and they want to rule the world. That's right: they want to rule the world. They hate freedom. They hate Christ. *They will fill the world with darkness* for a hundred years. (290; my emphasis)[6]

This Manichean worldview which places the US in a superior moral position is also evident in the reasoning of the entrepreneur Arnold Brighton, the fictional owner of the first radium paint company in Orange, New Jersey, who asks Fall for support in solving his problems with revolutionaries in Mexico: "I'll give now. Whatever amount you ask. Tell me where to send it. Just drop a few bombs on Mexico City – perhaps on their capitol and in the nicer parts of town – *I'm sure they'll see the light*" (292; my emphasis). That the bomb that detonates in Manhattan's Wall Street is linked by the narrative voice to darkness whereas American bombs dropped on the capital of a foreign country are supposed to be a means of making the local population 'see the light' shows the preposter-ousness of Brighton's stance and creates a heavily ironic juxtaposition which re-quires no further authorial comment in the novel.

As in these two instances, the novel constantly undermines the traditional association of light with notions of cultural and technological supremacy and of night with forms of backwardness and primitivism. That technological prog-ress and optimism can co-exist with forms of primitivism and savagery is dem-onstrated when the authorial narrator evokes the context of the 1920 presidential elections in which the Republican candidate Warren G. Harding, replacing the ailing Woodrow Wilson, won in a landslide victory. These elections were signifi-cant because they were the first ones in which women were allowed to vote in all 48 states. This progressive aspect which is linked to "great festivities and a gal-

---

6 Cf. also Fall's rhetorics on page 492.

vanization of energies throughout the land" (363) is sharply contrasted with the treatment of black voters:

> Blacks were not received quite so chivalrously at the polls [...] Two black churches were sacked, a black neighborhood was burned to the ground, and some thirty or sixty black people were killed, one of them strung up a telephone pole and hanged by the neck. (Rubenfeld 2011: 363)

The lynching of an African-American at a telephone pole links an object which symbolises dynamic technological progress and modern communication with pre-civilised murder and primitive racist impulses, and can be seen as a striking illustration of the dialectics of the Enlightenment which inspires the novel on many levels.

Detection and Psychoanalysis

In her study *Night Passages: Philosophy, Literature and Film*, Elisabeth Bronfen devotes a whole chapter to the nocturnal element in Freud's writings. She shows how Freud conceives of unconscious forces as agents which have retreated into a realm of darkness that cannot be illuminated by the light of reason:

> night implicitly assumes a plethora of positions in the cosmogenetic narrative Freud devises for the emergence of the psychic apparatus, first and foremost because it contains the unconscious, conceived as an internal dark site impenetrable to conscious insight. (Bronfen 2013: 88)

Thus, Freud's project of 'colonizing' the darkness of the mind, of investigating the recesses of the human psyche, of discovering its secrets and revealing its mysteries is indebted to the larger Enlightenment project of controlling the irrational and of aiding the powers of reason. The inclusion of a fictionalised version of Freud into a novel which combines the genres of historical thriller and (in the person of Jimmy Littlemore) police procedural is therefore a clever and not altogether far-fetched strategy. As in *The Interpretation of Murder*, the fictional Freud of *The Death Instinct* shares current insights and theories of the actual Freud with the police officer Littlemore and the gentleman detective Younger. Although the Freud passages in the later novel occupy less space than in the *Interpretation of Murder*, his investigative influence expands although his former disciple Stratham Younger has come to reject Freud's theories. The latter's growing impact can be attributed to two factors: on the one hand, he does not restrict himself to solving a single murder case, but is able to explain the obscure behaviour of a number of central characters. It is Colette Rousseau, Younger's battlefield acquaintance from World War I, and a fictional student of Marie Curie, whose enigmatic behaviour and wish to trace her alleged fiancée, a former German soldier named Hans Gruber, makes her a (recalcitrant) target for Freud's analytical skills. He also treats Colette's younger brother Luc who suffers from mutism after his and Colette's native village in France was raided by German soldiers. That Colette and Luc's behaviour is interrelated, the former wanting to take revenge on the man who killed her parents[7] and the latter being shocked by the fact that his father, with a gun to his head, revealed his family's place of hiding to the Germans, is ultimately exposed by Freud. But World War I's relevance to Freud's work is not limited to elucidating the personal traumata of individuals experiencing the horror of World War I. Rubenfeld's novel presents Freud at a decisive turning point in his work: perplexed by the phenomenon of war neuroses in which the patients re-enact experiences they had on the battlefield or in the trenches, Freud focuses on repetition as a means of understanding their behaviour. In *Beyond the Pleasure Principle* (1920), the treatise in which the historical Freud set out to solve this problem and which is frequently discussed in *The Death Instinct*, he states:

> The study of dreams may be considered the most trustworthy method of investigating deep mental processes. Now dreams occurring in traumatic neuroses have the characteristic of repeatedly bringing the patient back into the situation of his accident, a situation from which he wakes up in another fright. This astonishes people far too little. They think the fact that the traumatic experience is constantly forcing itself upon the patient even in his sleep is a proof of the strength of that experience: the patient is, as one might say, fixated to his trauma. (Freud 1955: 13)

Freud challenges this view which is in line with his original theory of the unconscious by reminding his readers of "the nature of dreams. It would be more in harmony with their nature if they showed the patients pictures from his healthy past or of the cure for which he hopes" (Rubenfeld 2011: 13).

Since the dreams of war neurotics suggest a deviation from the pleasure principle, Freud postulates a powerful force that exists independently of libidinous impulses: the death instinct that "would be concerned with the most universal endeavour of all living substance – namely to return to the quiescence of the inorganic world" (62).

---

7 It is Stratham Younger who completes the task Colette is unable to perform: he liquidates Hans Gruber and his friends in a killing spree which betrays a personality deeply affected by his war experience (cf. Rubenfeld 2011: 345).

At the beginning of *The Death Instinct*, the fictional Freud presents this new turn in his thinking to Stratham Younger in terms of a mystery that he has not solved, yet, and in terms of a darkness that has so far been impenetrable to analytic light: "I suspect there's something else. I sense it in Miss Rousseau's brother. I don't know what it is, yet. Pity he doesn't speak. Something dark, almost uncanny. I can't see it, but I can hear it. I hear its voice" (140).

On Younger's second visit to Vienna, Freud is able to articulate his thoughts on the death instinct more clearly and manages to explain through it Luc's mutism as well as the Wall Street bombing which he calls the "death instinct unbound. Freed from the life instincts, freed from the ideals by which the ego assesses its actions – conscience" (382). Freud's ground-breaking insight into the antagonism of life instincts and death instincts, which the novel turns into a structural principle, is accompanied by a – somewhat overdetermined – *mise-en-scene* which obliquely comments on Freud's role as psychoanalytic Prometheus. At the beginning of the scene in which he discloses his insights to Younger and Colette Rousseau, the electric lights in Freud's apartment – frequently unreliable in post-war Vienna – begin to flicker, but stay on (375). Yet, as Freud takes his listeners into the realms of mental darkness he claims to have discovered, the lights go dead, candles are lit, but Freud's cigar – in itself a symbol of phallic power and illumination – darkens the room with heavy smoke (377). Consequently, the act of shedding light onto the darkness of the death instinct is not an equivalent to the divine 'Let there be light' which substitutes order for chaos. Instead, it merely makes visible the terrible darkness that is formed by human aggression and destructiveness which Freud considers to be descendants of the death instinct. Unlike Sherlock Holmes in *The Hound of the Baskervilles*, Freud is not directly associated with darkness, but his act of evoking the forces of mental darkness seems to provide them with an energy which is as uncontrollable as the powers of evil evoked in Conan Doyle's novel. Freud's conjuring act places him in close proximity to the darkness he names in order to master it.

Radium, Illumination, and Enlightenment

By addressing radioactivity and the public discourse about it, Jed Rubenfeld introduces a second area of ground-breaking scientific discovery in his novel which, like Freudian psychoanalysis, can be considered one of the hallmarks of early twentieth century notions of 'modernity'. The novel constructs a symmetry between the two discoveries and their main representatives, even in the relationships with their brightest students: if the fictional Sigmund Freud was established as a father figure to Stratham Younger in *The Interpretation of Murder*, it is

Marie Curie who is now depicted as a mother figure to the orphaned Colette Rousseau.

After Wilhelm Roentgen's discovery of X-rays in 1895 and Henri Becquerel's discovery of radioactivity in 1896, it was Marie and Pierre Curie's isolation of polonium and radium in 1898 which spurned the public imagination and trust in the power of scientists to unveil the secrets of nature. Their story "congealed immediately into a widely told parable about dogged and clear-headed scientists pursuing the glimmer of knowledge, no matter what the obstacles" (Lavine 2013: 13). The quasi-religious admiration for radium as an almost divine source of light and energy is appositely captured in the 1904 comment "Radium: A Little Philosophy" in the *Richmond News-Leader:*

> And we are now treating it, handling it, using it, carefully, cautiously, observing, for all the service it may do to mankind. It seems to be the spirit of life itself. How strangely, marvelously, suggestive of the Great Original; of God tabernacled in the flesh; of Him who brought light and immortality to life, in whom was life, and the life was the light of men. (qtd. in Lavine 2013: 98)

According to Ross Mullner, radium quickly came to be seen as "an alchemist's dream come true" (1999: 10) and speculation about its further uses was endemic: "It was claimed, for example, that the energy from radium would replace natural gas and electricity" (ibid.). That these wild guesses were largely unfounded is emphasised by Matthew Lavine who points out that "radium's use as a light source was limited largely to places where electricity was too dear to use excessively, or absent entirely, as many houses and outbuildings still were in the 1920s" (2013: 96).

Still, unaware of the serious medical dangers that radium posed, the American public was interested in "ray-talk" (7) and in the array of radium products that were produced by companies suggestively named "Undark, Marvelite, and Radium LUMAnous Compound" (96). But the industrial exploitation of radium, which was hard to isolate from different types of ores, considerably raised the price of this element and made its medical use as a remedy against cancer incomparably more costly and difficult. This is one of Rubenfeld's interests in *The Death Instinct* when he sends Colette to the United States to raise money for the Marie Curie Radium Fund which has been established by American philanthropists and feminists. When the fund's chairwoman, Mrs Meloney, addresses her female audience in a church – the appropriate site for the precious item of worship – her lament about the scarcity of radium betrays a serious double bind:

> How outrageous it is [...] that Madame Curie [...] should for mere want of money be prohibited from continuing her investigations that have already led to the radium cure for our can-

cers, the radium face and hand creams that eliminate our unsightly blemishes [...] and the radium-infused waters that restore conjugal vitality to our husbands. (Rubenfeld 2011: 173)

For Mrs Meloney there is no contradiction in lionising the French woman scientist while at the same time praising the industrial products which are indirectly responsible for the limited availability of radium *and* for the proliferation of cancer and other diseases.

The latter aspect becomes a more central concern in the novel when Strathham Younger and Colette Rousseau gradually realise that radium is a two-faced element, able to cure cancer, but also capable of causing death, a clear allegory of Freud's discovery of the co-existence of life instincts and death instincts in the human psyche. The fictional Mme Curie addresses this issue in the following terms:

> 'Some think that radioactivity may be the long-sought fountain of youth,' Madame Curie went on. 'Unquestionably it has curative power. But radium is also one of the most dangerous elements on earth. Its radiation seems to interact in some unknown fashion with the molecular structure of life itself. (Rubenfeld 2011: 413–414)

This insight – which the real Marie Curie managed to downplay or ignore until her death of anaemia or leukaemia (cf. Grady 1998) in 1934 – is pivotal to the third mystery (apart from the terrorist attack and the war crime) which the novel introduces: the lethal work of the (female) painters who applied radium paint to watch dials in a New Jersey factory run by Arthur Roeder, whose fictionalised equivalent bears the telling name of Arnold Brighton. According to Claudia Clark, the so-called radium girls "were the first industrial victims of radium poisoning; indeed, they were among the first victims of any form of radioactivity" (Clark 1997: 2). The workers' exposure to the radioactive luminous paint was extreme because they were taught to lick the paint brushes with their tongues in order to create a finer point, which was necessary to paint the small dial figures. When the first workers and ex-workers of the company fell ill, suffering from anaemia, the growth of tumours, necrosis, and many other related symptoms, Roeder (and others with him) emphatically denied a connection to the work in their factories. This connection was established by doctors and law courts in the 1920s and compensation payments were made to the (surviving) victims.

The strong ambivalence of radioactivity as a light source is illustrated in two episodes located in the novel's initial and final chapters: when Colette and Luc Rousseau are abducted from their hotel room, Colette uses her case filled with radioactive material in order to give directions to Younger and Littlemore, who are following them with a radiation detector: "Every sample in Colette's case is radioactive,' said Younger. 'Their car is leaving a trail of radioactive particles like breadcrumbs. We can't see them. But this thing can – if we hurry'" (Rubenfeld 2011: 49). The traditional association of light and detection is maintained through Colette's sophisticated plan which dovetails with the admiration for radium and luminescence shared by the general public.

The second episode functions as an epiphany on several levels. Arnold Brighton, Arthur Roeder's fictional alter ego, who is first established as a philanthropist and entrepreneurial provider of the new source of light during his appearance at the Marie Curie Radium Fund lecture, turns out to be the epitome of darkness and deadliness. He is also involved in the conspiracy of Senator Fall and other Republican senators who instigated the Wall Street bombing in order to provoke a war with Mexico, a country rich in ores for the procurement of radium. After Colette has realised the full extent of radium's lethal properties during a tour of Brighton's factory (474–475) and tries to escape from Brighton and his bodyguard, she turns off the factory's master light switch, "plung[ing] the factory into darkness" (482). In a reversal of the detective plot logic which would stage the positive character as the source of illumination and elucidation, it is Brighton who lifts up a "glass measuring cup of radio-luminescent paint [...], glowing greenish yellow, casting an eerie light on his nose and chin" (482), in order to create new light. When Colette manages to throw the cup's content into Brighton's face, he literally merges with his product and becomes a quasi-gothic figure. In a travesty of his previous function as modern lightbringer he turns into his own uncanny double, a modern Lucifer, "his face a glowing chartreuse orb, his eyes starkly white by contrast" (484). As a result, the progressivist discourse about the potential of radium as a cure-all and scientific Holy Grail is revealed to be a powerful myth, obscuring radium's deadliness by mesmerising the public with a seductive, greenish light: a 'deadly glow' (cf. Mullner 1999) which represents Enlightenment's dark side.

Conclusion

As I argued in this paper, *The Hound of the Baskervilles* and *The Death Instinct* can be read as powerful illustrations of light which inadvertently, but inevitably, evoke the forces of night. In this respect, both texts can be compared to the famous lines which John Milton penned in order to evoke the realm of hell and in which the light of hellfire magnifies the overpowering presence of eternal darkness and makes it "visible":

A Dungeon horrible, on all sides round
As one great Furnace flam'd, yet from those flames
No light, but rather darkness visible
Serv'd only to discover sights of woe,
Regions of sorrow, doleful shades, where peace
And rest can never dwell, hope never comes
That comes to all... (Milton 1989: I, ll 61–67)

In *The Hound of the Baskervilles* the ambivalence of (figures of) light and darkness is coupled with the novel's narrative and generic fluctuation, with Sherlock Holmes trying to provide closure to the overwhelming experience of the nocturnal and primitive he managed to keep at bay. His "disclosure of hidden motives and unperceived facts is organized around visual metaphors ('Retrospection' and 'point-of-view') that frame the work of detection in familiar ocularcentric terms" (Smajic 2010: 2), producing an act of containment which the novel's overall structure denies.

In *The Death Instinct*, it is the multilayered detective plot in unison with the romance plot (centred around Younger and Colette Rousseau) which seeks to exorcise the nocturnal element from its conclusion. When Jimmy Littlemore, correcting his former sceptical view of the new decade, states, "Something in the air. The twenties may not be as bad as I thought" (Rubenfeld 2011: 525), his wish to see the silver lining is implicitly challenged by the information that a postmodern reader would add to the dangers mentioned in the novel: the end of the Golden Twenties in economic disaster; the looming of an even more disastrous world war at the end of the following decade; 9/11, which is conjured by the September bombing of 1920 and which is also replayed in the discussions about an unjustified war of aggression in Mexico; and the civilian and military dangers of radioactivity. That Colette Rousseau's exposure to radioactivity as a long-standing assistant to Mme Curie could result in long-term effects, or that Stratham Younger's uncured war trauma (also reminiscent of more recent wars) might produce more violent outbreaks than the one represented in the novel, links the characters' fates to the more general elements of darkness and gloom that an early 21st century reception perspective undoubtedly constructs.

In both novels, the professional and amateur detectives and scientists who attempt to explore and master the nocturnal spheres of the human psyche, of dark places and dark secrets, rely on sources of light as technology and as metaphor. What most of them fail to understand is their fundamental implication in the darkness they help to create,[8] a darkness which feeds back on their own position in the texts, transforming these figures of light into liminal figures, go-betweens who are suddenly placed in the darkness they sought to control.

Works Cited

Bronfen, Elisabeth. 2013. *Night Passages: Philosophy, Literature, and Film*. New York, NY: Columbia University Press.

Clark, Claudia. 1997. *Radium Girls: Women and Industrial Health Reform 1910 – 1935*. London: University of North Carolina Press.

Clausson, Nils. 2005. "Degeneration, *Fin-de-Siècle* Gothic, and the Science of Detection: Arthur Conan Doyle's *The Hound of the Baskervilles* and the Emergence of the Modern Detective Story". *Journal of Narrative Theory* 35.1: 60 – 87.

Doyle, Arthur Conan. 2003. *The Hound of the Baskervilles* (1902). Ed. Christopher Frayling. London: Penguin.

Frame, Paul. 2007. "Radioluminescent Paint". *Oak Ridge Associated Universities,* 10 August 2007. <http://www.orau.org/ptp/collection/radioluminescent/radioluminescentinfo.htm> [accessed 7 April 2015].

Freud, Sigmund. 1955. *The Standard Edition of the Complete Psychological Works of Sigmund Freud*. Vol. XVIII. Ed. James Strachey. London: The Hogarth Press.

Grady, Denise. 1998. "A Glow in the Dark, and a Lesson in Scientific Peril". *New York Times* October 6. n. pag.

Horkheimer, Max and Theodor W. Adorno. 2002. *Dialectic of Enlightenment: Philosophical Fragments*. Redford City, CA: Stanford University Press.

Kayman, Martin A. 2003. "The short story from Poe to Chesterton". In: Martin Priestman (ed.). *The Cambridge Companion to Crime Fiction*. Cambridge, MA: Cambridge University Press. 41 – 58.

Lavine, Matthew. 2013. *The First Atomic Age: Scientists, Radiations, and the American Public, 1895 – 1945*. New York, NY: Palgrave Macmillan.

Melbin, Murray. 1987. *Night as Frontier: Colonizing the World After Dark*. New York, NY: The Free Press.

Milton, John. 1989. *Paradise Lost* (1667). Ed. Christopher Ricks. Harmondsworth: Penguin.

Mullner, Ross. 1999. *Deadly Glow. The Radium Dial Worker Tragedy:* Washington, DC: American Public Health Association.

Otter, Chris. 2008. *The Victorian Eye: A Political History of Light and Vision in Britain, 1800 – 1910*. Chicago, IL: University of Chicago Press.

Rubenfeld, Jed. 2011. *The Death Instinct* (2010). London: Headline Publishing.

Smajic, Srdjan. 2010. *Ghost-Seers, Detectives and Spiritualists: Theories of Vision in Victorian Literature*. Cambridge, MA: Cambridge University Press.

---

8 Both texts therefore illustrate the basic thesis developed by Adorno and Horkheimer in their *Dialectic of Enlightenment* (orig. 1944; trans. 1972/2002).

Thoms, Peter. 2002. "Poe's Dupin and the power of detection". In: Kevin J. Hayes (ed.). *The Cambridge Companion to Edgar Allan Poe*. Cambridge, MA: Cambridge University Press. 133–147.

Stella Butter
The Blackout of Community:
Charlotte Jones' *The Dark*

The modern Western world is unthinkable without electric light. Electric illumination is bound up with modes of industrial production, the organisation of work, lifestyles, and fantasies of panoptic control, to name just some elements on the long list of how electric light is crucial for modern living. Many cultural theorists have been quick to draw attention to how electric light is enmeshed with processes of modernisation. Walter Benjamin (1974: 49), for example, famously described how the shock of electric light in the city, which had previously only known gaslight, dramatically changed the cityscape in the 19th century and, by doing so, rendered the flaneur out of place. In the 21st century, the most effective way of demonstrating the cultural significance of electric light is arguably the staging of a blackout. In this article, I engage with a contemporary British play that does precisely this. Funny lights, dodgy wiring and finally "wham ... a blackout" (Jones 2004: 42) feature prominently in Charlotte Jones' *The Dark*.[1]

At the heart of Jones' play is an exploration of community in contemporary Britain. We encounter six characters living in "a typical terraced street of two-up, two-down houses" (2004: 3). This physical proximity does not, however, translate into a feeling of community among the neighbours. The dramatic flickering of electric lights in this modern living space can be seen as a psychological comment on dysfunctional relationships and the pervading atmosphere of violence and alienation within society. Jones' play highlights the metaphoric qualities of light and darkness by connecting the level of illumination with the psychological landscapes of characters. At the same time, the play draws attention to the "thing-power" (Bennett 2010: 2) of light by showing how the power cut makes a difference in social interaction. In my article, I discuss how the notion of community staged in *The Dark* is informed by both the metaphoric quality of light and its agency. Given the detailed stage directions regarding the use of lighting in the play, special attention will be paid to how this theatrical dimension shapes the play's depiction of community.

---

1 Jones' *The Dark* is, of course, not the only British play to exploit the dramatic potential of a power cut for the stage. Peter Shaffer's *Black Comedy* (1965), for example, makes use of a blackout for farcical effects. Its theatrical lighting is, however, markedly different to that of Jones' play because artificial light is indicated by "[c]omplete darkness" (Shaffer 1981: 143) and the failure of electricity through "[b]rilliant light" (146).

The Metaphoricity of Light/Dark: Communal and Individual Malfunction

The Dark introduces the topic of community by granting the audience access to the home life of six characters who are immediate neighbours. Six rooms on stage, which are "divided loosely by paper-thin walls[,] [...] represent in a highly stylised way both the rooms of one house and three houses in a row" (Jones 2004: 3). The first six scenes of the play show the inhabitants of these houses going about their daily activities and interacting with family members in their homes. In contrast to Western ideals of home, which conjure up visions of an "embryonic community" (Douglas 2012: 51) promising warmth, safety, mutual understanding, and support in times of need, Jones' play presents home spaces as insecure worlds. Even before the power cut, there is a lurking sense of crisis due to displays of hostility and the reoccurring conversational topics of crime and things being wrong. The power cut brings this crisis to a head as conflicts are brought out into the open. However, darkness is not only crisis realised, but also enables moments of communal bonding as the neighbours come together in one of the homes before the return of electric light causes them to scatter and go their own ways again.

The play's focus on how home spaces are embedded within a neighbourhood encourages the audience to think about scales of home: how does the experience and structure of home life connect to larger scale units, such as one's neighbourhood and nation? The question of what form communal life takes is hence not restricted to the family or neighbourhood as an object of literary analysis, but expanded to the nation as homeland. The issue of scale is foregrounded when characters wonder, after the electric lights went funny, whether "the whole street's affected? Maybe it's not just us" (Jones 2004: 7). This correspondence between micro- and macrostructure is heightened through parallels between the characters' home life and events presented on national television. A breaking news story on TV deals with how a man brutally murdered his wife and two children with a hammer before committing suicide. This event haunts the play because one of the inhabitants of the terraced houses, Brian, a husband and father, is also contemplating committing this crime himself.

By presenting home as a place of media consumption (e. g. television, internet), home becomes a "phantasmagoric place, to the extent that electronic media of various kinds allow the radical intrusion of distant events into the space of domesticity" (Morley 2000: 9). The traditional notion of a strict public/private divide, which allows for the idea that home is a refuge from the public sphere, is hence undermined. The flickering electric lights in the play, which culminate in a black out, further strengthen the idea of interconnectivity by implying that home spaces are part of a network. Currents of electricity flowing through a network of cables render each home part of an interconnected and dynamic whole. Taking its cue from the marked spread of technological and media networks in modernity, *The Dark* uses the electric network as a model to map both the 'wiring' of the social body or nation and that of the individual who is part of this networked society. Each node of the nationwide network(s) turns out, on closer inspection, to be a further network. *The Dark* hence locates network structures on different scales, ranging from society to the workings of individual minds.[2]

A strong focus is thereby on gauging the relationship between the individual and society: Jones' play addresses the crucial question of whether the networked nation or society allows for the experience of "a 'caring-and-sharing' community" (Bauman 2001: 111). While both 'society' and 'community' are forms of "associative life" (Delanty 2003: 32), it is only the latter term that has, the sociologist Zygmunt Bauman notes, a "warm feel" (2001: 3) to it. The ideal of community (and one might add 'home') promises to grant "people what neither society nor the state can offer, namely a sense of belonging in an insecure world" (Delanty 2003: 26). The yearning for community in contemporary society is therefore, according to Gerard Delanty, best understood "as a response to the crisis in solidarity and belonging that has been exacerbated and at the same time induced by globalization" (2).[3]

The mapping of social spaces in *The Dark* foregrounds "dodgy connection[s]" (Jones 2004: 8) and suggests that "complete rewiring" (Jones 2004: 10) may be necessary to transform contemporary networks of social relations into communal ones. The malfunction of the electric light in the modern living space is a metaphoric comment on dysfunctional community. The ideal

---

2 The use of networks or webs as a metaphor to understand units on various scales is already prominent in Victorian literature as the example of George Eliot's *Middlemarch* (1871/72) shows (cf. Miller 1992; Otis 2001). On the network as a key metaphor of modernity and a model for mapping social relations, cf. Böhme (2004).

3 This is not to say that the ideal of a 'caring-and-sharing community' is unproblematic. Critics have been quick to point out the blind spots that arise when conceptualising community exclusively in terms of a warm inner circle of belonging: "There is a price to be paid for the privilege of 'being in a community' – and it is inoffensive or even invisible only as long as the community stays in the dream. The price is paid in the currency of freedom, variously called 'autonomy', 'right to self-assertion', 'right to be yourself'. Whatever you choose, you gain some and lose some. Missing community means missing security; gaining community, if it happens, would soon mean missing freedom" (Bauman 2001: 4). On the ongoing debate on different conceptualisations and assessments of community in sociology and philosophy, cf. Delanty (2003) and Rosa et al. (2010).

of community in the context of this play refers to experiencing a sense of belonging and support. Elsie, who is of the older generation with her 70 years of age, laments the loss of community in the neighbourhood:

> This street never used to be like this. Everyone looked out for everyone else. [...] Now I don't know half of them. Sooner gouge their eyes out than look at you. Cut out their tongues rather than give you the time of day. (Jones 2004: 15)

The imagery of physical mutilation gives an impression of the pervading atmosphere of violence in the play, which counteracts the ideal of supporting and caring for each other.

The loss of community is not only visible in the neighbourhood, but also holds true for the home as an 'embryonic community'. Isolation, alienation, and an atmosphere of menace pervade each of the home spaces depicted. There is no intimacy between family members in the sense of cognitive or emotional closeness. Physical expressions of caring, such as affectionate embraces, are also not displayed.[4] This lack of intimacy undermines the ideal of family life. In contemporary Western culture, 'doing family' is seen as overlapping with practices of intimacy, i.e. practices that "enable, generate and sustain a subjective sense of closeness and being attuned and special to each other" (Jamieson 2011: 1). One way of building intimacy is "through a dialogue of mutual self disclosure between equals, revealing inner qualities and feelings, simultaneously generating a self-reinforcing narration of the self" (2). In Jones' play, the inability of achieving intimacy is linked to the failure of communication.

Language is rendered problematic with the very first words that are spoken by the characters. Each of the six rooms is lit up consecutively to show the characters living in their home spaces. When all the cells are lit "the characters speak/type at once, and as such their words are indistinguishable" (Jones 2004: 5). This collective babbling on the level of neighbourhood ties in with the failure of communication on the lower level unit of the family. The teenager Josh, for example, shuts himself into his room and refuses to speak to his parents. The interaction between Elsie and her grown-up son John, to offer a second example, is strained by her suspicion that the charges of paedophilia against him may be true. The isolation and alienation between the characters are visualised during the power cut when they "bump into each other in the dark, as if they were bumping into furniture" (30).

The events in the play imply that it is not only the network of social relations that needs to be rewired, but also the wiring within the individuals. *The Dark* fea-

---

4 On these different dimensions of intimacy, cf. Jamieson (2011).

tures characters who harbour "bad thoughts" (Jones 2004: 26) so that physical violence may erupt at any moment.[5] John, Elsie's grown-up son, for example, dreams about killing his mother and 'murderously' tells her how far she pushes him (cf. 56). Louisa, a married woman in her thirties, ponders whether life would be easier if her baby were dead so that she could finally stop agonising over the possibility of cot death. The malfunction of individual wiring may have far-reaching effects precisely because the subjects are nodes within a network. This danger becomes especially manifest in Brian's description of his traffic accident:

> **Brian** I'm a lorry driver, long-distance. I'm not now – I'm on the sick, but I used to be so – you know – up in my little cabin, music, driving all over the land. [...] A friendly chat here and there. Tales from the road, you know the sort of thing, innocent. Then, wham, one day I have a blackout. [...] Like a sledgehammer through my brain. All the wiring went. [...] I lost control. [...] Do you know where I ended up?
> **Janet** Right by a railway line.
> **Brian** [...] Do you know what time it was? Four o'clock in the afternoon – it was the school train I would have hit. (Jones 2004: 42–43)

The marked presence of a material network, namely the railway, in Brian's description of the accident gestures once again to a model of society as an interconnected network. The interplay between part and whole in the network means that the 'blackout' of individual units may spread along various lines of connection and hence generate system-wide effects. In this case, Brian was just "[i]nches away from a major catastrophe" (43). At the same time, the nodes of the network, namely the subjects themselves, appear as a bodily network of electric circuits ('wiring') so that a mise-en-abyme structure is introduced. The network structure of the individual unit is replicated on a higher level.

The use of lighting in Jones' play further emphasises that the human body and brain are to be understood in terms of an electric network. The final scene of the play depicts Barnaby, Louisa's husband, falling asleep. The stage directions describe how his drifting asleep is to be visualised through the use of lighting: "He starts to nod off. [...] He wakes himself up. The lights lower and raise three times as his head nods and then jolts up" (82). The ensuing "Blackout on all the rooms" signals his deep sleep. This staging of Barnaby's falling asleep by means of flickering electric light points to the currents of electricity flowing through the human body, namely through the neural network of the brain

---

5 Violence is clearly gendered in *The Dark*. In one of the climactic scenes, two men (Brian and John) appear to be on the verge of killing women (cf. p. 56). This constellation conforms to the coding of violence as masculine and the victim position as feminine in patriarchal society. On gender and violence in literature, cf. Bach (2010).

and, by extension, through the whole body's network of nerves. The analogy between the individual as an electric network and a larger social whole as a network explains why the metaphoric quality of light/darkness in the play pertains to both the quality of social interaction and to the psyche of each individual.

One of the key 'dodgy connections' that Jones' play targets is the relation between adults and children. The contemporary culture of fear regarding children (see below) is a lurking presence in Brian's description of his blackout with its spectre of dead children. Brian perceives the potential harm he could have wrecked as a fall from innocence (cf. 42). The fear and anxiety surrounding childhood is markedly brought to the fore through the issue of paedophilia in the play. John admits his paedophilic leanings for young boys and hates himself for them. He refuses to give in to his urges and instead tries to exorcise his paedophilic fantasies during the blackout:

> These are my worst thoughts. Thoughts of young boys. Boys of fourteen, fifteen. I send them into the net. I scatter them into the world. There's no power tonight. It's safe. What I think – what I write – will disappear. Nobody will see my thoughts, nobody will read them. So they will evaporate. Yes. (Jones 2004: 52)

While John "choose[s] not to" (61) become a 'monstrous paedophile' (cf. ibid.), the interaction between fourteen year old Josh, who is Brian's son, with paedophiles on the internet endows the threat of child abuse with added urgency. All in all, Jones' play is riddled with numerous references to the victimisation of children, be it through murderous fathers or parents who shake their baby to death.

With this intense focus on the child as a possible victim, *The Dark* participates in the child-panic that is the sign of contemporary times. As Helen Freshwater explains,

> anxiety about the experience of childhood in Britain seems to have intensified in the twenty-first century, and the pervasiveness of these anxieties leads Libby Brooks to conclude in her 2006 publication, *The Story of Childhood: Growing Up in Modern Britain*, that '[...] Childhood has become the crucible into which is ground each and every adult anxiety – about sex, consumerism, technology, safety, achievement, respect, the proper shape of life. This is a time of child-panic'. (Freshwater 2013: 170 – 171)

The devastating effects of this hysteric "fear that children will be abducted, murdered by paedophiles, or commit violent crimes themselves" (169) is shown by means of the self-destructive behaviour of Josh, who turns himself into a nocturnal creature as a survival strategy:

Stop crying, baby [i.e. Louisa's baby]. Don't cry. Don't be frightened. They teach you that. [...] From the moment you're born. FEAR, press, SEND! [...] You're like wide open when you're born – just accepting it all, you know, and then they throw all this shit at you – and slowly they close you off. Then they start thinking bad thoughts about you. [...] They want to turn you into their worst fears. (Jones 2004: 27)

In this passage, Josh describes the psychological damage he suffered due to the pervasive culture of fear regarding child abuse. He describes how he "used to be scared of the dark" (27) because he thought there was "a man in the shadows who was going to hurt [him]" (ibid.). The series of prohibitions the adults issue to protect their children turn into an instrument of hurt themselves. Josh's coping strategy with his intense fear of the dark is to 'invite the man in the shadows in' (cf. ibid.). He not only actively seeks contact with paedophiles in the internet, but wants to become "nocturnal" (28) himself by actively "pedd[ling] terror" (ibid.). He is so successful with his transgressive behaviour that his own parents become afraid of him. Josh's sense of safety, his warding off the ever present danger of becoming a victim himself, depends on other people being scared of him (cf. 53).

The overall impression that Jones' play conveys is that of a crisis. This sense of crisis has to do with the characters' feeling of helplessness in the face of contingency. Brian's traffic accident, the inexplicable cot death of Louisa's first baby, and Josh's deep-seated fear of becoming a victim of child abuse all point to uncontrollable elements in daily life. This list may be easily expanded. The fact that Elsie, for example, worked for "Emergency service" (33) and wakes up with the routine phrase on her lips "Which service do you require? [...] Ambulance? Fire or Police?" (ibid.) emphasises the idea that hazard is woven into our lives. The blackout is a metaphoric expression of this idea: "No one has power" (30).

The characters' sense of helplessness in an insecure world increases due to the lack of communication and emotional support. Brian, for example, thinks about killing his family "because he loved them. He couldn't show it in any other way [...]. He'd forgotten all the other ways. Things had got so bad he thought that it would be better to take them with him" (79). It is his wife Janet, who, after the power cut, gives voice to what is preying on her husband's mind in an understanding way, as the passage I just quoted shows. Moments of understanding between individuals offer hope in the play:

Janet We won't need rewiring, then?
Brian No. (Jones 2004: 79)

In the case of Janet and Brian, the flash of understanding between them is also expressed through the physical gesture of a caress. Their moment of closeness can be described as physical, cognitive, and emotional intimacy.

The darkness, which the power cut brings, triggers catalytic events and conversations as characters deal with their worst fears and nightmares. Louisa, for example, was afraid to bond with her newly born baby for fear of another cot death. This is also why she refuses to give her baby a name. Louisa's fear of losing her baby takes on manifest shape when Josh enters her apartment during the blackout and threatens to kill her child: "I could hurt her. I could shake her. I could throw her against that wall. [...] She needs to learn there's so much evil out there" (51). This genuine threat to her baby rallies Louisa to insist on the strength of her child and its capacity to survive. On the one hand, the dark intensifies Louisa's 'loss of power' because she is confronted with her worst nightmare: her inability to save her child from death. On the other hand, she regains a sense of agency by persuasively arguing for the strength of her baby and how she and her husband will be good parents (cf. 51). By doing so, the possibility that her child will live and grow-up becomes real for her. It is due to this catalytic event that Louisa is finally prepared to bond with her baby so that she and her husband Barnaby can now give it a name: Dot.

A similar emotional roller coaster ride can be sketched for the other characters. Janet, for example, finally vents her "sense of awfulness" (74) by storming into her son's room, smashing up his computer with her husband's hammer, all the while screaming

> I KNOW WHAT YOU DO! I KNOW, JOSH! GOING OUT AT NIGHT. TERRORISING THE WORLD. YOU MONSTER! HOW COULD YOU! WHY ARE YOU LIKE THIS?! YOU LITTLE FUCK! YOU – EVIL – LITTLE – YOU – HOW COULD THIS HAPPEN? (Jones 2004: 75)

Josh, in turn, is so shaken by the events of the night that he drops his adopted façade and costume, i.e. his "balaclava" (63) as a scary 'nocturnal creature'. These events include both his mother's violent outburst and his interaction with John. Josh had tried to exorcise his own nightmare by getting John to sexually molest him during the blackout. Under Josh's aggressive pressure, John does own up to having paedophilic desires, but he adamantly refuses to act on these yearnings and to follow Josh's script. Instead, he expresses understanding for Josh's actions: "You don't know who to be, do you? Poor, poor boy. You don't know who to be" (63). Addressed in this way, the teenager drops his 'nocturnal' stance and starts speaking like an 'innocent little boy' again (cf. 63, 76). In a similar manner, Josh spontaneously hugs his father to assuage his bewilderment after his mother's violent outbreak.

While Jones' play offers redemptive moments, it eschews glib happy endings. On the one hand, the play gestures towards the possibility of hope and rejuvenation by showing acts of intimacy, care, and affection between the characters. While tending to John's sling after the end of the power cut, Elsie emphasises, "The darkest hour is just before dawn" (82). This implies that the alienation and isolation of the characters, their 'darkest hour', will come to an end because communal relationships are forged. On the other hand, the depiction of Brian and Barnaby in the final moments of the play renders Elsie's statement highly ambivalent. The literal blackout may be over at that moment, but the 'darkest hour' is still very much present when the audience sees how Brian "clutches his heart. He appears to be in the throes of a heart attack" (ibid.). Given the emphasis on networks in the play, this heart attack or crisis of (blood) circulation within the network of veins can be read as a renewed metaphoric reference to the still ongoing malfunctions within the network of social relations.

In contrast, a silver lining shows itself in Barnaby's case because "his vigil [is] finally over" (ibid.) insofar as he no longer worries over the possibility of another cot death. His family seems to be safe. Jones' play concludes with Barnaby falling asleep, thereby murmuring the name of his daughter: "Dot. Dot. Dot" (ibid.). While the act of his falling asleep signals closure (the end of his vigil), his words, however, undermine the very notion of closure by gesturing to the open-ended nature of the play. Three dots in a written text signify that something is left out. This back and fro between 'darkest hour' and dawn, pessimism and hope, is continued when the flickering lights in the final minutes of the play bring a renewed "Blackout on all the rooms" (ibid.).

Up until now, I have concentrated on the metaphoricity of light and (electric) networks in *The Dark*. The next section expands the discussion of communal relations by looking at the depicted interplay between what may be called '(atmo) spheres' and the thing-power of light.

(Atmo)Spheres: Co-Existence and the Thing-Power of Light

When analysing how *The Dark* engages with the topic of community, it is helpful to work with a distinction between the perspective of the observer and that of the characters immersed in the modern world. As the previous discussion has shown, the individuals depicted in Jones' play suffer from feelings of isolation and alienation in their everyday lives. The textual strategies of Jones' play are geared towards counterbalancing this focus on isolation by raising the audience's awareness of interconnectivity between individuals. The *leitmotif* of networks belongs to these strategies. Another strategy is the use of theatrical space with its distinct atmosphere(s).

The choreography of the characters' spatial movements draws attention to co-existence as the fundamental state of being. The stage directions make clear how this is achieved. As the six rooms on stage represent "both the rooms of one house and three houses in a row", the "characters will use all the rooms as if they were their own, if necessary walking through occupied rooms without seeing the other occupants" (3). This means that the seemingly self-enclosed room an individual dwells in literally contains the presence of others. The use of space in *The Dark* visualises what Martin Heidegger termed 'being-with' (*Mitsein*): being-in-the-world means being-with-others. In Jones' play, the individual hence does not appear as autonomous or "absolutely detached for-itself" (Nancy 1991: 3). Instead, an "ontological 'sociality'" or "being-in-common" (28) is given prominence. This (re)conceptualisation of the individual is of crucial importance for community thinking because, as the philosopher Jean-Luc Nancy explains, "one cannot make a [communal] world with simple atoms. [...] There has to be an inclination or an inclining from one toward the other" (ibid.). Community requires that the individual perceives and affirms the ontological dimension of *Mitsein*.[6] The staging of space in *The Dark* encourages the audience to embrace such a stance.

The movement of the characters through "occupied rooms" transforms the "six cells" (Jones 2004: 5) into 'consubjective space'. The philosopher Peter Sloterdijk coined this term in order to express that being-in-the-world means being situated within a dyadic or multiple space of relations, in which the self is only one of many poles (cf. 2011: 541). Sloterdijk refers to these spaces of relations as

---

6 The philosopher Jean-Luc Nancy goes a step further in his argument by reconceptualising 'community' to designate the ontological level of *Mitsein*. He rejects all notions of community based on shared commonalities such as race, ethnicity, class, religion, values, or norms because the positing of a shared identity could lead to authoritarian forms of community that rigidly exclude internal heterogeneity. While Nancy rightly warns of the dangers inherent in establishing commonalities as a basis for community, his ontological redefinition of community has the drawback of divorcing 'community' from empirical forms of associative life with their concrete power hierarchies and political battles for inclusion and exclusion. Nancy hence neglects, his critics emphasise, the role of community as a "concrete element of politics" (Spitta 2013: 298; my translation). As noted above, *The Dark* foregrounds *Mitsein* through its use of space in order to surmount an isolationist stance of the individual. While awareness of co-existence is a pre-requisite for establishing communal relations, Jones' play also implies that community requires more than *Mitsein*, namely the experience of solidarity, care, and mutual understanding between different selves embedded in power relations.

spheres in order to emphasise how moods, emotions, and dynamic interactions colour the atmosphere of these con-subjective spaces (cf. 28, 46). The performance of *The Dark* stages these six cells as spheres whose atmosphere is profoundly shaped by the level of illumination: "The lights flicker again. They [i. e. the characters.] are all found in varying states of bewilderment. The baby stops crying. The music stops" (Jones 2004: 5). The play of light influences the atmosphere of these cells as the references to mood ("bewilderment") and soundscape ('stop crying') emphasise. Most importantly, the audience also experiences these changes in the atmosphere of the theatrical space. This experience may encourage the audience to ponder how they, too, are enclosed within an atmospheric space that divides and connects subjects.

By foregrounding consubjective space, *The Dark* also draws attention to the "ecstatic" (Sloterdijk 2011: 84) existence of the self. The self is not, Sloterdijk explains, an impermeable self-enclosed entity. Instead, "the relationship between human subjects sharing a field of proximity can be described as one between restless containers that contain and exclude one another" (85). The subject is "surrounded, encompassed, disclosed, breathed-upon, resounded-through, attuned and addressed" (541). In the anonymous apartment house of Jones' play, for example, each of the characters is attuned to micro-sonospheres, feels addressed by them, and contributes to these. A concrete example of this is provided when Josh turns down his music to better hear Louisa's baby cry and starts addressing it. Moreover, the audience can literally see the six cells with their inhabitants as relational spaces that contain and exclude one another. The characters use the rooms of the others so that these spaces are contained or shared within their space. At the same time, there is also an element of exclusion because, within the fictional world, they are still within the space of their separated apartment and immersed within its specific micro-atmosphere.

The "ecstatic entwinement of the subject" (87) within spheres becomes even more pronounced in *The Dark* due to its specific pattern of elaborate interconnectivity between the characters. It is from the privileged position of an observer that this interconnectivity may be identified and traced. The audience finds, for example, characters echoing each other's statements, speaking in chorus, and using identical objects within their interior spaces. This means that

> [e]very subject in the real consubjective space is containing, in so far as it absorbs and
> grasps other subjective elements, and contained, in so far as it is encompassed [...] by
> the circumspections and arrangements of others. (Sloterdijk 2011: 87–88)

Consubjective spaces erode the inside-outside distinction because the self is perceived as not something exclusively 'inside a single container' in the sense of psychological interiority, but dispersed and created within spheres, and hence inside multiple containers. The characters in *The Dark* not only unwittingly share the interiority of their domestic spaces with subjects living in other apartments. The larger consubjective space of the apartment house is also portrayed as 'absorbing and grasping their subjective elements' when things they have said in the privacy of their home are repeated verbatim by other characters in their flat. The scenes in which the characters, unbeknownst to them, speak in a chorus are perhaps the clearest example of how the play stages the individuals as subjects that are contained and encompassed by (the voices of) others. While the characters themselves remain oblivious to their shared interiority, the play potentially raises the audience's awareness of how the climactic conditions of spheres are created through socially embedded ecstatic subjectivities, spatial arrangements, media, and technology, especially lighting.

The raising of the audience's awareness regarding interconnectivity or being-in-spheres can be described as the epistemological function of the play. As scholars like Rita Felski insist, literature is a potential and valuable source of knowledge precisely because it uses artistic means to "expand, enlarge, or reorder our sense of how things are" (2008: 83). In the case of *The Dark*, the aesthetic strategies encourage the audience to perceive existence as co-existence. The form of knowledge conveyed by *The Dark* is hence "more akin to […] 'seeing as' rather than 'seeing that', learning by habituation and acquaintance rather than by instruction" (93).

This epistemological function of Jones' play arguably serves a sociological function. By raising awareness of interconnectivity, *The Dark* works against indifference as a mode of 'being-with-another' in favour of being attuned to one's relation to other people. The development of the plot points to a shift from egocentrism to communal relations. It is during the power cut that the characters start interacting with each other and finally introduce themselves as neighbours. All of the characters eventually make their way to the apartment of Janet and Brian. It is there that "[p]eople talk in cross-currents – the whole room is talking" (Jones 2004: 70). While some characters speak at cross purposes, there is also a sense of disclosural intimacy that allows for at least a moment of bonding. Louisa, for example, for the first time speaks about how she randomly sent dozens of faxes to complete strangers informing them of the death of her baby Jacob. She did this because she could not bear the idea of people going about their daily business as if Jacob's death had never happened. The blackout within the six terraced houses triggers events and interactions that allow the characters at least briefly to move out of metaphoric darkness. This is indicated through the stage directions shortly after the blackout: The characters start to "slowly […] talk their way out of the darkness. Softly, starting to overlap [i. e. characters' voices], it should sound almost like a prayer" (29). The reference to prayer endows the move out of metaphoric darkness, the surmounting of isolation and alienation, with a religious dimension so that moments of care and affection between characters are coded as redemptive.

The Dark not only establishes metaphorical meanings of illumination and its absence, but also draws attention to the thing-power of light. As outlined above, the power cut in *The Dark* literally makes a difference in how the characters interact. Before the power cut, the people in the six terraced houses were intensely aware of each other's goings on because they could hear each other through the thin walls, but there was no social intercourse. The fact that the neighbours only start to directly engage with each other in the course of the power cut foregrounds the role of light as an 'actant'. As Jane Bennett explains, an actant is "neither an object nor a subject but an 'intervener' [...] [;] by virtue of its particular location in an assemblage [...] [it] makes the difference, makes things happen, becomes the decisive force catalyzing an event" (Bennett 2010: 9). This notion of an actant is informed by Bruno Latour's concept of distributed agency. Instead of positing a strict subject/object divide with agency exclusively attributed to the subject, proponents of distributed agency insist that "agency always depends on the collaboration, cooperation, or interactive interference of many bodies and forces. A lot happens to the concept of agency once nonhuman things are figured less as social constructions and more as actors [...]" (Bennett 2010: 21).

The notion of distributed agency goes hand in hand with network thinking because actants are seen as part of heterogeneous assemblages. "Assemblages are ad hoc groupings of diverse elements" (23–24) with a decentralised structure and whose effects are emergent properties. Bennett discusses the electrical power grid as a prototypical example of an assemblage:

> It is a material cluster of charged parts that have indeed affiliated, remaining in sufficient proximity and coordination to produce distinctive effects. The elements of the assemblage work together, although their coordination does not rise to the level of an organism. Rather, its jelling endures alongside energies and factions that fly out from it and disturb it from within. And [...] the elements of this assemblage, while they include humans and their (social, legal, linguistic) constructions, also include some very active and powerful nonhumans: electrons, trees, wind, fire, electromagnetic fields. (Bennett 2010: 24)

Bennett teases out the specific actants involved in the electric grid by concentrating on the North American blackout on 14 August 2003 as a case study. Electricity features as one of the nonhuman actants in the electric grid, whose other actants include electric companies in different American states, the Federal Energy Regulatory Commission, and members of Congress who subscribed to a neoliberalist belief in market self-regulation (cf. 25 – 28). The blackout hence appears as the emergent effect of a "human-nonhuman assemblage" (28).

Jones' play refrains from tracing the actants involved in generating the depicted blackout. It does, however, encourage the audience to adopt a view of distributed agency by repeatedly emphasising the thing-power of light in combination with a focus on networks. Another clear example of the thing-power of light is offered when the lights suddenly go on. All of the neighbours, who are sitting and chatting in Janet and Brian's apartment, suddenly "rush homewards" (Jones 2004: 77). "They all start to drift away to other rooms. To the light" (78). The lighting of the spheres in which the characters live and move hence makes all the difference for communal interaction. As Janet aptly puts it, "We must do this again. [...] Not wait for a power cut for the next time" (78). The implication is that the deepening of relations with one's neighbours would never have taken place without the power cut. The characters are embedded within an assemblage of human and non-human actants (e. g. light). The presence or absence of light in this dynamic network changes its configuration: its literal currents (i. e. electricity) and metaphoric flows (e. g. flow of communication). By staging the level of illumination as a catalytic force, Jones' play suggests an "[a]gentic capacity" (Bennett 2010: 9) of light.

The metaphoric and agentic dimensions of light are closely intertwined in the play. In metaphoric terms, the blackout references the characters' experience of radical contingency and concomitant feeling of powerlessness. A traditional subject-centred notion of agency is, indeed, questioned by staging the agentic capacity of light. It is important to note, however, that *The Dark* equally highlights the agency of humans and their ability of making a difference in terms of shaping their own lives and that of others. *The Dark* does not give up the idea of human agency as such, but instead conceptualises the subject as part of a network of distributed agency.

All in all, *The Dark* offers a multi-facetted exploration of how light features as an actant in communal interaction. While the play is sceptical about achieving a sense of belonging and bonding in the modern world, it does hold this vision up as an ideal. Most importantly, it draws on strategies that may help to raise the audience's awareness of interconnectivity, which may, in turn, help foster communal relations. The 'blackout of community' in the title of my paper is a reference to this double movement. On the one hand, the play diagnoses the 'blacking out' of community in the modern world. Atomisation and not community seems to be the order of the day. On the other hand, the literal blackout, i. e. the loss of electric light, functions as a trigger for the development of communal interaction in the course of the play. In exploring the role of electric light as an actant, *The Dark* is notable for the full use it makes of theatrical lighting so that the audience members can themselves experience how lighting contributes to creating a specific (atmo)sphere within the playhouse. Perhaps the sphere of the darkened auditorium is even perceived as a communal space due to the shared witnessing of the events on stage. If yes, then this transitory community is likely to scatter once the theatrical lights go on again just like the characters in the play did after the end of the power cut. Thus, the social interaction preceding and following the performance of the play demonstrates on an extratextual level the role of light within a complex assemblage of human and non-human actants that was foregrounded within the storyworld.[7]

Works Cited

Bach, Susanne (ed.). 2010. *Gewalt, Geschlecht, Fiktion: Gewaltdiskurse und Gender-Problematik in zeitgenössischen englischsprachigen Romanen, Dramen und Filmen*. Trier: wvt.

Bauman, Zygmunt. 2001. *Community: Seeking Safety in an Insecure World*. Cambridge: Polity 2001.

Benjamin, Walter. 1974. "Der Flaneur" (1937/38). In: Walter Benjamin. *Charles Baudelaire: Ein Lyriker im Zeitalter des Hochkapitalismus*. Ed. Rolf Tiedemann. Frankfurt/Main: Suhrkamp. 33–65.

Bennett, Jane. 2010. *Vibrant Matter: A Political Ecology of Things*. Durham: Duke University Press.

Böhme, Hartmut. 2004. "Einführung: Netzwerke. Zur Theorie und Geschichte einer Konstruktion". In: Jürgen Barkhoff, Hartmut Böhme, and Jeanne Riou (eds.). *Netzwerke. Eine Kulturtechnik der Moderne*. Cologne: Böhlau. 17–36.

Delanty, Gerard. 2003. *Community*. London: Routledge.

Douglas, Mary. 2012. "The Idea of a Home: A Kind of Space". In: Chiara Briganti and Kathy Mezei (eds.). *The Domestic Space Reader*. Toronto: University of Toronto Press. 50–54.

Felski, Rita. 2008. *Uses of Literature*. Malden, MA: Blackwell.

Freshwater, Helen. 2013. "Children and the Limits of Representation in the Work of Tim Crouch". In: Vicky Angelaki (ed.). *Contemporary British Theatre: Breaking New Ground*. Houndmills: Palgrave Macmillan. 167–188.

Jamieson, Lynn. 2011. "Intimacy as a Concept: Explaining Social Change in the Context of Globalisation or Another Form of Ethnocentrism?". *Sociological Research Online* 16.4. <http://www.socresonline.org.uk/16/4/15.html> [accessed: 15.02.2014].

Jones, Charlotte. 2004. *The Dark*. London: Faber and Faber.

Miller, Hillis J. 1992. "Optic and Semiotic in Middlemarch" In: John Peck (ed.). *Middlemarch: George Eliot*. Houndmills: Macmillan. 65–88.

Morley, David. 2000. *Home Territories. Media, Mobility and Identity:* London: Routledge.

---

7 I would like to thank Stefan Glomb and Marcus Menzel for their helpful feedback on an earlier version of this article.

Nancy, Jean-Luc. 1991. *The Inoperative Community.* Minneapolis, MN: University of Minnesota Press.

Otis, Laura. 2001. *Networking. Communicating with Bodies and Machines in the Nineteenth Century.* Ann Arbor, MI: University of Michigan Press.

Rosa, Hartmut, Lars Gertenbach, Henning Laux, and David Strecker. 2010. *Theorien der Gemeinschaft zur Einführung.* Hamburg: Junius.

Shaffer, Peter. 1998. *Four Plays: The Private Ear/The Public Eye/White Liars/Black Comedy.* Harmondsworth: Penguin.

Sloterdijk, Peter. 2001. *Spheres.* Vol. 1: *Bubbles: Microspherology.* [German 1998]. Los Angeles, CA: Semiotext(e).

Spitta, Juliane. 2013. *Gemeinschaft jenseits von Identität? Über die paradoxe Renaissance einer politischen Idee.* Bielefeld: Transcript.

Murat Sezi

Genre, Gender, Mythology: Functions of Light and Darkness in Terry Pratchett's *Feet of Clay* and *Thud!*

> The compulsive elimination of darkness in and since platonic philosophy, its separation and negative allocation as, among others, hell (the 'hidden'), its equation with evil as well as the equally compulsive attempts to maintain a God that is purified of all dark marks and in all senses of the word a luminous and therefore good God, in short: all attempts to rob the darkness of its right and understand it purely negatively as an absence of light could not remove it. (Thieme 2008: 47; my translation)

Although Thieme's remarks point to a philosophical and theological history in Western culture that has 'favoured' light over darkness, understanding light and darkness as complements instead of opposites also has a long-standing tradition which can be traced back to Greek mythology and the Bible. And while contemporary literature is still under the influence of these traditions, advances in technology and the changing landscape of cities have extended the relationship between light and darkness from metaphysical, conceptual, and spiritual concerns to the realm of real societal issues.

This is interesting for literature and literary studies because it offers authors a variety of influences as well as real-world models to choose from in their portrayal of darkness and light and utilise them stylistically and thematically. The case for fantasy literature is somewhat peculiar because it is primarily oriented towards the past (Attebery 1992: 87) and therefore, presumably, less able to implement said technological advances. For that reason, it needs to rely more strongly on its literary predecessors and the light/darkness relationship in terms of a concept or metaphor. However, this does not negate its potential for addressing real-world issues, and this relationship is, furthermore, not as black and white as one might suppose. While it is true that – in heroic fantasy in particular – the light vs. darkness dichotomy is often merely a stand-in for good vs. evil, there are still numerous other ways to portray this relationship and the spectrum of meanings connected to it.

Writers and readers are aware of the powerful connotative, metaphorical, and symbolic potential connected to the terms light and darkness and make use of them in their process of creating meaning. However, they also warrant contextualisation. For the present study, taking genre into account is highly important for the way in which meaning is created when considering these terms and their associated word fields. For example, Thieme has pointed out that:

the etymological relationship in the Indo-European languages between 'light', 'saying', 'seeing', 'knowing', and 'truth', between light and word leads from the (unavoidable) metaphorical use of the words for light to the development of an ontology and epistemology that is ultimately dominated by light. (Thieme 2008: 47; my translation)

Conversely, one could argue that darkness is associated with ignorance, deceit, and so forth. But if genre is taken into account, the matter may not be as simple as associating light with positive terms and darkness with the corresponding antonyms. The two novels examined here – *Feet of Clay* and *Thud!* – draw upon elements of crime and fantasy fiction, often parodying the conventions of these genres (James 2004: 199). It is my contention that light and darkness have specific uses and meanings within these genres, which has to do with their respective traditions, tropes, and plot lines. To provide an example: When the police officers in *Thud!* characterise their progress in the investigation as being "still in the dark" (127) as far as the crime is concerned, this is true on a literal as well as on a metaphorical level. On the one hand, they are conducting their investigation in the underground tunnels of a dwarf mine; on the other, they have not discovered any clues yet. This is an issue which was pointed out by Farah Mendlesohn when she noted that "in fantasy literature obvious metaphors may be explicitly literalized" (2012: 126). In the case of *Thud!*, while the police procedural is – primarily – a mimetic form, the metaphor above becomes literalised due to the fantasy nature of the text.

This essay posits that Pratchett's utilisation of light and darkness allows him to create a semantic space which accomplishes three things. One, it defamiliarises the light and darkness relationship from known myths and integrates it into invented fictional mythology in order to create a credible culture and belief system. Two, it employs light and darkness in a fashion which situates the texts within their respective genres, for example through the use of metaphorically coherent language. And three, as an extension of these terms, it creates literal and metaphorical visibility and invisibility to showcase gender issues.

At this juncture, it is opportune to present a short overview of *Feet of Clay* and *Thud!* They are the 19th and 34th entries of Terry Pratchett's *Discworld*, a series of humorous fantasy novels that began in 1983 with the publication of *The Colour of Magic* and, with its latest entry in 2013, *Raising Steam*, now spans 40 novels. Although there are recurring settings, characters, and story arcs, each entry can be read as a standalone novel. Spatially, the stories are set on the Discworld, a world that consists of a disc which is upheld by four elephants who are in turn standing on a gigantic turtle. The series is highly metafictional and intertextual, drawing from sources as diverse as world mythology, Shakespeare, and contemporary popular culture.

The two novels discussed here belong to a larger story arc commonly referred to as the City Watch series.[1] All of these novels begin with a crime and are, for the most part, set in Ankh-Morpork, the major metropolis of the Discworld. Subsequently, the City Watch, Ankh-Morpork's police force, investigates and eventually solves this crime. In terms of a literary model, they are similar to the police procedural (James 2004: 196).

In *Feet of Clay*, several murders are committed in Ankh-Morpork, and the city's patrician, Lord Vetinari, is poisoned. While it is first suspected that the city's golems are responsible for the murders, it later turns out that a vampire called Dragon King of Arms was poisoning Vetinari and planning to install a puppet king in his place. A major issue of the novel is free will, shown through the self-determined actions of the golems who were hitherto thought to be mindless labour machines (cf. Butler 2007: 148).

Thud!, on the other hand, focuses on racism and religious conflict. The anniversary of a historic battle between dwarfs and trolls, which is named after its location (Koom Valley), is approaching, and a leader within the dwarf community is murdered, presumably by a troll.[2] It eventually emerges that this dwarf was killed by other dwarfs, subsequently releasing an ancient spirit called the Summoning Dark. The plot is resolved when Commander Vimes of the City Watch defeats this ancient spirit and an artefact reveals that a dwarf and a troll leader of old had intended for dwarfs and trolls to live peacefully alongside one another (cf. Butler 2007: 368).

Thud!: Contrasts of Light and Darkness in Dwarf Culture and Mythology

Thud! begins with a creation myth which tells of the creation of the first man, dwarf, and troll:

> And in the twilight of the mouth of the cave, the geode hatched and the Brothers were born. The first brother walked towards the light, and stood under the open sky. Thus he became too tall. He was the first Man. He found no Laws, and he was enlightened.

---

1 The other novels which belong to this arc are: *Guards! Guards!* (1989), *Men at Arms* (1993), *Jingo* (1997), *The Fifth Elephant* (1999), *Night Watch* (2002), and, to a lesser degree, *Snuff* (2011).
2 Trolls and dwarfs are generally portrayed as enemies in the Discworld novels.

> The second Brother walked towards the darkness, and stood under a roof of stone. Thus he achieved the correct height. He found the Laws Tak had written, and he was endarkened.
>
> But some of the living spirit of Tak was trapped in the broken stone egg, and it became the first troll, wandering the world unbidden and unwanted, without soul or purpose, learning or understanding. Fearful of light and darkness it shambles for ever in twilight, knowing nothing, learning nothing, creating nothing . . . (*Thud!* 7)

This account implements several aspects commonly found in creation myths. The type of creation above is defined as follows:

> The cosmic egg from which the universe was born, often from which mankind emerged, or from which the creator of the universe and mankind emerged: a concept of the ancient cosmogonies of India, Egypt, Greece, Phœnicia, etc., also found in the mythologies of many primitive peoples. (Leach and Fried 1972: 1184)

This can include the separation of one thing (here, the geode) into several. Furthermore, this passage utilises the concept of defamiliarisation. While the reader has just been informed that man 'walked towards the light', 'stood under the open sky', and 'was enlightened', acts to which we ascribe positive values, he does not find any laws. Meanwhile, the process of being 'endarkened' is said to lead to lawfulness and correctness, expressed through height. The trolls, on the other hand, are 'unbidden and unwanted, without soul or purpose, learning or understanding'. Their place in the cosmogenic order is described as 'twilight', implying that they are caught between, but not truly a part of either light or darkness. Elisabeth Bronfen has characterised cosmogenetic narratives as follows:

> Cosmogenetic narratives revolve around the notions of formless darkness informing the beginning of all things. The world takes shape only in contrast *to* and separation *from* the deep darkness from which it has emerged, engendering an incessant interplay of day and night, light and shadow, becoming and passing away. (Bronfen 2013: 29; emphases in the original)

In the Bible, for instance, "[t]he first work of creation was the separation of light and darkness, which were interfused in the beginning" (Chevalier and Gheerbrant 1996: 602). And the *Dictionary of Biblical Imagery* notes that "God's first creative act is to produce light and separate it from darkness, with overtones of light's conquering darkness (Gen 1:4–5)" (Ryken et al. 1998: 191). So while light and darkness are separated in the dwarfish creation myth as well, darkness and not light is assigned primacy in the order of things.

This creation myth outlines separation and disunity between dwarfs, humans, and trolls, though the suggested inferiority of the trolls is much more important. At the same time, the fact that all three races come from the same source and are labelled 'Brothers', mirrors the original biblical interfusion of light and darkness, an aspect which is also implemented in resolving the novel's plot. At this point, consideration will be given to how this creation myth and its treatment of light and darkness form a basis for dwarf society, customs, and beliefs.

The beginning of the novel does not establish a conflict between light and darkness at all, but between traditional dwarf culture and the modernity of the city of Ankh-Morpork. As Vimes, the head of the City Watch begins his investigations into the murder of a dwarf religious leader, he observes the deep-downers, a group of what are essentially dwarfish religious extremists who are preaching "the superiority of dwarf over troll [...] and [to] remove trollkind from the face of the world" (*Thud!* 37).

Shortly thereafter, Vimes remembers an earlier occurrence: "Vimes closed his eyes and recalled that little figure, dressed in heavy black leather and hooded so that he would not commit the crime of seeing daylight" (38). Again, there is a defamiliarisation strategy at work here. While readers are presumably familiar with the veil worn by women in some Muslim cultures, which prevents the wearer from being seen, the hood here is supposed to prevent the wearer from seeing. But even if they differ in function, it evokes a recognisable image for the reader. Furthermore, it is an innocuous passage like this one which allows for demonstrating societal issues current at the time of the publication of the novel. As Andrew Butler has pointed out, "[t]he novel was timed perfectly for its portrayal of **racism** in an era when multiculturalism was very much under debate – the book anticipated rather than drew on the July 7 2005 bombings" (2007: 368; emphasis in the original).

This is accomplished by establishing the dwarfs as immigrants to Ankh-Morpork and having humans and trolls comment on their backwardness, the fact that they came from mountains and caves, and their 'inferior' height. The analogy here is that the dwarfs represent immigrants to a Western metropolis. Meanwhile, Ankh-Morpork is depicted as a place of modernity and enlightenment, but also as one of crime, decadence, and one which is perceived to be lacking in decency and morals. All of these are things dwarfs stand against – after all, they are the ones who are 'endarkened' and have access to the laws.

To these dwarfs light – metaphorically as enlightenment, concretely in terms of daylight – and not darkness is a danger and an intrusion. Therefore, the biblical notion that "light symbolizes understanding, darkness represents ignorance (Ps 82:5)" (Ryken et al. 1998: 192), is turned on its head. Not only does this reverse the classic light/darkness relationship in order to characterise dwarf culture, it also exemplifies the idea that whether darkness and light are good or bad depends on, in a very definite sense, point of view.

This notion has direct bearings on what constitutes the right way of behaving and dressing for dwarfs. In the following passage, city dwarfs, accustomed Ankh-Morporkians, are contrasted with the deep-downers:

> This was not the time to be a *d'rkza*. Strictly speaking, most Ankh-Morpork dwarfs were *d' rkza*; it meant something like 'not really a dwarf'. They didn't live deep underground and come out only at night, they didn't mine metal, they let their daughters show at least a *few* indications of femininity, they tended to be a little slipshod when it came to some of the ceremonies. But the whiff of Koom Valley was in the air and this was no time to be *mostly* a dwarf. So you paid attention to the grags.[3] (*Thud!* 77; emphases in the original)

Essentially, this is a prescriptive definition of what a dwarf should be. It includes living underground, coming out only at night, and adhering to dress codes, which indicates patriarchal structures, especially through the phrase 'let their daughters'. Jacqueline Simpson, who extensively treats dwarf culture in her text *The Folklore of Discworld*, has pointed out that

> dwarfish identity is not defined by mere genetics and size, but by a whole complex culture of laws, taboos, customs, moral principles and traditional knowledge. It is not precisely a religion, but it is as vital to their sense of selfhood as any religion could be. (Simpson 2009: 65)

It is noticeable that the 'correct' way of living is linked with darkness, night, and hiding from sight. Deviating from these guidelines entails a verbal form of punishment by being labelled a 'd'rkza' – 'not really a dwarf'. Further, from the viewpoint of the grags, the 'ideal dwarf' is equated with living in a mine, not working under the open sky: "Somewhere down there in the dark was true dwarfishness" (*Thud!* 84). Ergo, darkness and dwarfish identity are inexorably linked. Furthermore, Ankh-Morpork as the setting enables pitting old-fashioned and modern dwarfs against one another. Thereby, the contest between light and dark is extended to differences within dwarf society as well, which, in turn, is made visible by the various light and dark contrasts within dwarf culture itself, a few of which will now be highlighted.

As Vimes begins the investigation of the murder, he is greeted by a dwarf named Helmclever, who claims that his name means "daylight face" (85), because he takes care of things which need doing above ground. While it is unclear how he acquired this name, it can reasonably be surmised that his name, in the context of what has been considered thus far, should be read as a telling name

---

3 Grags are the extremist leaders within dwarf society.

signalling deceitfulness. The encounter with Helmclever then leads to Vimes meeting with the deep-down dwarfs:

> He'd met deep-down dwarfs before. They'd been weird, but he'd been able to deal with them. The Low King[4] was a deep-downer, and Vimes had got on with him well enough, once you accepted that the fairytale dwarf in the Hogfather[5] beard was an astute politician. He was a dwarf with vision. He dealt with the world. Ha, 'he'd seen the light'. But those in the new mine … He hadn't even seen them, even though they were sitting in a room made brilliant with hundreds of candles. That seemed odd, since the grags themselves were completely shrouded in their pointy black leather. But maybe it was some mystic ceremony and who'd look for sense there? Maybe you got a more holy dark in the midst of light? The brighter the light the blacker the shadow? (*Thud!* 106)

The phrases 'he was a dwarf with vision' and 'he'd seen the light' are not purely humorous, but mean what they conventionally signify: ambition, clarity, and enlightenment. As outlined, however, these are not regarded as positive traits within dwarf culture, at least as interpreted by the deep-downers opposing the low king who, incidentally, is female (Gallardo C. 2007: 332). The candles, on the other hand, are there to keep the darkness away. They signal a state of fear, which might lead one to conclude that these ultra-religious dwarfs are hypocrites, but it also reveals that light is part of their mythology as well, pointing to an ambiguity of light and darkness also found in Greek and Christian cosmogony. Vimes' notion of 'a more holy dark in the midst of light' in particular must not only be understood as humorous or ignorant, but as the idea that light and darkness function as supplements instead of opposites here.

In this context, the comments of a dwarf named Ardent on the king of dwarfs are also worth noting. He characterises her as

> wishy-washy. Dangerously liberal. Shallow. He has seen the light … Different worlds, commander. Down here, it would be unwise to trust your metaphors. To see the light is to be blinded. Do you not know that in darkness the eyes open wider? (*Thud!* 96)

The meanings of light and darkness are again reversed, and his comment on "your metaphors" is metafictional, addressing the reader as much as Vimes. The last aspect of light in dwarf mythology are the so-called 'vurms', fluorescent creatures which feed on the darkness. Within the novel, they serve as a contrast to the varied forms of dark in dwarf mythology. With respect to the crime genre,

---

4 The king of dwarfs.
5 The Discworld version of Father Christmas or Santa Claus.

they also function as clues or guides for the watch, because they glow in the dark.

Invisible Females? Dress Codes in Dwarf Culture

In this section, invisibility and lack of visibility are treated as extensions of the metaphoric complex around darkness or absence of light. It is demonstrated how they are implemented to showcase gender issues, specifically within dwarf culture. First, however, a few general remarks regarding the treatment of sex and gender within the Discworld novels need to be made.

As Ximena Gallardo C. notes:

> In general, Pratchett exposes the absurdities of gender determinism by exploring them in cultures parallel to our own, such as **dwarf** culture in the **Discworld** novels. [...] However, as satire necessarily addresses stereotypical attitudes and behaviors found in our own cultures, some of his work seems to replicate sexist viewpoints uncritically, especially in its representation of female characters. (Gallardo C. 2007: 331; emphases in the original)

She goes on to point out that "[i]n Pratchett's works, many notable female characters create a niche for themselves in male-dominated societies, but only a few truly challenge the status quo for all women" (Gallardo C. 2007: 333).

Challenging the status quo, however, is the case for the dwarf Cheery Littlebottom and, to a lesser degree, her watch colleague Angua von Uberwald, a female werewolf. Gallardo C. describes dwarf society in the Discworld novels as essentially genderless (331). Visually, male and female dwarfs appear to be the same – both wear beards, for instance. This allows for comedy when it leads to confusion among non-dwarf species. At the same time, however, "it is socially restrictive for those dwarfs who would like to be openly female" (ibid.). This introduces another problematic issue, namely that Cheery strives for a kind of femininity that includes make-up, boots, and a skirt, wanting to free herself from the trappings of a masculinity which is just as stereotypical and includes drinking beer, singing about gold, and fighting (cf. ibid.). However, the confines of such a gender model also allow Pratchett to create a space where serious issues such as patriarchy can be talked about. This is especially apparent through cultural components; for instance, female dwarfs are expected not to use overt displays of femininity such as high heeled shoes or make-up. Ergo, labelling dwarf society genderless is somewhat of a misnomer; as Gallardo C. herself points out, "dwarfs are considered 'he' by default" (ibid.). To put it succinctly, there is an absence of public acknowledgement of femininity in dwarf culture (Simpson 2009: 70).

At the beginning of *Feet of Clay*, Cheery conforms to dwarf norms by hiding her femininity until she is confronted by Angua about it. Following this, Cheery confesses to Angua her longing for the type of femininity described above, to which Angua responds:

> Look, there's plenty of women in this town that'd love to do things the dwarf way. I mean, what are the choices they've got? Barmaid, seamstress[6] or someone's wife. While *you* can do anything the men do ...' 'Provided we do only what the men do,' said Cheery. [...] 'I can't hold an axe!' said Cheery. 'I'm scared of fights! I think songs about gold are stupid! I hate beer! [...] I saw a girl walk down the street and some men *whistled* after her! And you can wear *dresses!* With *colours!*' 'Oh, dear.' Angua tried not to smile. 'How long have lady dwarfs felt like this? I thought they were happy with the way things are ... 'Oh, it's easy when you don't know any different,' said Cheery bitterly. 'Chainmail trousers are fine if you've never heard of lingerry!' 'Li—oh, yes,' said Angua. 'Lingerie. Yes.' She tried to feel sympathetic and found that she was, really, but she did have to stop herself from saying that at least *you* don't have to find styles that can be easily undone by paws. (*Feet of Clay* 113; emphases in the original)

On a surface level, the statements by Cheery seem like longings for a type of femininity that is, from the reader's point of view, as clichéd as it is outdated. However, this needs to be understood as much in terms of the gender binary described above as it does in terms of the setting, since "Ankh-Morpork is quasi-medieval, Victorian, *film noir* and/or modern as the needs of the novels require" (Lee 2007: 37; emphasis in the original). Hence, while Cheery's statements may not be modern or empowering against the background of the 21st century, they are coherent and progressive within the confines of the text.

It is also notable that Angua does not join Cheery in her elatedness. As an experienced, city-accustomed woman, she is beyond the needs which the recently arrived and uncertain Cheery outlines, but also recognises new issues that their fulfilment would create. Hence, Pratchett allows multiple voices on the subject to be heard and refrains from painting a picture that is black and white.

Moreover, Cheery addresses Angua's question through acknowledging the power of social conventions by stating that 'it's easy when you don't know any different'. Finally, this passage utilises genre to outline difficulties females of fantastical races have to deal with: for Cheery, it is a social paradigm; for Angua, physical limitations.

The socially dictated absence of femininity in dwarf society can be traced to problems of visibility. Recall that Cheery attempts to hide the fact that she is female – her response to Angua pointing out her 'secret' is met with bewilderment:

---

6 In Ankh-Morpork, seamstress is a euphemism for prostitute.

"How could you tell?' he said. 'Even other *dwarfs* can't tell! I've been so careful!'"
(emphasis in the original). The 'he' is not a typo; until this point in the novel, the
narrator has been employing a strategy to lead the reader to believe that Cheery
is a man: She is always referred to as a 'he' until confronted by Angua (cf. 112).

At a later point in the novel, visibility is again a focal point. In conversation
below, Angua is talking to her fellow officer Carrot:

> When they were out in the fog Carrot said, 'Do you think there's something a little bit ... *odd*
> about Littlebottom? 'Seems like a perfectly ordinary female to me,' said Angua. '*Female?* He
> *told* you he was female?' 'She,' Angua corrected. 'This is Ankh-Morpork, you know. We've
> got extra pronouns here.' [...] 'Well, I would have thought she'd have the decency to keep it
> to herself,' Carrot said finally.' I mean, I've got nothing against females. I'm pretty certain
> my stepmother is one. But I don't think it's very clever, you know, to go around drawing
> attention to the fact.' [...] 'There'll be trouble when the other dwarfs notice,' said Carrot.
> 'I could almost see his knees. *Her* knees.' 'Everyone's got knees.' 'Perhaps, but it's asking
> for trouble to flaunt them. I mean, *I'm* used to knees. I can look at knees and think, "Oh
> yes, knees, they're just hinges in your legs", but some of the lads—' Angua sniffed. 'He
> turned left here. Some of the lads *what?*' 'Well ... I don't know how they'll react, that's
> all. You shouldn't have encouraged her. I mean, of course there's female dwarfs, but ... I
> mean, they have the decency not to show it.' (*Feet of Clay* 267; emphases in the original)

It is notable that their conversation is embedded into the fog, linking setting and
conversational subject matter. Carrot exposes the bigotry of the dwarf culture attitude to female dwarfs; the repetition of the word 'decency' is particularly striking, evoking the historical as well as current component of many cultures where
women have to or had to cover specific parts of their body. It is also not inciden-
tal that Carrot should be the one to make these statements, as he is characterised
as a very liberal person within the context of the series, demonstrating that even
liberal people can hold bigoted views.

Cheery follows Angua's advice and decides to wear a skirt, boots and put
on make-up. However, it is important to point out that this does not resolve
the issue. On the one hand, in other novels of the series, female dwarfs follow
Cheery's lead. However, both Angua (cf. *Thud!* 89) and Cheery are met with resistance for openly showing their femininity. This is a central point, because
while it does indicate progress, it also shows that it is an ongoing struggle.

Finally, the real-world comparisons which Jacqueline Simpson has drawn in
this regard are worth considering:

> It is fascinating to compare the way Discworld dwarfs view femininity with the rules, taboos
> and superstitions about women in many Earthly societies, past and present. At first glance,
> they seem to be opposites. Dwarfs expect females to conceal their gender, to dress exactly
> like males, to be warriors, miners, blacksmiths and so forth, just like males. On Earth, on

the contrary, societies and religions which feel strongly about questions of gender abominate the idea of a woman dressing like a man. They expect her to wear distinctively female clothing, obeying rules as to what is or is not 'modest': the most important concerns usually being the length of the skirt and how much of the hair, head and face should be concealed. In extreme cases, women end up looking more like small perambulating tents than human beings. So, although their garb proclaims their gender, at the same time it hides it, as surely as that of a Discworld she-dwarf. (Simpson 2009: 72)

This is a clear example for the opportunities in terms of defamiliarisation offered by fantasy literature. Simpson's comparisons, which she identifies as opposites only on a superficial level, indicate that there is actually no difference between the prescriptiveness in terms of clothing and displaying gender in the fictional dwarf society compared to some of our real-world societies.

In the next section, it will be outlined how aspects of invisibility and visibility not only serve to showcase gender issues, but also contribute to shaping genre.

Shades of Grey: Issues of Visibility in *Feet of Clay*

With her *Rhetorics of Fantasy* (2008), Farah Mendlesohn provided theorists and critics with a structuralist toolkit for the analysis of fantasy literature. The question she posits is as simple as it is crucial: How is the reader of the fantasy text positioned in relation to the fantastic within the text (cf. XIV)? In her study, she derives four main forms of fantasy: portal-quest, immersive, intrusion, and liminal. For the purposes of this essay, it is the second and the third which are interesting.

As Mendlesohn herself notes, the City Watch novels are immersive fantasies (cf. 91). Central elements of this type of fantasy are the creation of a complete world, imperviousness to external influence and the reader sharing the assumptions of the fictional world as well as the position of its protagonists (cf. 59). The intrusion fantasy, on the other hand, is characterised as follows: "[T]he world is ruptured by the intrusion, which disrupts normality and has to be negotiated or defeated, sent back whence it came, or controlled" (115).

The core argument in this regard is that while *Feet of Clay* and *Thud!* are immersive fantasies, both feature an intrusion as described above and that, furthermore, Pratchett gives shape to these intrusions through light and darkness. In this section, the meaning spectrum of these terms is extended to encompass the intrusion in *Feet of Clay:* fog. This fog at the same time illuminates and conceals, while also influencing the nature of both light and darkness.

This is central because the events of *Feet of Clay* are almost entirely framed through an elaborate use of fog, and since artificial lighting is scarce in Ankh-Morpork, the fog lends a nocturnal quality to the day, limiting vision and perception, invoking a darkness-like state. Additionally, the importance of the term 'fog' itself is marked by its frequency and its recurring positions within the text,[7] appearing once or multiple times on 37 pages in total, which account for about ten percent of the novel's length.[8] Fog is often mentioned at the beginnings or ends of paragraphs, prominent positions within the text to which readers are inclined to pay more attention.

The *leitmotif* of the novel is (in-)visibility in a literal as well as in a metaphorical sense. This can already be identified in the novel's prologue:

> It was a warm spring night when a fist knocked at the door so hard that the hinges bent. A man opened it and peered out into the street. There was mist coming off the river and it was a cloudy night. He might as well have tried to see through white velvet. But he thought afterwards that there had been shapes out there, just beyond the light spilling out into the road. A lot of shapes, watching him carefully. He thought maybe there'd been very faint points of light ... (*Feet of Clay* 9)

Even though the passage above is set at night-time and darkness is therefore to be expected, it is still useful for illustrating how it establishes mood, tone, and theme of the novel. The mood moves from pleasant ('warm spring night') to a feeling of unease, while the observer's vision is hindered by elements of nature (mist and clouds). Though the uncanny is delayed at first, it returns in a subdued form of horror when the 'shapes' are remembered. The light is scattered and does not provide adequate visual support. The 'very faint points of light' are the golems' burning eyes, serving to establish the importance that visibility is going to have. Shortly afterwards, the text emphasises the turning of the seasons: "The mist of spring became the fog of autumn [...]. Autumn fog pressed itself against the midnight window panes" (13). This is the first indicator that the fog is going to act as an intrusion in the novel; however, it is not fully evolved

---

7 The relative frequency with which fog is mentioned as well as its metaphorical importance is quite evident in the newsgroup discussion "Fog and FoC" on *The L-Space Web*. For example, the importance of fog was outlined by forum poster 'Miq'. In particular, he/she draws attention to its frequency, its connection to light, and psychological effects on the characters (cf. Miq 2000).
8 Mentions of fog can be found on the following pages: 13, 15, 49 120, 121, 126, 147, 148, 150, 154, 156, 157, 158, 159, 192, 194, 195, 198, 204, 205, 207, 257, 272, 274, 278, 283, 292, 299, 302, 306, 334, 337, 341, 342, 370, 382, 401.

yet and can only 'press against the windowpanes' but not penetrate them. This changes as the novel progresses; the following passage in particular marks a turning point:

> The fog was rising fast. All morning it had hung around in alleys and cellars. Now it was moving back in for the night. It came out of the ground and up from the river and down from the sky, a clinging yellowish stinging blanket, the river Ankh in droplet form. It found its way through cracks and, against all common sense, managed to survive in lighted rooms, filling the air with eye-watering haze and making the candles crackle. Outdoors, every figure loomed, every shape was a menace ... (*Feet of Clay* 120)

This passage needs to be understood not only in terms of its actual content, i.e. that fog is spreading throughout the city, but also in regards to what it signifies in terms of genre. The fog is personified, evidently growing, and dangerous. The fact that it 'manages to survive in lighted rooms' underpins the notion that this fog is supernatural. It is also not just impervious to light, but even attacks it ('making the candles crackle'). Finally, its effects on visibility are explicated, as the air is filled with 'eye-watering haze' and everyday objects and shapes acquire a threatening nature.

At this juncture it should be noted that though the fog – in Mendlesohn's terms that which disrupts normality – is not the villain but rather intrudes upon the world and frames the events of the story. Significantly, the real villain is characterised through the interplay of light and darkness as well. Unknowingly, both the reader and Vimes are confronted with him early on in the novel, when Vimes visits him about his family's coat of arms:

> The hall inside was as quiet and dark as the yard had been full of light and noise. There was the dry, tombstone smell of old books and church towers. Above him, when his eyes got used to the darkness, Vimes could make out the hanging flags and banners. There were a few windows, but cobwebs and dead flies mean that the light they allowed in was merely grey. (*Feet of Clay* 42)

This passage creates a (metaphorical) transition from the realm of light into the realm of darkness, with light and noise being contrasted with darkness and silence. The light is not 'clean', but filtered (grey), obscuring his vision. Furthermore, we are informed that "[h]e couldn't see the figure clearly. The light came from a few high and grubby windows, and several dozen candles that burned with black-edged flames" (49). This is an instance where absence of sufficient light and visibility merge with the crime genre, for Vimes cannot identify the figure, thereby muddling his view as investigator, which is also complicated by the fact that Vimes is not there in his professional capacity, but as a private person.

During the visit, Vimes and Dragon King of Arms engage in a conversation about the coat of arms belonging to the family of an Ankh-Morpork candle manufacturer, which shows a "lampe au poisson (fish shaped lamp)" (55). This is resolved as a multi-lingual play on words, as the candle manufacturer turns out to be producing poisonous candles at Dragon's behest (367). Beyond that, this passage plays with conventions of the crime genre: The overconfident, Bond-like villain relies on Vimes' 'lack of vision', in a literal as well as a metaphorical sense, for Vimes is on the whole characterised as a rational man who believes in what he *sees*. Additionally, he is a policeman who loves the chase, knowing the city by the feel of the streets and through his boots. In the following, it is outlined how this reliance on non-visual senses contributes to solving the crime and thereby dispelling the intrusion. However, it must be emphasised that this is not an intended effort; rather, I suggest that the fog cannot or will not retreat until the crime is solved.

Even though he is no longer obligated by his duties to do so,[9] Vimes decides to set off alone on night patrol (147). Because he has already returned his professional clothes, he is not wearing his police boots, and therefore borrows a pair from a nearby palace guard, pointing out to him that a good policeman needs to be able to think with his feet. Hence, the theme of lack of visibility is brought together with what Vimes regards as a necessary, non-visual skill of a good policeman (148).

Vimes' patrol eventually turns into a chase when he spots a golem; at this point in the investigation, these are still the prime suspects for the murders. The chase itself is fairly uneventful, but does culminate in the following climax:

> Around him, the world became a crystal of horror, the special horror that has nothing to do with fangs or ichor or ghosts but has everything to do with the familiar becoming unfamiliar. Something fundamental was wrong. [...] Two red points of red light flared in the fog above him. (*Feet of Clay* 154)

Here, the intrusion manifests itself: the world turns into the uncanny, 'the familiar becoming unfamiliar', and into a fundamental sense of wrongness:

> A sense of wrongness, therefore, when it bears in upon the protagonist of a fantasy text, generally signals not a threat from abroad but the apprehension of some profound change in the essence of things, though perhaps initially signalled in terms that evoke supernatural fiction. (Clute and Grant 1999: 1038)

---

9 In *Feet of Clay*, Vimes is supposed to marry and retire from the watch. Though he does marry, he does not retire and is even promoted at the end of the novel.

The passage above depicts just such a change in 'the essence of things', a concept related to but not the same as an intrusion. Additionally, a psychological sense of horror is introduced, which is relevant when considering Vimes' connection with darkness in the novel *Thud!*.

At the end of the novel, Vimes again meets with Dragon: "Dragon King of Arms stepped into his library. The dirt of the small windows and the remnants of the fog made sure there was never more than greyness here, but a hundred candles yielded their soft light" (*Feet of Clay* 383). The intrusion is retreating; there are merely 'remnants of the fog' and the candles provide weak light. Dragon's home is still identified by relative darkness, however. Vimes defeats Dragon with the help of light – garlic-infused candles – which he had lit beforehand to weaken him. But Vimes is still lacking an admission of his crimes as well as a witness:

> 'Trying to trick me into admission, Mr Vimes?' 'Oh, I had *that*,' said Vimes. 'When you looked straight at the candles.' 'Really? Ah-ha. But who else saw me?' said Dragon. From the shadows there was a rumble like a distant thunderstorm. 'I Did [sic!],' said Dorfl.' (*Feet of Clay* 391)

Vimes points out that he knew Dragon was guilty when he looked at the candles – confirming Vimes' suspicion that Dragon is a vampire (ergo, the creature of darkness is betrayed by light), but Dragon asks who saw him, at which point the golem Dorfl steps out of the shadows and into the light to serve as witness. As Vimes concludes, "Only crimes could take place in darkness. Punishment had to be done in the light. That was the job of a good watchman [...]. To light a candle in the dark" (393). This quote exemplifies two things. One, it refers to the literal and metaphorical meanings of light and darkness within the crime genre. Secondly, that the job of a watchman is not merely to solve the crime, but also to provide hope, outlining their social importance; the idiom 'it is better to light a candle than curse the darkness' here serves as a literalised metaphor.

The intrusive fog disappears after Dragon is brought to justice. This is a case in point for the argument that even though there is no *causal* connection between intrusion and resolution, they are still connected through the workings of the types of fantasies outlined at the beginning of this section, while also merging fantasy and crime. However, it is crucial to note the discrepant awareness between character and reader: while we are able to perceive the fog as an intrusion, the characters are not.

Vimes in the Dark

In *Thud!* there is a move from a perceived intrusion (light) on behalf of the dwarfs to a personified intrusion (dark) in the form of the ancient spirit called the Summoning Dark, which is awoken by the dwarfs and thereafter attempts to enter the city of Ankh-Morpork by penetrating Vimes' mind. *Thud!* is frequently interrupted by passages where we see this personified dark in action and/or are privy to its thoughts. The Summoning Dark, however, is more than a mere personification. Consider the following quote: "'It's as if he had his own Summoning Dark in his head,' said Bashfulson. 'In a way, perhaps, we all have, commander. Or something similar'" (*Thud!* 318).

These remarks by the dwarf Bashfulson to Vimes are similar to Bronfen's interpretation of the Hegelian conception of the subject in relation to darkness: "The thinking subject is not the bearer of a light of reason that counteracts an impenetrable darkness. Instead, the thinking subject carries this darkness within, in the sense of a mental/spiritual night" (Bronfen 2013: 70).

The Summoning Dark is much more strongly personified and closer to an actual villain than the fog in *Feet of Clay* because it is a sentient actor, if still a supernatural being. In the context of genre, however, it does not constitute a villain in the sense that it commits crimes, but is more like an absolute evil, similar to Sauron in Tolkien's *The Lord of the Rings*.

Its first appearance is described as follows: "The creature swam through a mind. [...] It looked like a city" (*Thud!* 128). The most sensible reading here is that the Dark is trying to enter Vimes' mind, here equated with Ankh-Morpork, which makes sense given his knowledge of the city.

After several such attempts on part of the Summoning Dark, a showdown between them takes place when his investigations lead Vimes to Koom Valley.[10] Similar to *Feet of Clay*, Vimes becomes a metaphorical agent of light: as a member of the watch it is his job to defeat evil (in this case darkness) and bring the truth to light. As he notes earlier in regards to the crime: "Someone killed four of *our* dwarfs, not some crazy rabble-rouser, and left them down there in the dark. I don't care who they are, they're going to be dragged into the light. It's the law. All the way to the bottom, all the way to the top" (249; emphasis in the original).

This is another instance where an idiom ('truth to light') is literalised. However, as Elisabeth Bronfen noted, "[...] the human subject must first experience the abyss within the soul before he or she can discover the light of Truth"

---

10 To reiterate, this is both the name and the place of the historic battle between dwarfs and trolls.

(2013: 194). As Vimes comes to Koom Valley, he is guided by the Dark which has now managed to enter his mind. He also begins to understand the true meaning of the Dark:

> There was a bigger cave here, so big that the blackness in it seemed to suck all the light from the match, which scorched his fingers and died. The heavy darkness closed in again, like curtains, and now he knew what the dwarfs meant. This wasn't the darkness of a hood, or a cellar, or even of their shallow little mine. He was a long way below the ground here, and the weight of all that darkness bore down on him. (*Thud!* 384)

Here, the Dark overwhelms Vimes and drives him to madness, and it is only his ambition to read a bedtime story to his son that manages to keep him sane.

How Vimes manages to defeat the Darkness is not told. However, the text provides some clues. When Vimes recovers, he sees the following:

> There were more stars now, drifting along the walls. The vurms were moving with a purpose. Overhead they had become a glowing river. Although they were flickering a little, the lights were also coming back on in Vimes's head. He peered into what was now no longer blackness but merely gloom, and gloom was like daylight after the darkness that had gone before. (*Thud!* 390)

The fact that the 'vurms were moving with a purpose' signifies that they are fulfilling their role within dwarf mythology. In the Discworld novels, mythology is not abstract and passive but something that manifests in reality. It could even be argued that it is the vurms which give Vimes his strength back, counteracting the Dark; they are flickering while he is recovering. Finally, the darkness changes into gloom, which Vimes by contrast evaluates as daylight. While we do not see how Vimes actually defeats the Dark – and it later turns out that he has no memory of the event – we do see that the Summoning Dark is banished to "*Night, for ever*" (396; emphasis in the original) and when it asks its adversary who he/she/it is, is met with the following reply:

> 'He created me. Quis custodiet ipsos custodies? Who watches the watchmen? Me. I watch him. Always. You will not force him to murder for you. [...] I am not here to keep darkness out. I'm here to keep it in.' There was a dink of metal as the shadowy watchman lifted a dark lantern and opened its little door. Orange light cut through the blackness. 'Call me ... the Guarding Dark. [...] The Summoning Dark backed desperately into an alley, but the light followed it, burning it. (*Thud!* 397)

Vimes has created something akin to a guardian angel, unknowingly though actively furthering dwarf mythology. The slogan "who watches the watchers?" – originally from Juvenal ("Satire VI", l. 347) and also utilised in Alan Moore's *Watchmen* (Chapter VI Page 15 Panel 6) – undergoes a switch: The Guarding

Dark turns out to be a saint for the watchmen. It also strengthens the idea that light and darkness are not opposites, but complements within dwarf mythology and confirms Bronfen's notion of the relationship between the subject and the darkness as outlined previously.

To close this section, the question of the relationship between the solving of the crime and the defeat of the intrusion needs to be revisited. The novel's resolution is marked by the following passage, where Vimes witnesses the Summoning Dark dissolving into light: "He rolled over and saw, fading in the middle of the air, a crude drawing of an eye with a tail. It dwindled into nothing, and the all-enveloping darkness slowly gave way to flames and the light of the vurms" (*Thud!* 398).

As mentioned, the darkness in *Thud!* is much closer to a villain than it is in *Feet of Clay*. Within this text there is then, as opposed to *Feet of Clay*, not only a causal relation between the two, but also an active defeat of the intrusion on part of the protagonist, whereas in *Feet of Clay* the fog as intrusion merely disappears once the crime is solved.

Conclusion

"You can take a dwarf out of the dark, but you can't take the dark out of a dwarf. *Those symbols are very old. They have real power.* Who knows what old evils exist in the deep darkness under the mountains? There's no darkness like it" (*Thud!* 262; my emphasis).

This passage exemplifies the opening remarks of this essay in regards to the power which darkness and light continue to embody in contemporary (fantasy) literature, as well as the degree of flexibility they possess in terms of their implementation in texts. The novels discussed here continue this literary, artistic, and philosophical tradition, but also manage to infuse them with new meanings.

One of the most notable issues in this regard was established in the last section of this essay, namely that light and darkness as parts of the fictional mythology in these texts are not static but active, bearing on the lives of the characters. Furthermore, a strategy repeatedly used in the novels is one of inversion and reversal in order to defamiliarise, in the most literal sense taking that which is familiar and presenting it to the reader in a novel and creative way. This became perhaps most apparent when the visual presentation of females in dwarf culture and its similarities to real world cultures and customs were considered.

In terms of the invented mythology, it is noteworthy that it manages to incorporate both traditions with regard to the relationship between light and darkness, namely as opposites and as complements. The functions and implementations of light and darkness in this fictional mythology and culture are not only varied, but invested with a variety of meanings.

On the other hand, Mendleson's category of the intrusion fantasy proved especially fruitful for the analysis presented, not merely in terms of how light and darkness contribute to it, but also in terms of the genre mixing that is evident in the two texts discussed. It was particularly striking that both texts are immersive fantasies which feature intrusions. However, these intrusions are embedded and resolved in very different ways. Furthermore, within both texts there is a movement from obscuration (darkness) to revelation (light), which obviously fits with the genre of crime, more pointedly the solving of a crime in order to provide closure, but also with the genre of fantasy, in terms of light conquering darkness and confirming the biblical: "And the light shineth in darkness; and the darkness comprehended it not" (*King James Version*, John 1:5).

Works Cited

Attebery, Brian. 1992. *Strategies of Fantasy.* Bloomington, IN: Indiana University Press.

Bronfen, Elisabeth. 2013. *Night Passages: Philosophy, Literature and Film.* Trans. David Brenner. New York, NY: Columbia University Press.

Butler, Andrew M. 2007. "*Thud!* (2005)". In: Andrew M. Butler (ed.). *An Unofficial Companion to the Novels of Terry Pratchett.* Oxford: Greenwood World Publishing. 368–369.

Chevalier, Jean and Alain Gheerbrant (eds.). 1996. "Light". *The Penguin Dictionary of Symbols.* Trans. John Buchanan-Brown. London: Penguin. 600–606.

Clute, John and John Grant (ed.). 1999. "Wrongness". *The Encyclopedia of Fantasy.* New York, NY: St. Martin's Press. 1038–1039.

Gallardo C., Ximena. 2007. "Sexism". In: Andrew M. Butler (ed.). *An Unofficial Companion to the Novels of Terry Pratchett.* Oxford: Greenwood World Publishing. 331–333.

James, Edward. 2004. "The City Watch". In: Andrew M. Butler, Edward James and Farah Mendlesohn (eds.). *Terry Pratchett: Guilty of Literature.* 2nd ed. Baltimore, MD: Old Earth. 193–216.

Juvenal. 2011. "Satire VI". *The Satires.* Trans. A. S. Kline. <http://www.poetryintranslation. com/PITBR/Latin/JuvenalSatires6.htm> [accessed 14 April 2015].

Leach, Maria and Jerome Fried (eds.). 1984. "World Egg". *Funk & Wagnall's Standard Dictionary of Folklore, Mythology and Legend.* New York, NY: Harper Collins. 1184.

Lee, Zina. 2007. "Ankh-Morpork." In: Andrew M. Butler (ed.). *An Unofficial Companion to the Novels of Terry Pratchett.* Oxford: Greenwood World Publishing. 35–39.

Mendlesohn, Farah. 2008. *Rhetorics of Fantasy.* Middletown, CT: Wesleyan University Press.

Mendlesohn, Farah. 2012. "Thematic Criticism." In: Edward James and Farah Mendlesohn (eds.). *The Cambridge Companion to Fantasy Literature.* Cambridge, MA: Cambridge University Press 2012. 125–133.

Miq. 16 Dec. 2000. "Fog and FoC". *The L-Space Web*. <http://www.lspace.org/fandom/afp/timelines/discussions/fog-and-foc.html> [accessed 14 April 2015].

Moore, Alan. 2008. *Watchmen*. New York, NY: DC Comics.

Pratchett, Terry. 1997. *Feet of Clay*. London: Corgi.

Pratchett, Terry. 2006. *Thud!*. London: Corgi.

Ryken, Leland, James C. Wilhoit and Tremper Longman III (eds.). 1998. "Darkness". *The Dictionary of Biblical Imagery*. Downers Grove, IL: InterVarsity Press. 191–193.

Simpson, Jacqueline. 2009. *The Folklore of Discworld. Legends, Myths and Customs from the Discworld with helpful Hints from Planet Earth*. London: Corgi.

The Bible. Authorized King James Version with Apocrypha. 2008. Eds. Robert Carroll and Stephen Pickett. Oxford: Oxford University Press.

Thieme, Klaus. 2008. "Worte des Lichts – Licht der Worte. Anmerkungen zur Geschichte des Lichts". In: Christina Lechtermann and Haiko Wandhoff (eds.). *Licht, Glanz, Blendung: Beiträge zu einer Kulturgeschichte des Leuchtenden*. Berlin: Peter Lang.

Tolkien, J. R. R. 2012. *The Lord of the Rings*. (1954–55) New York, NY: Mariner/Houghton Mifflin Harcourt.

Susanne Bach

Twenty Thousand Lights Hanging from the Ceiling: Ecocatastrophe in Karen Thompson Walker's *The Age of Miracles*

The rising and setting of the sun is a central parameter of life on Earth: the circadian rhythm influences animals, plants, and unicellular organisms alike. It affects human beings physiologically and psychologically, and the exposure or lack of exposure to sunlight has a profound impact on the hormonal regulation of sleep and mood. In social terms, too, its impact is profound: the rhythm of day and night lends shape to many aspects of social organisation:

> As the earth spins, the shadow moves around, and since a cycle of light and darkness was present when life began it gave its pulse as an inheritance to living things. One-celled creatures have twenty-four-hour cycles. Complex animals and plants have internal daily rhythms that are paced by light. We inherited the tempo too. Our body's physiology is attuned to sunlight's comings and goings, and we have established separate phases of labor, leisure, and rest in our daily round. Family life, work, mental alertness, sexual interest, and the conduct of business all fill a timetable synchronized with the turns of the globe. (Melbin 1987: 1)

Radically challenging or altering that rhythm would entail catastrophic consequences for the micro-, meso-, and macro-levels of societies. Karen Thompson Walker's *The Age of Miracles* explores and illustrates this threatening scenario in its dire details. The 2012 novel belongs to the group of ecocritical and/or apocalyptic works of fiction, a genre which has been gradually progressing to a seat in the front rows of academic interest. Or, as Volkmann et al. put it in a recent study, nature has long been of "paramount importance" in literary studies (2010: xi); and ecological – and thus often ethical (cf. Cohen 2004; Zapf 2008) – concerns have for an equally long time found their way into the pages of novels and plays. The "'nearly ubiquitous cultural fascination' with the hostile and deadly elements of the natural world and the threat which they pose to human life" (Hillard qtd. in Curry 2013: 40) was and is a strong peg to hang a story on.[1] Wojcik contends correctly that narratives "about the end of the world have existed since the beginning of recorded history" (1997: 5). Only that – in postmodern times and contrary to, for instance, the New Testament version – fictional apoc-

---

1 Cf. Ahearn 1996; Rosen 2008; Seed 2000. For a discussion on the definition of apocalypse as a critical term see Wojcik (1997: 11–13).

alypses nowadays are often "meaningless" and "unredemptive" (1; 211), they do not offer "a new heaven and a new earth" (*King James Version*, Rev. 21:1).

In the following I would like to analyse a dystopian, apocalyptic novel that questions something ubiquitous on a global scale; something which is as firmly rooted in the sphere of nature as it is in the sphere of culture; something which is completely taken for granted: light.

Natural Light and Darkness vs. Artificial Light and Darkness

Karen Thompson Walker's debut coming-of-age novel *The Age of Miracles* speculates what would happen if Earth's rotation were

> for some reason [to decelerate drastically]. [...] The days and nights get longer – by the end of the book there are six-week periods of daylight, then darkness. The birds, whales and grasses start to die; radiation increases as the magnetosphere undergoes irreversible change. (Priest 2012)[2]

Praised as "one of this summer's hot literary reads" in *The New York Times* (Kakutani 2012), the story is rendered in retrospect by Julia, a first person narrator, and eleven years of age when the events described in her memoir begin to unfold. Situated at its centre is the description of a chronobiological catastrophe, i.e. the lengthening of days and nights, which entails drastic changes in – among others – social, medical, cognitive, linguistic, and environmental respects. On that account, the treatment of natural and artificial light becomes one of the work's focal points – one could justifiably call light the second protagonist of Walker's novel.

In *The Age of Miracles*, days finally last up to six weeks. The duration and quality of the 'new' natural light affects society in its core. First of all, it divides society into two distinct groups: those who live by the traditional 24-hour-regime come what may, and the others who try to adapt as much as possible to the new situation. As a consequence, social ties like friendships and family bonds are questioned or shattered. The societal division affects everyone living on 'real time', because access to schools, doctors, mechanics, stores, gyms, restaurants, and cinemas is determined and restricted by those living on the 24-hour-sched-

---

2 Priest criticises the novel: "[s]cientifically, much of this is a bit suspect as well as being inconsistent" (Priest 2012), but this does not concern my research focus.

ule (cf. Walker 2012: 146). Later on in the novel, exposure to the sun causes immediate and severe burns (and other symptoms such as nausea and dizziness); consequently, people go out only during night time, and take vitamin D supplements in order to prevent a deficiency. Food has to be produced at extremely high costs: "Industrial farms were guzzling up electricity at an impossible rate. The twenty thousand lights that hung from the ceiling of just one greenhouse could eat up in half an hour as much power as most families used in a whole year" (224). The economic consequences are drastic: in the US, grapes cost 100$ a pound, power failures and power shortages become the norm (cf. 309 – 311), famines are predicted for developing countries, and "[b]illions of dollars had drained from the markets" (239).

In this work of fiction, the perception of one of our most basic divisions, day and night, light and darkness, is questioned, threatened, and alienated. The growing dependence on artificial light (due to the long darkness periods and due to the fact that all food has to be produced in greenhouses) is thus as foregrounded as are the associated psychological, ecological, and sociological consequences. This is literally visible at first sight, as the immediate paratextual presentation of the novel already draws attention to light as a topic. The front section of the dust jacket, designed by Matt Johnson, seems faded, as if it had been exposed to light for too long. The edges of the title's letters – in an angry red – seem blurred, and the dust jacket photograph underneath, depicting a rural US-American village, seems blurred in the centre, too, as if an amateurish photographer with little talent had taken that shot against the sun. Turning the book around, the reader realises that the dust jacket photograph seen as a whole shows, in a Magritte-like twist, the village simultaneously in day- *and* in night-time,[3] thus foreshadowing the paradoxical division of society into two groups living on different time lines but still within the same time-frame and the same place. The last 'night time' house of the dust jacket is illuminated from within, with artificial light, anticipating the 'aquarium' image the narrator will later use.[4] The book's first page – sporting praise from two other writers – looks prematurely aged, as if taken from a 19th century book; it is of a brownish hue, and the edges seem frayed, the letters of praise themselves already faded. If one re-

---

3 In a painting by René Magritte, *The Empire of Lights* (1954), it is day and night at the same time.

4 Cf. "On dark days like that one, the library windows looked lit up like an aquarium, the inhabitants on display for all the other kids to see" (Walker 2012: 275). Another reading would state that it pictured the house of Julia's music teacher whose windows manage "to glow against the darkness" (136). Since the teacher is living at the margins of society, the placing of her house at the extreme end of the photograph would make sense, too.

moves the dust jacket, the novel's cover is of a pristine white – which makes sense because the jacket was allegedly used to block light's damaging access to the cover. In short: The book's cover, printed in 2012, looks aged and severely damaged by exposure to light.

Having thus been alerted to the relevance of light, the reader can hardly be surprised by the fact that natural and/or artificial light is mentioned on virtually every page. Light permeates every action and nearly every paragraph of *The Age of Miracles*, and its mentioning, relevance, and function can be divided into several clusters. The treatment of light is intimately connected with a discussion of topics such as time,[5] psychology, human relationships, with metaphors, and the plot structure itself; it is woven into questions of ambiguity, of artificiality, of religion and science, of order and stability, and of the global chronobiological catastrophe as such. It reflects the proleptic style of the narration and it focusses the readers' attention onto the socio-political consequences. In the following, I will take a closer look at these analytical parameters and relevant clusters. I will start out with the central concern of artificial and natural light, and then move on to connected topics and problems.

Artificial Light Objects

Initially, the signs of the catastrophic lengthening of days and nights are not of the expected magnitude and visibility: "There was no footage to show on television, no burning building, no twisted metal or scorched earth, no houses sliding off slabs. No one was wounded. No one was dead" (Walker 2012: 13). The catastrophe they – as Californians – expected was another: "The Big One" (11), an earthquake. Their preparations thus proved inadequate: "we kept batteries in our flashlights and gallons of water in our closets" (11). All the time, they had worried over the wrong things: "the hole in the ozone layer, the melting of ice caps, West Nile and swine flu and killer bees" (37); people had been more concerned with the visible realities of "weather and war" (1).

The population literally arm themselves with artificial sources of light: "double-A batteries [...] [for] three flashlights [...], a mini arsenal of light" (25). These artificial light sources gain the significance of weapons against the looming disaster; Julia's mother nervously tests her flashlights by repeatedly switching them on and off, dumping "the old batteries out of each barrel and replac[ing] them

---

5 Of course, the following aspects are all closely connected. For simplicity's sake, I have separated them.

with new ones, as if arranging ammunition in a set of guns" (26). Artificial sources of light, controlled by others, cannot be trusted anymore. Streetlights come on in the evening, since they are set to a timer, but, as the narrator remarks dryly, "the sun continued to shine" (28). So eventually, they are being switched off, which causes a weird, pre-light pollution scenario: "[...] the neighborhood remained submerged in the dark. It was a new kind of darkness for me, a thick country black, unseen in cities and suburbs" (34). When switched on again, streetlights only manage to tint faces "yellow" (127), a skin colour normally connected with jaundice.

Light pollution as such is mentioned, too. However, in the context of the novel it evokes a sense of nostalgia rather than being a reason for scientific concern: "[...] streetlights [...] had been specially designed for dimness .... *Light pollution*, they called it. But what were those astronomers staring at anymore, now that the real action was happening down here?" (Walker 2012: 127; emphasis in the original).

Strangely enough, however, despite the mélange of old and newer forms of lighting – candles and flashlights, the sun's rays and industrial floodlight –, people in Julia's society hardly ever get adequate light. There is often either too little or too much light. At the same time, some lights lose their original meaning or function. Porch lights, for instance, symbols of the familiar and of home, go "unnoticed" (128) under the new conditions, or they only function as meeting places for "gnats" (278).

In certain areas, artificial lighting is desperately reinforced:

[...] we discovered that workmen were installing stadium lights all over campus. Under the floodlights,[6] the faded green walls – painted, rumor had it, with surplus paint from the marine base up the coast – looked like those of a prison. So much that seemed harmless in daylight turns imposing in the dark. What else, you had to wonder, was only a trick of light? (Walker 2012: 129)

Not only the psychological insight into the fine layers of perception is of interest, but also the mismatched half-association of floodlights with darkness. For Julia, most likely, artificial light is not seen as 'real' light anymore, and whatever is not natural light turns in her dichotomic way of thinking into 'no light', and thus darkness. Only her beloved music teacher's window does seem positively animated by artificial light, it glows "*against* the dark" (136; my emphasis).

The longer the days and nights become, the more intensive and numerous do the attempts at lighting – and darkening – become: "[we] purchased sunlamps

---

6 Floodlights are only ever mentioned again with reference to burials. Cf. Walker (2012: 345).

and installed blackout curtains" (144). Gardens sport artificial turf and "giant sunlamps" (224), often "hidden among the branches" (248). Technical equipment copies the natural: "A special device, part sunlamp, part alarm clock, was supposed to mimic the effect of sunset with the slow fade of its bulb" (148), and teenagers stand around a lamp "as if it were a campfire" (249).

Rich people equip their houses with Baudrillardian simulacra which imitate the natural circadian rhythm and natural light:[7] dimmers set to a clock to "mimic the effects of sunrise and sunset", blackout shutters, a "tanning bed", and a "greenhouse" (247). Julia and other children look up to "glow-in-the-dark star stickers" on their bedroom ceilings (125) or send notecards which shimmer "with van Gogh's *Starry Night*" (152).

Perception of Light

The perception of light changes under these new conditions and sometimes comes to carry negative connotations. The blueish light emanating from the television set, for instance, suddenly appears "sickly" (34). The "white light" of a computer screen throws Julia's mother's "features into unflattering relief" (196). Seth, Julia's friend, looks older in candlelight (309) and the windows of the lighted library turn into "an aquarium, the inhabitants on display for all the other kids to see: here the most exotic fish, the lonely, the unloved, the weird" (275).

Darkness comes to carry positive aspects more often than before: it "endowed us, too, with certain special abilities. What was possible in the darkness never would have worked in the light" (251). Only in "low light" (310) does the narrator dare to tell Seth a secret, and it is during night time and in the "pitch-black waters" (311) of a Jacuzzi that they exchange their first kiss. Darkness later on represents even freedom and health since it becomes near-lethal to walk around in daylight. During bright light periods, people have to remain indoors (cf. 320).

But darkness still can be scary. Faced with "pre-historic dark" due to a power cut, Julia and Seth metaphorically jump back and forth through several stages of the history of artificial light within minutes:

---

7 "The real is produced from miniaturized units, from matrices, memory banks, and command models – and with these it can be reproduced an indefinite number of times. It no longer has to be rational, since it is no longer measured against some ideal or negative instance" (Baudrillard 1983: 3).

We scoured the house for flashlights. We bumped into each other in our blindness and ran into the walls. We broke a lamp and laughed for a long time. Seth lit candles with one of his father's lighters. We carried them around like torches, our faces shadowy in the flame light. We wondered if it might last forever, the age after electricity. (Walker 2012: 309)

Thoughts and actions suddenly are associated with qualities of light. Rendered from the narrator's perspective, guilt and embarrassment can "radiate off [...] skin" (235). A secretly bought first bra "radiates from deep within" a bag (209). Objects that can reflect light become highly important to Julia; she seems to be obsessed by them, be it the "sequined flip-flops" (48) of a friend, her mother's "crystal earrings" swaying and "her bare shoulders" shimmering slightly "in the light from a new bronzing powder she's dusted on her skin" (181), or the "glittery dress" of a friend's mother (244). The neighbour's roof "sparkles with a dozen solar panels" (142) (whose only function, by the way, was to provide the energy necessary for the growing of marijuana, planted and consumed to make the new life more bearable; cf. 162). Snow makes the street appear "sparkling" (313). An accident is represented by "sequins of glass" (183) and a car's mirrors "glinting in the sunshine" (185). Even a soccer ball is able to "shimmer" (352).

Some lights carry memories of times gone by, "colored Christmas lights blinked as usual" (165) – but they are not the same anymore: in a semblance of synaesthesia Julia thinks she can "hear the inner workings of those lights, a tiny, metallic clicking" (170).[8] These formerly 'magic' lights are now exposed as an electrical illusion that used to create a certain atmosphere which now is only experienced in its artificial quality.[9] "A cinnamon Christmas candle" (171) cannot save the mood; Julia keeps her eyes fixed on the flame, most likely in order to avoid seeing what is happening around her: not only the dissolution of her family but also the dissolution of culture as she – and the reader – knows it. The "climate change is", as Curry states in her study *Environmental Crisis in Young Adult Fiction*, "envisaged as [...] an immediate and devastating shattering of cultural norms" (2013: 18). Aligned with this process – the loss of cultural meaning – is the loss of an aura, reminiscent of the general paradigm shift which Walter Benjamin diagnosed in his 1936 essay "The Work of Art in the Age of Mechanical Reproduction":

---

8 Light can also be heard, for instance, in the "buzz of fluorescent lights" (Walker 2012: 208). The young narrator dreams of a rural commune's quiet, associated with natural light: "... how quiet that thick desert darkness must have been with only the stars to light the land" (237). For her, the "glittering of stars" is "soundless" (309).
9 The same is true for New Year firecrackers which are lit in broad daylight (Walker 2012: 189).

During long periods of history, the mode of human sense perception changes with humanity's entire mode of existence. The manner in which human sense perception is organized,
the medium in which it is accomplished, is determined not only by nature but by historical
circumstances as well. (Benjamin 1936)

Colour

Colour, too, acquires new connotations, since a lack of light makes "all the colors
of the spectrum [collapse] to a few dusky grays"; the sky turns "a brackish evening blue" (Walker 2012: 66–67), and "a row of brand-new stainless-steel appliances" gleam sadly "in the moonlight" (233). Julia notices the absence of light
and colour much more than ever before. In a longer passage about her friend
Gabby, she points out in a verbal orgy of black the "second coat of black polish
on her fingernails" (119–120), a "glossy, grim black", her "dyed black hair",
"charcoal eyeliner", the music in her room emanating from "two big black speak-
ers", "black ink on her desk" and the fact that she likes "going out in the dark"
(120–121). Rather ostentatiously drawn, Gabby is the antagonist to the light-seek-
ing narrator. Their houses are the same models "but reversed. Her bedroom was
the same bedroom as mine, the dimensions exactly equal. [...] Grown under similar conditions, we had become very different, two specimens of girlhood, now
diverging" (121).

As opposed to Gabby's 'blackness', in Julia's perception, events are prominently noticed by their light and colour. A police raid on the neighbour's
house is at first just a "sweep of the headlights, [...] red lights flashing noiseless-
ly" (161). The face of a person witnessing the night scene is "lit red by the
lights" (161). Desire infuses objects with special light and colour; after not having
had a grape for a very long time, Julia notices these fruits in the kitchen of a rich
friend: "[...] on the countertop *shone* a deep glass bowl full of green grapes" (242;
my emphasis).[10]

But humanity has larger problems than a pubescent girl fascinated by light
and colour:

All across America, giant greenhouses were swallowing up the open-air fields of our farms.
Acres and acres were put under glass. Thousands of sodium lamps were giving light to our
tomato plants and our orange trees, our strawberries and our potatoes and our corn. (Walker 2012: 224)

---

10 These are the last grapes she will ever eat. Later, memories of this and of other sensations
will fade: "the sound of Sylvia's piano [...] the sensation of sunshine on my face, the taste of
strawberries, the squish of a grape in my mouth" (356).

This of course has financial ramifications which even a teenager is able to comprehend (cf. 239). In the long run, there are power outages, and light as well as energy need to be rationed: "No lights after ten P.M. No air-conditioning unless the temperature exceeds eighty-eight degrees" (311).

Light and Time

Light in the novel is intimately connected to time, as is evident by now. The instinctive equation of light with day, and of darkness with night, gets disrupted by the ongoing deceleration of the Earth's rotation; therefore the established connection of the one with the other does not hold true anymore. "Like a tumor blooming beneath the skin" does the extra time bulge animatedly "from the smooth edge of each day" (1). With the loss of natural light's regularity – the rising sun does not indicate morning anymore –, the feeling for time does not come naturally any more either; humans now completely depend on clocks and watches. After the US decide to live according to "clock time" (114), Julia clears her nightstand of books so that she can "see [her] alarm clock", and she also pulls her "grandfather's pocket watch" out of a drawer (114).[11] Along with the necessity to tell time by 'artificial' means (after all, at 3 a.m. the sun might be up) comes the necessity of creating and using artificial light – and artificial darkness.

Light and Psychology

Light and day, darkness and artificial light serve as points of reference for the description of psychological effects. Night shift workers in *The Age of Miracles* are among the first to become alert to the emerging catastrophe: "[...] the night work-

---

11 She learns that not only light and time are connected, but that they are also intimately interwoven with space; they are "inseparable" (Melbin 4): Julia's father explains that with the help of her new telescope she will not see the stars "as they are today but how they were thousands of years ago. [...] That's how far away they are; even the light takes centuries to reach us" (Walker 2012: 123). And similar to the story her father told about the stars' light, the two teenage lovers, Julia and Seth, later in the novel want to leave a mark in wet cement knowing that they may soon be dead (357): their names, the date and the words "We were here" (369). In a similar vein, but on a grander scale, humankind devises a rocket, the "*Explorer*", which carries "information about our planet and its people" into "in some distant realm of the universe" (366), with the implicit caveat that mankind might not be alive anymore by the time other beings encounter the rocket.

ers, the graveyard shifters, the stockers of shelves, the loaders of ships, the drivers of big-rig trucks" (2) notice the changes first. And the psychologically troubled are aware of the looming disaster, too, since the "sleepless and the troubled and the sick [...]" are "accustomed to waiting out the night [...]" (ibid.), the lengthening of which extends their insomniac ordeal. Later on, psychological and psychopathological responses to the lengthening process and the necessity to use artificial light sources increase. Julia observes that her mother – like herself – develops a "persistent churning of her mind on a single subject" and a "low tolerance for uncertainty" (30). To Julia herself it seems "that dangers lurked everywhere" (32). But, later on, people get used to the new conditions; they grow "more accustomed to the small terrors of life" (151), and "boredom develop[s]" (154). The slow death of "native plant species" from "insufficient light", for instance, is noticed only very much in passing (228). An unconscious re-programming of values takes place: instead of indicating danger, "[wild]fires only added to our enjoyment. They meant that we were living in important times" (248).

Old associations, perceptions, and connotations are jeopardised, judged from a psychological perspective. The grown-up Julia, later in the novel intending to become a doctor, tells us at the end of her tale:

> Five thousand years of art and superstition would suggest that it's the darkness that haunts us most, that the night is when the human mind is most apt to be disturbed. But dozens of experiments conducted in the aftermath of the slowing revealed that it was not the darkness that tampered most with our moods – it was the light. (Walker 2012: 175)

Light, its presence and its absence, influences relationships. As the balance of light and darkness is changing, human relationships are subject to a new balance, too. The adolescent Julia elaborates on this with examples taken from her own sphere of experience, illustrating the sociological and psychological ramifications of the changes in her world:

> What I understood so far about this life was that there were the bullies and the bullied, the hunters and the hunted, the strong and the stronger and the weak, and so far I'd never fallen into any group – I was one of the rest, a quiet girl with an average face, one in the harmless and unharmed crowd. But it seemed all at once that this balance had shifted. [...] [A]ll the hierarchies were changing. (Walker 2012: 52)

According to Elizabeth K. Rosen, the "apocalyptic impulse is, in effect, a sense-making one" (Rosen 2008: xiii) and therefore it comes as no surprise that adolescent attempts at sense-making conflate with the apocalypse's power of making, distorting, altering, and destroying sense. Julia's old world is turned upside-down due to the shifting of Earth's balance: her father is caught cheating on his wife, and her best friend Hanna, after having been evacuated with her parents, returns completely changed and their friendship is terminated in a painful manner, while the rest of the world is "going to shit" (Walker 2012: 215). Julia falls in love with Seth, and since both live in times of shifting values and parameters, their relationship is valued as a safe haven against the crises on all levels of society.

Light and Religion

With the world "going to shit" (215), people turn to religion, as already hinted at by the title (*The Age of Miracles*)[12] and as indicated on the back cover blurb ("Something God-awful is happening"). God, according to the Christian Bible, created Heaven and Earth, and divided day and night:

> And God said, "Let there be light," and there was light. God saw that the light was good, and he separated the light from the darkness. God called the light "day," and the darkness he called "night." And there was evening, and there was morning – the first day. (Gen. 1:3 – 5)

In turn, such a disaster on a global scale has repercussions in religious respects, too. It is difficult for Jews to keep the Sabbath if the day lasts for an unpredictably long time (cf. Walker 2012: 23). Born-again Christians "were making their final arrangements, hoping at any moment to be summoned from their beds, leaving behind empty houses and piles of crumpled clothing where their bodies once stood" (87). Immigrants from "North Africa and the Middle East" go off the clock "for religious reasons" (202). The Mormons leave for Salt Lake City because they expect Jesus' "next return to earth", whereas the "bloodless breed of Lutherans [...] harbored no clear vision of the end of the world" (31). Jehovah's Witnesses stay home to prepare and pray (52). But it is obvious that they do not find a

---

12 From Latin *miraculum*, i.e. 'object of wonder'. In this novel, the title refers 1) to unexpected events in the life of adolescent Julia from the surprising invitation to a party (Walker 2012: 240 – 242) to falling in love with Seth, etc.; 2) to changes that befall the adolescents: "This was middle school: the age of miracles ..." (56); 3) to the global changes mentioned which come as a surprise to everyone; 4) to miracles which will not come about, as in the case of corn growing without light (cf. 262); 5) to natural miracles such as snow in April (313) or the reappearance of the sun after long hours of darkness (68); 6) to man-made miracles in medicine (cf. 365); 7) to miracles some Christians believe in (87 – 88); and 8) to despair and / or to challenging God (a man throws himself in front of a car, "bent on suicide or miracle" (182)).

satisfactory answer to the questions posed by the catastrophe. Later, for instance, the Mormons will return from Utah, not having been met there by the Messiah, and just get on with their lives.

All forms of (religious) prophecies flourish, events are read as signs which simply need decoding. At school, children excitedly spread the gossip that in 1562 "a scientist named Nostradamus had predicted that the world would end on this exact day" (56). A woman proselytising in the streets shouts at Julia: "And the Lord God said, 'On that day, I will make the sun go down at noon and darken the earth in broad daylight'" (78). Neither Julia nor her mother can remember whether this is from the Bible or not.[13]

Some of the novel's characters revert to older forms of superstition as a would-be safeguard against fate. Julia starts to believe in omens (269). In the face of a catastrophe, her father insists on their wiping their feet on the doormat which the narrator reads as a ritual that "could ensure [their] safe passage" (21). Superstitions in themselves quickly adapt to the new circumstances: suddenly it is regarded "good fortune for a birthday to land on a dark night" (228). "Although current fatalistic beliefs and behavior often concern the role of fate in individual life", Daniel Wojcik comments aptly, "apocalyptic thinking conceptualizes fate as a cosmic, controlling power that determines history and the future of the earth and humanity" (1997: 19–20). Individual acts of superstition then can be seen as the attempt to create a personal counter-force directed against this impersonal, determining agent of fate.

Light, Science, and Order

Not only do religions flourish, the complex of the prolonged daylight and its consequences becomes an object of science. Attempts are made at classifying, analysing, and measuring the problem. Satellite maps are being consulted (Walker 2012: 24), charts of the day's sunrise and sunset (7) are debated, and scientists strive to explain environmental phenomena on TV (14). Schools, as influential socialising institutions, try to deal with the changes in a scientific, matter of fact, and pedagogical way: they instruct the children to make new sundials (57), they keep updating the solar system displayed on a classroom wall (60), and read a short story in class in which a young girl has to wait seven years to see the sun shine again (232).

---

13 It is: Amos 8:9.

People try to deal with the developing catastrophe in various ways. Most see the circadian rhythm as a guarantee of order and stability. However, even before the onset of the catastrophe, there were deviations from the majority's idea of a 24-hour-cycle. In "northern Scandinavia, the icy slopes of Siberia, the Inuit villages of Canada and Alaska [...] *night* and *day* had always been abstract. Morning did not necessarily bring with it the light. And not all the nights were dark" (107; emphases in the original). The same is true for Julia's whole family. The narrative proper starts – not arbitrarily – with a teenage sleep-over.[14] Sleep-overs are not primarily connected with sleep; Julia's mother is regularly sleepless, and her father, a medical doctor, often works night shifts at the hospital.

The novel *The Age of Miracles* does and does not foster simple binary divisions. Apart from working with literal and metaphorical black and white divisions, it also explores the realms of ambiguity and liminality. Light's ambiguous qualities are referenced early on. Light is not only something that all characters are missing sorely during their long nights, it is also qualified as potentially harmful early on. Children are told to apply sunscreen (6) and not to look directly into the sun since she 'ruins' the eyes (25). Julia's father, while driving his car, can only glance up "through the windshield at the sun" (55). In order to see Hanna's eyes, Julia has to squint because the day turns "brighter by the minute" (131). Sleep masks go "on backorder for months" (147), school buses and houses are equipped with blackout shades (319); amusement parks and malls close during daylight days (319). Sun-glasses come in "oversize" (289). Julia and Seth are hit by "the worst" (333) sunburn of their lives after a single excursion into daylight, having been burnt right through their clothes (335). "Solar storms" rage all summer (348). In the end, houses are coated with "thick steel sheeting" and "sun-proof shutters" (368). At the same time, however, sunrise "after so many hours in the dark" is greeted with "euphoria" (281).

Light and Language

Light also serves as an all-encompassing metaphor, simile, and means of comparison. With so many changes in the novel caused by light, by its presence and absence, its sources and ambiguities, it seems logical that light also features

---

14 Night, darkness, and bodily proximity set the expositional parameters of female bonding with Hanna, her best friend, of separation from the adult world, and of a sphere of their own. The exclusive secrecy of night that the two girls share is betrayed by Hanna's defection: during one night, a boy climbs into her bedroom and kisses her (cf. Walker 2012: 132), thus disrupting the female bond.

strongly in language. According to the narrator, families try to flee from the catastrophe like "small animals caught suddenly under a light" (3), thus belittling and reducing them. However, in contrast to animals, *homo sapiens* is not adequately attuned to nature any more, since it is, in fact, cats, and not humans, who sense "the change" (7) first.

The object of Julia's teenage love, Seth Moreno, is "a blinking light" in her head (49). Suddenly, a "thin circle of light" after darkness becomes valuable "like a diamond on a ring" (68). In contrast, other well-known similes are doomed, for instance *dark as night*, "as we used to say" (250). Instead, neologisms come to the fore, for instance "*aurora medius*" for the Northern Lights which have "swooped down" (321) nearly to the equator.

Language as a way of access to and making sense of reality is affected not only by a change in metaphorical usage but also by other linguistic side effects. Old associations are separated: When the United States agree to revert to the 24-hour regime, this immediately means that they "would fall out of sync with the sun almost immediately. Light would be unhooked from *day*, darkness unchained from *night*" (111; emphases in the original).

The dissolution of natural boundaries and the disruption of time's and light's predictable course is reflected in the first person narrator's proleptic style, announcing, for instance, that "there were those that *would later claim to have recognized* the disaster before the rest of us did"; a "hastily arranged press conference" is "*now* infamous" (2; my emphases), "all these years later" (5). Simultaneously, two different time levels are present – the narrator's 'then' (as teenage girl) and her 'now' (as grown up student) –, parallel to the existence of two different time communities within in the novel's depicted society, and also parallel to the "before" (7) the ecocatastrophe and the 'after' for the world population.

Light and Sociopolitics

The changes in the lengths of daylight and night time also effect changes in the sociopolitical set-up of the country: reminiscent of the American Civil War, in which seven Southern states seceded from the Union, the population is split in those still adhering to a 24-hour-cycle, and those in accordance with the new length of days. An alternative, and literally closer to home, would be an analogy founded on the 1960s and 1970s hippie communes of California. In *The Age of Miracles*, there are "new colonies" sprouting "from the sand in the desert", one with the telling name Circadia (Walker 2012: 199). Most of them are communes living according to the natural light-darkness rhythm, but others are also founded on religious beliefs: "[...] everyone was Jewish and everyone agreed on the Sabbath: sundown to sundown on every seventh day" (218). Individual support of the one group or the other is easily discernible: "[...] while the neighbors' windows glowed all day, [Sylvia] left hers unlit, as if she'd learned to sleep for twenty hours or more in a row" (201). Deviant behaviour is so threatening world-wide that "[c]ertain countries in Europe had made it more or less illegal to live the way Sylvia did" (202). Curfews in Paris (after all, the cradle of the Enlightenment, which takes on particular significance when considered in relation to the novel's plot) are being followed by riots (cf. 202).

The adherence to real time as opposed to clock time divides society in its core. At this point, Bloch's idea of the simultaneity of the non-simultaneous becomes tangible,[15] namely the "two dimensions of time occupying a single space" (144). Julia elaborates: "Most everything ran on the clock" (and thus on man-made and controllable time), not just the schools "but the doctors and the dentists and the mechanics, the grocery stores and the gyms, the restaurants and the movie theatres and the malls" (147). So, Earth is not the "redemptive, sublime entity of the romantic tradition" (Curry 2013: 40) anymore, but the place where a neo-Darwinian fight for the survival of the fittest and a division of the species seems to start taking place: "[...] these real-timers seemed very different from us, their customs incompatible with ours. They were widely regarded as freaks. We did not mix" (Walker 2012: 154–155).[16] Later on in the novel, the narrator even looks out for facial and bodily differences which would finally confirm the development of a second, separate human species even down to what Julia herself calls the 'molecular', 'atomic' level (cf. 287).

The group of time outcasts seems to be put in the position of scape-goats having to bear the brunt of ostracising measures, starting with the decoration of their houses with toilet paper (155–156) or the cutting of their power lines (202–203). The narrator quickly understands the psychological mechanisms hidden behind this marginalisation:

---

15 Orig.: "Gleichzeitigkeit des Ungleichzeitigen"; cf. Dietschy et al. (2012: 591).

16 Society's dissolution and a Darwinian fight for the survival of the fittest is mirrored by some animals taking over human territory: sand crabs exist under a "soggy carpet", starfish cling to "granite countertops", and sea anemones live "in the sinks" (Walker 2012: 157). There are "creatures at the bottom of the ocean that can live without light. They've evolved to thrive where other animals would die" (251). This Darwinian fight erupts on the global scale: "Famines were predicted for Africa and parts of Asia. 'These countries simply lack the financial resources to adapt' [said the head of the Red Cross]" (224). I am aware of the fact that the term 'survival of the fittest' was coined by Herbert Spencer – and not by Charles Darwin – as early as 1852; but this debate does not contribute in a vital manner to my argument.

The real-timers made the rest of us uncomfortable. They too often slept late while the rest of us worked. They went out when everyone else was asleep. They were a threat to the social order, some said, the first small crumbles of a coming disintegration. (Walker 2012: 163)

But at the same time, by their example they are able to provide mankind with new biomedical insights because human "circadian rhythms were turning out to be vastly more malleable then anyone had previously thought" (237).[17]

Conclusion

As stated before, in this novel, light, both in its natural and artificial form, functions as a protagonist. Because of the new circadian rhythm of Earth, mankind's control and dominance are threatened, and all other rhythms and areas of life in turn are upset or endangered. Easy equations lose their validity. Light is not only good, darkness is not only dangerous. Seen from a teenager's perspective, the new situation in *The Age of Miracles* represents ecological issues which humankind, with its unquestioned and taken for granted control over artificial light, seems to be not quite aware of. Often, eco-fiction focusses on man's detrimental impact on nature, be it pollution, atomic power, or the meddling with DNA. *The Age of Miracles*, for a change, does not directly blame mankind for the circadian catastrophe; instead, it shows them as the victims of a natural development and puts them in a situation comparable to the one the dinosaurs were in 66 million years ago. These huge animals, now extinct, allegedly could not survive as a species because of their low adaptability to changes in their environment.

The Age of Miracles re-evaluates light in biological, ecological, psychological, epistemological, medical, societal, individual, environmental, and linguistic terms – just to mention the most prominent factors. Natural and artificial light's ambiguous qualities are foregrounded: both are essential to our survival, and yet, both can seriously harm us, each in their own way. Artificial light cannot truly replace natural light, and vice versa, for obvious reasons. Light is a vital factor in everything we do and everything we see, it is a major force pertaining to control. It is illusionary to believe that mankind is in charge ("[...] fill the earth and subdue it"; Gen. 1:28) just because we are allegedly not dependent upon the natural givens of night and day any more.

The ending also addresses larger issues of implied theological criticism, of theodicy. God's creation of light and darkness, and thus of day and night, is

---

17 However, they are doomed: there is a limit to the adaptability of the human body (cf. Walker 2012: 354).

out of control; and the survival of his creatures, men and women, is at stake. Similar to Mary Shelley's *Frankenstein* (1818), a novel that critically featured a creator who left his new-born being to his own devices, the Christian God's division of day and night malfunctions in *The Age of Miracles*, and there are no signs of his benevolent intervening. The novel repudiates the claim of a permanently ordered and durable creation. The title's miracles become rare in the end, and the protagonist Julia has to put hope over experience and probability. Only a miracle will save her – and mankind.

Works Cited

Ahearn, Edward J. 1996. *Visionary Fictions: Apocalyptic Writing from Blake to the Modern Age.* New Haven, CT: Yale University Press.

Baudrillard, Jean. 1983. *Simulations.* Trans. Paul Foss, Paul Patton and Philip Beitchman. Los Angeles, CA: Semiotext[e].

Benjamin, Walter. 1936. "The Work of Art in the Age of Mechanical Reproduction". Transl. Harry Zohn. <https://www.marxists.org/reference/subject/philosophy/works/ge/benja min.htm.> [accessed 27 May 2015].

Cohen, Michael P. 2004. "Blues in the Green: Ecocriticism Unter Critique". *Environmental History* 9.1: 9–36.

Curry, Alice. 2013. *Environmental Crisis in Young Adult Fiction.* Houndmills: Palgrave Macmillan.

Dietschy, Beat, Doris Zeilinger, and Rainer Zimmermann (eds). 2012. *Bloch-Wörterbuch: Leitbegriffe der Philosophie Ernst Blochs.* Berlin: De Gruyter.

Joshua, Suka. 2007. "An Ecocritical Investigation on Margaret Atwood's Futuristic Novels". In: Nirmal Selvamony Nirmaldasan and Raysom K. Alex (eds.). *Essays in Ecocriticism.* Chennai: OSLE India. 207–215.

Kakutani, Michiko. 2012. "Normalcy Grinds to a Halt. 'The Age of Miracles,' Debut Novel by Karen Thompson Walker". *The New York Times* 18 June. <http://www.nytimes.com/2012/06/19/books/the-age-of-miracles-by-karen-thompson-walker.html?pagewanted=all&_r=0> [accessed 27 May 2015].

Magritte, René. 1954. *The Empire of Lights.* <http://en.wikipedia.org/wiki/The_Empire_of_Lights#/media/File:The_Empire_of_Light_Guggenheim.jpg> [accessed 31 May 2015].

Melbin, Murray. 1987. *Night as Frontier. Colonizing the World After Dark.* New York, NY: The Free Press.

Priest, Christopher. 2012. "The Age of Miracles by Karen Thompson Walker – Review". *The Guardian* 13 July. <http://www.theguardian.com/books/2012/jul/13/age-of-miracles-karen-walker-review> [accessed 25 May 2015].

Rosen, Elizabeth K. 2008. *Apocalyptic Transformation: Apocalypse and the Postmodern Imagination.* Lanham: Lexington Books.

Rueckert, William. 1978. "Literature and Ecology: An Experiment in Ecocriticism". *Iowa Review* 9.1: 71–86.

Seed, David (ed.). 2000. *Imagining Apocalypse: Studies in Cultural Crisis*. Houndmills: Macmillan Press.

Shelley, Mary. 1996. *Frankenstein* (1818). Ed. by J. Paul Hunter. New York, NY: Norton & Company.

The Bible. Authorized King James Version with Apocrypha. 2008. Eds. Robert Carroll and Stephen Pickett. Oxford: Oxford University Press.

Volkmann, Laurenz, Nancy Grimm, Ines Detmers, and Katrin Thomson (eds.). 2010. "Local Natures, Global Responsibilities: An Introduction". *Ecocritical Perspectives on the New English Literatures: ASNEL Papers 15*. Amsterdam: Rodopi. xi–xvii.

Walker, Karen Thompson. 2012. *The Age of Miracles*. London: Simon and Schuster.

Wojcik, Daniel. 1997. *The End of the World as We Know It. Faith, Fatalism, and Apocalypse in America*. New York, NY: New York University Press.

Zapf, Hubert. 2008. "Literary Ecology and the Ethics of Texts". *New Literary History* 39.4: 847–868.

Folkert Degenring

On Behalf of the Dark? Functionalisations of Light Pollution in Fiction

The notion that light might constitute a form of pollution is a relatively recent one: the *Oxford English Dictionary Online* added the above definition as a draft addition to the lemma 'light' only in June 2013. And certainly, an expression that brings together the terms 'light' and 'pollution' grates. That this should be the case is not entirely surprising, given the dominantly positive connotations of the noun 'light' and the overwhelmingly negative connotations of the word 'pollution'. In this chapter, I will try to trace the historical development of the term and examine some definitions that try to define light pollution from a number of different angles, including astronomical, ecological, cultural, medical, and legal perspectives. I will then discuss the question to what degree the term and the concept have entered literary discourse and how its effect can be quantified. Finally, I will try to demonstrate the scope of functionalisations of the term in literary texts, providing brief examples from across a broad range of genres.

Light Pollution: Origins, Definitions, and Meanings

Light shapes our perception of the world in a literal and physical sense, but also metaphorically; light and darkness are part of an extended complex that informs language and culture on many different levels. Despite some ambivalence, light is predominantly assigned positive attributes in this complex (cf. Bach and Degenring 2015; cf. the introduction to this volume). Against this background, thinking about light in terms of pollution is counterintuitive. However, natural darkness has become something of a rarity in many parts of the world today. This is certainly the case in urban centres of industrialised societies, where only the very brightest stars can be seen in the night sky, if any at all. Voicing concern over this development may be variously countered by pointing towards the necessities of economic development or public safety, or derided as hopelessly 'romantic', but for some years now, studies have shown that the ubiquitous and permanent illumination of the night has negative ecological and medical implications, even if the potential effects and interconnections are not yet fully understood (cf. Narisada and Schreuder 2003; Hölker et al. 2010; Meier et al. 2015).

The *Oxford English Dictionary Online* provides the following definition and information concerning the historical usage and sources of 'light pollution':

> **light pollution,** *n.* (the presence of) artificial light with harmful or undesirable effects; *esp.* the brightening of the night sky by street lighting, floodlights, neon signs, etc., which reduces the visibility of celestial objects or changes the behaviour of living organisms.
>
> 1968 *Capital Times* (Madison, Wisc.) 20 July (Editorial page) Mercury vapour [sic] lamps ... produce an unnatural appearing light. Some lean towards green, some towards yellow green, and some towards pink. Light pollution!
>
> 1971 *Science* 5 Feb. 461/1 The amount of 'light pollution', as the astronomers refer to the interfering city glare, is still far less in the Tucson area.
>
> 1995 *Beyond Horizon* (U.S. Environmental Protection Agency) 15/2 Increasing light pollution is found to be seriously disruptive to many species' physiology and behavior.
>
> 2010 D. A. Rothery *Planets: Very Short Introd.* i. 3 Before the curses of light pollution and smog, people were more familiar with the night sky than they tend to be today. (*OED Online*)

It is interesting to note that the earliest source the *OED Online* provides, a letter to the editors concerning the choice of public street lamps in Madison, WI, appears to use the term light pollution as an aesthetic judgement, and it is worth considering the letter in its entirety:

> [Madison, July 17th] I wish to make a few comments in regard to street lamps.
>   The first street lamps undoubtedly produced some form of firelight such as oil or kerosene lamplight. This type of light is rich in visible red, yellow, and orange as well as infrared. The lamplight which most closely approximates, and in addition is brighter than, natural firelight is that light which is produced by the tungsten filament lamp.
>   Mercury vapor lamps are even more intense and perhaps more economical to operate but they produce an unnatural appearing light. Some lean towards green, some towards yellow green, and some towards pink. Light pollution!
>   Instead of choosing one type of lamp for the entire city, consideration could be given to the esthetic [sic] qualities as well as the intensity of light desired for different locations, such as: main thoroughfares, quite residential areas, park areas, etc.–John Gangstad (1968: 28)

The full letter corroborates the initial impression. The commentator objects to contemporary street lamps because the light they provide may be too intense depending on the area where they are employed. The main objection, however, is that the colour of the light they emit appears to be 'unnatural' when compared to the spectrum emitted by 'natural firelight'. Street lighting here is to be considered as a pollutant, then, not because it is potentially harmful or undesirable per se, but because it deviates from the commentator's aesthetic ideal.

Gangstad's letter may be one of the earliest sources for the term 'light pollution' in print, but strong aesthetic objections to certain forms of lighting can be traced to almost a century earlier. In 1878, before he became a major literary figure, Robert Louis Stevenson wrote a short piece on the subject, "A Plea for Gas Lamps", which was later published as part of the collection *Virginibus Puerisque* (1881). In the essay Stevenson constructs a persona who considers the plight of his ancestors from the perspective of the 'age of gas lamps' in a quasi-historical retrospective, and then goes on to consider what future developments might entail. At the beginning of his discourse, the narrator-persona establishes that "[c]ities given, the problem was to light them" (288). The problem of appropriate illumination, then, is one that derives from the social context of the city, just as in the case of Gangstad's letter to the editors.

The evaluation of changing lighting technologies in Stevenson's text appears enthusiastic at first:

> When gas first spread along a city, mapping it forth about evenfall for the eye of observant birds, a new age had begun for sociality and corporate pleasure-seeking, and begun with proper circumstance, becoming its own birthright. The work of Prometheus had advanced by another stride. Mankind and its supper parties were no longer at the mercy of a few miles of sea-fog; sundown no longer emptied the promenade; and the day was lengthened out to every man's fancy. The city-folk had stars of their own; biddable, domesticated stars. (Stevenson 1881: 291)

When considering what future developments may replace gas lighting, however, the tone changes dramatically:

> The word ELECTRICITY now sounds the note of danger. In Paris, at the mouth of the Passage des Princes, in the place before the Opera portico, and in the Rue Drouot at the *Figaro* office, a new sort of urban star now shines out nightly, horrible, unearthly, obnoxious to the human eye; a lamp for a nightmare! Such a light as this should shine only on murders and public crime, or along the corridors of lunatic asylums, a horror to heighten horror. To look at it only once is to fall in love with gas, which gives a warm domestic radiance fit to eat by. (Stevenson 1881: 295)

The 'lamp for a nightmare' which Stevenson refers to here is a Jablochkoff candle, named after its inventor. The principle of the arc light, i.e. that an electric current flowing through two coal electrodes causes an extremely bright arc of light to appear between them, had first been described by Humphrey Davy in 1800. It was not until the 1870s, however, that arc lights were developed for commercial use and that they were used for the lighting of public spaces in major

European cities (cf. Schivelbusch 1988: 56). In 1878 experimental arc street lights appeared in London and Paris, where Stevenson witnessed them (Brox 2010: 103). The domestication of "the wildfire of the storm" (Stevenson 1881: 295), i.e. electricity, evident in the arc light appears as hubris which threatens to have, just like Prometheus' theft of the fire, dire consequences: the night, which has just been won for mankind from blackness and goblins through the "mild lustre" (296) of gas lamps, will be lost to the "blinding ugly glare" (295) of the new light (cf. Bach and Degenring 2015: 59).

Negative evaluations of, and aesthetic objections to, nocturnal illumination appear to run counter to its cultural association with the divine and its overwhelmingly positive connotations. However, both in the case of Stevenson's essay and Gangstad's letter, the objections are brought forward not against light in general, but against very specific light sources and lighting technologies. In both instances, the light sources in question are described as inherently unnatural, or even a perversion of nature. In Gangstad's case, the objectionable light is constructed as deficient because its appearance deviates from "natural firelight" (1968: 28). In Stevenson's case, it is constructed not just as deficient because it lacks the "warm domestic radiance" (1881: 295) of gaslight but as a perversion of nature: the use of the "wildfire of the storm" (ibid.) for the purpose of illumination overturns the natural order.

While Stevenson's condemnation of arc lights thus appears to be an attack on the use of electricity for lighting purposes, reactions to other contemporary electric lighting technologies do not follow this example. On September 5, 1882, for example, the *New York Times* reports on the reactions in its own newspaper office to the incandescent light bulbs installed in the building, which had been switched for the first time on the previous evening:

> It was a light a man could sit down under and write for hours without the consciousness of having any artificial light about him …. The light was soft, mellow, and grateful to the eye, and it seemed almost like writing by daylight to have a light without a particle to flicker and with scarcely any heat to make the head ache. The electric lamps in THE TIMES Building were as thoroughly tested … as any light could be tested in a single evening, and tested by men who have battered their eyes sufficiently by years of night work to know the good and bad points of a lamp, and the decision was unanimously in favor of the Edison electric lamp and against gas. (qtd. in Brox 2010: 122–123)

Here, Edison's electric light bulbs are described as superior to gaslight for similar reasons as Stevenson's denouncement of arc lights: the quality of the light and its steadiness is perceived to be much closer to natural daylight.

"In the course of the nineteenth century, the value placed on light as a guarantor of public morals, safety and order decreased as lights actually became brighter" (1988: 133–134), writes the historian of culture and technology, Wolfgang Schivelbusch, in *Disenchanted Night: The Industrialization of Light in the Nineteenth Century*,[1] his seminal study of the artificial illumination of the night. If, in times before the general availability of comparatively cheap and reliable light sources, light in domestic, as well as in public contexts, was considered rare and precious (cf. Brox 2010: 122–123), then it must appear paradoxical that the 19th century's realisation of the "[u]topian dream of nights lit up as bright as day [...] transformed into the nightmare of a light from which there was no escape" (Schivelbusch 1988: 134). That lighting might be used not to facilitate pleasure and extend the range of activities that are possible at night but to discipline instead was recognised as early as 1845 by the French historian Jules Michelet, who comments on the effect of bright gaslight in factories:

> These newly built big halls, flooded by brilliant light, torture eyes accustomed to darker quarters. Here there is no darkness, into which thought can withdraw, here there are no shadowy corners in which the imagination can indulge its dreams. No illusion is possible in this light. Incessantly and mercilessly, it brings us back to reality. (Michelet qtd. in Schivelbusch 1988: 134)

And while the diagnosis of a shift in the meaning of light at night from guaranteeing the individual's safety towards light allowing the "total surveillance by the state" (ibid.) in the 20th century is perhaps too harsh an assessment, it can be demonstrated that in crime and spy fiction around 1900, light and lighting technologies are linked to the themes of surveillance and control. That objections to and criticism of specific forms of light and light sources should become more frequent as nocturnal illumination becomes more intense, common, and ultimately ubiquitous, however, appears evident.

Against this background it is clear that the valuation of nocturnal illumination is historically changeable. It is true that critical voices do appear to be comparatively rare and isolated, but they do exist well before the time electric light becomes as dominant and ubiquitous in nocturnal lightscapes as it is today. The perception of unwanted side effects of specific lighting techniques as a form of pollution, however, does appear to be a phenomenon that develops only in the second half of the 20th century. And whereas earlier objections to specific forms of lighting appear to be mostly – if not exclusively – founded on aesthetic grounds, attitudes begin to change in the 1960s and 1970s. This is not to say

---

1 Translated from the German original, *Lichtblicke: Zur Geschichte der künstlichen Helligkeit im 19. Jahrhundert* (1983).

that aesthetic objections disappear, of course, but rather that new critical voices are added which begin to establish and popularise the term 'light pollution'.

During that time, professional astronomers in the US started lobbying for legislation to limit nocturnal illumination levels in order to be able to conduct their research in locations which were increasingly affected by the growth of urban areas and public and private lighting. In a 1971 *Science* magazine news item entitled "Star Bright, Street Light, Which Will They See Tonight?", Robert J. Bazell reports on a campaign by astronomers in the Tucson, AZ area to establish a light control ordinance. The report contents that astronomers would ideally like to locate their observatories "as far as possible from civilization so that the skies they observe could remain dark and free from air pollution"; however, since "they require supplies and technical assistance, the astronomers must compromise and locate the facilities near commercial centers" (461). Bazell continues to write that the observatories in the area are particularly affected by "two types of light": ultraviolet light emitted predominantly by mercury vapour lamps and "general glare", emitted by all kinds of light sources (ibid.). Citing an astronomer, the associate director at Kitt Peak National Observatory, Arthur Hoag, as a source, Bazell explicates the correlation between air pollution and the adverse effects of light on astronomy: "Both [types of light] are scattered in the air by particulate matter; thus air pollution and light pollution are closely related" (ibid.).

The news item introduces the term 'light pollution' into scientific discourse. A more comprehensive definition of astronomical light pollution was to follow in *Science* two years later in an article by Kurt Riegel (1973), but Bazell's text has the merit of making clear that light pollution is not merely the concern of astronomy but a multi-dimensional phenomenon by drawing attention to the ecological dimension of light pollution through linking it with the pollution of the air. And indeed, ecologists became interested in the phenomenon not long after astronomers. Travis Longcore and Catherine Rich, in "Ecological Light Pollution" (2004), for example, point out that their discipline has considered the problem of light pollution at least since the 1980s, even though it has not been quick to adopt the term:

> We describe artificial light that alters the natural patterns of light and dark in ecosystems as 'ecological light pollution'. Verheijen (1985) proposed the term 'photopollution' to mean 'artificial light having adverse effects on wildlife'. Because photopollution literally means 'light pollution' and because light pollution is so widely understood today to describe the degradation of the view of the night sky and the human experience of the night, we believe that a more descriptive term is now necessary. (Longcore and Rich 2004: 191)

Beyond the astronomical and the ecological dimension, the news item in *Science* touches upon a third aspect associated with light pollution: the legal dimension, which in the text is rhetorically linked with the other two, and to great effect. By setting the astronomers' campaign to influence local legislation against the background of the link between light and air pollution, the problem of one relatively small group becomes an issue that concerns the whole of the scientific community as well as the general public.

What Bazell and his contemporaries were not aware of is another dimension: the medical one. Medical publications have suggested that exposure to light at night and certain illnesses may be linked since the early 1990s, and more recent research appears to confirm this suspicion. In 2013, Jounhong Cho et al., for example, in a so-called 'brief communication' in *Sleep Medicine*, draw attention to the phenomenon of light pollution by stating:

> Exposure to light at night is now considered to be ordinary. Artificial light certainly has beneficial aspects; it has extended the length of productive days of work and recreational activities. However, when it becomes unreasonably excessive, it can be considered as light pollution, negatively affecting human physiology. It may disturb circadian organization; influence neuroendocrine systems; and cause many diseases, such as obesity, diabetes mellitus, depression, and even cancers. (Cho et al. 2013: 1422)

Cho et al. point out that when it comes to the effects of nocturnal light on human beings, light pollution is frequently literally home-made:

> Artificial lighting also is commonplace in bedrooms, and individuals with poor sleep hygiene often deliberately or unintentionally fall asleep with lights on. For example, one may fall asleep late night with the television light on, and children who are afraid of the dark may ask their parents to keep their lights on during sleep. (Cho et al. 2013: 1422)

Abraham Haim and Boris Portnov discuss potential effects on human health in greater detail in their 2013 monograph, *Light Pollution as a New Risk Factor for Human Breast and Prostate Cancer*, calling light at night (LAN) a "potential risk factor for human breast and prostate cancers [...] which can be termed 'light pollution' or even 'light toxicity'" (2013: 1). They posit that exposure to light at night (LAN) may pose a cancer risk because it disrupts the production of melatonin, a neuro-hormone, and ultimately reach the conclusion that

> [c]onsidering LAN as a source of environmental pollution and a source of toxicity is a challenge to our way of thinking. As we stated already in this chapter, we do not want to live in the dark 'pre-Edison' world. Therefore, we need to implement dramatic changes in thinking paradigms. Realizing the negative effects of LAN should help decision-makers to support the development of a holistic approach helping to deal with the problem at large. Therefore, environmental considerations, together with economic and sociological factors, should be considered before introducing new technologies, which, at first glance, may sound environ-

mentally friendly, but, at the end of the road, may be proved hazardous to the environment and to human health, with a wide range of negative socio-economic implications such hazards may entail. (Haim and Portnov 2013: 144)

Haim and Portnov's conclusion not only draws attention to the medical side of light pollution, but also points towards the socio-economic dimension, likening the situation to that of cigarette smoking in the mid-20th century (cf. ibid.).

The economist Terrel Gallaway, in "On Light Pollution, Passive Pleasures and the Instrumental Value of Beauty", considers the socio-economic dimension as well, if from a different angle. Rough estimates, he writes, show that "light pollution in the United States wastes \$6.9 billion worth of energy per year, generating 66 million metric tons of CO_2," (2010: 73). The main drive of his argument is less of an economical one, however, but centred on the cultural values the unpolluted night sky offers, including aesthetic and inspirational ones. What is more, Gallaway argues that the "night sky is somewhat like a museum of cultural and natural history. Those who care to can see the same planets, constellations, and asterisms that have been enjoyed for countless generations" (75). Light pollution is thus shown to constitute a pollution of humanity's cultural heritage. Despite it being a "passive pleasure", as a source of beauty, the night sky is "fundamental to human welfare and the recreation of community" (ibid.) and should be valued accordingly.

Light Pollution, Literature, and Literary Studies

In summary, then, light pollution is a phenomenon that has an astronomical, ecological, legal, medical, socio-economic, aesthetic, and cultural impact. In other words, it is not a problem that can be adequately studied from the perspective of a single discipline alone, but calls for a wider-reaching approach. In "The Dark Side of Light: A Transdisciplinary Research Agenda for Light Pollution Policy", members of the 'Verlust der Nacht' (Loss of the Night) research consortium in Germany[2] explain:

Given the dramatic increase in artificial light at night (0 – 20 % per year, depending on geographic region), we see an urgent need for light pollution policies that go beyond energy

---

2 The 'Verlust der Nacht' (Loss of the Night) transdisciplinary research consortium was funded by the German Federal Ministry for Education and Research (BMBF) from 2010 to 2013 and consisted of 14 interconnected sub-projects. Their website, http://www.verlustdernacht.de/, provides information on their research, access to a number of publications, and links to other research and information platforms.

efficiency to include human well-being, the structure and functioning of ecosystems, and inter-related socioeconomic consequences. Such a policy shift will require a sound transdisciplinary understanding of the significance of the night, and its loss, for humans and the natural systems upon which we depend. Knowledge is also urgently needed on suitable lighting technologies and concepts which are ecologically, socially, and economically sustainable. Unless managing darkness becomes an integral part of future conservation and lighting policies, modern society may run into a global self-experiment with unpredictable outcomes. (Hölker et al. 2010: 13)

If a thorough understanding of the effects of night-time illumination requires a transdisciplinary research effort because it affects the natural just like the cultural sphere, then surely it is not just the natural sciences but the humanities as well who must contribute. But what might the specific contribution literary studies can make to the research agenda look like? I believe that an answer must involve at least four dimensions:

The first concerns the descriptive dimension of literature. The assumption is that individual and collective attitudes and values of the production context of literature will always manifest themselves in literary texts, if sometimes through an absence rather than a presence. In other words: literary discourses and non-literary discourses interact, even though literature is never merely a straightforward reflection of extraliterary reality but always creates its own literary reality. The extra- and intraliterary sphere can be correlated, however, and literature can thus be used to trace and re-construct societal attitudes to light, night, and illumination.

Secondly, and with the same underlying assumption, the descriptive function of literature implies that it has an archival function as well. By looking at the historical treatment of light, night, and illumination in literature, literary scholars can contribute to an understanding of how societal attitudes have changed and evolved over time.

Thirdly, literature has a normative function. The underlying assumption is that literature is not only influenced by social conventions but that it also shapes them by providing an illustration of, and model for, what is considered good and proper behaviour. Literature does not directly determine its readers' world-view, of course. However, it does not merely entertain either but also affects its readers emotionally and cognitively, even if not all readers are affected in the same fashion or to the same degree. That fictional narratives do have an impact beyond being mere entertainment is something literary scholars have always been convinced of. But exactly why and how this should be the case has not necessarily been examined very closely, let alone explained systematically, by literary studies. For some years, however, the topic has received increased attention from other disciplines and its importance has been highlighted. For example, psychologists Melanie Green, Jeffrey Strange, and Timothy Brock, in their introduction to *Narrative Impact: Social and Cognitive Foundations*, stress that the "impact of public narratives can be, and has been enormous beyond reckoning" (2002: 2). And the cognitive psychologists Tobias Richter, Markus Appel, and Frank Calio, measuring narrative impact on readers experimentally, state in a 2014 essay: "A growing body of evidence indicates that mass-mediated stories can not only influence how we judge features of the outside world but also affect how we perceive ourselves" (182).

Fourthly, literature has an experimental function. Literature is not only a space in which subjective and collective experiences as well as societal attitudes manifest themselves, it is also a space in which thought experiments can be conducted. Literature is the realm of both the 'as if' as well as the 'what if', and it can examine the consequences of current phenomena taken to extremes, it can speculate on future developments, and it can break the laws of extraliterary reality in order to consider old and new issues from innovative angles.

It is evident, then, that literature and literary studies have much to contribute to a multi- and transdisciplinary study of light pollution. In the context of the pressures that the humanities face in times of public spending cuts and public debates concerning their utility in many countries, this might appear like relegating literary studies to the status of a secondary or ancillary discipline. I do not believe that this is the case: I believe that it highlights that literature is a valuable resource for understanding complex phenomena in its own right. Accessing this resource is not trivial, however. An adequate understanding of what literature has to say about what lies outside literature, what new and different perspectives and insights it has to offer, is only possible on the foundation of a thorough knowledge of literature itself, its evolution, its internal organisation, how it works, and as a work of art.

Light Pollution in Literature: A Quantitative and Qualitative Approach

Against this background, I will address two questions. First, has the concept of light pollution explicitly entered literary discourse, and if so, to what extent? And second, if the phenomenon has entered literary discourse, how is light pollution functionalised in literary texts?

Trying to answer the first question is easy and difficult at the same time. It is easy in the sense that, formally speaking, identifying one literary text in which light pollution is directly referenced is sufficient for a positive answer. It is difficult in the sense that if waiting to simply stumble across a reference is not an option, a more planned search methodology is required, particularly if the objective is to gain an understanding not just if, but to what degree the concept can be traced in literature.

Until relatively recently, such an undertaking would have involved a major and concentrated research effort. With the advent of large-scale digital initiatives (LSDIs) like Google Book Search, however, the process has become relatively easy and straightforward, perhaps even deceptively so. Numerous critics have voiced concerns over the effects projects like Google's have on the way research is conducted in the humanities. Paul Gooding, for example, formulates two major concerns:

> First, there is the concern that quantitative analysis has inadvertently fed a culture that favours information ahead of traditional research methods. Second, little information exists about how LSDIs are used for any research other than quantitative methods. (Gooding 2013: 425)

Gooding goes on to stress that the use of quantitative methodology in the humanities is not problematic per se. He cites Franco Moretti's *Graphs, Maps, Trees: Abstract Models for Literary History* (2007) as an example that successfully uses 'distant reading' to develop visualisations in aid of a better understanding of literary history: "graphs of the growth of the novel in various countries; maps that show the nature of space in narrative; and trees that demonstrate the taxonomy of novelistic genres" (Gooding 2013: 427). Gooding identifies as problematic not those approaches which, like Moretti's, are aware of the methodological limitations of quantitative analysis, but those which uncritically adopt quantitative perspectives and use admittedly sophisticated computational methods "to justify the marginalization of close reading in the humanities" (ibid.). It seems undeniable, however, that the very large scale text collections which have been produced in recent years offer new and fruitful research perspectives for the digital humanities (cf. Juola 2013; Jockers 2013: 24–32), even though far from all methodological issues have been resolved.

Keeping in mind that this approach is not without conceptual and methodological problems, I have decided to use the Google Ngram corpus in order to approach an answer to the question whether light pollution has entered literary discourse (cf. Michel et al. 2010). Google's Ngram viewer is a publically available tool that allows for an easy and quick search of the various corpora that form the Google Ngram Corpus.[3] It will return graphs that show the relative frequency of

---

3 The Ngram Viewer can be accessed at https://books.google.com/ngrams. The website provides

the n-gram in relation to the corpus as a whole. In the following I will present the results of searches that have been conducted using the English 2012 corpus.[4] This corpus contains n-grams from some 4.5 million books published in English all over the world and over 468 billion tokens (Lin et al. 2012: 170).

A search for the bi-gram 'light pollution' and variants with different capital- isations yielded the result that until the 1920s the bi-gram does not appear in the corpus at all, and that its relative frequency begins to rise sharply in the 1970s (Figure 1).[5]

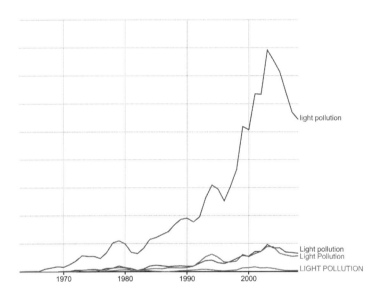

Figure 1: relative frequencies of 'light pollution' in the eng_2012 corpus

basic information on its functions and search syntax, and links to more detailed explanations as well.

4 Version and file name googlebooks-eng-all-20120701.

5 All figures have been generated using Google's Ngram Viewer. For the sake of visual clarity the timeframe has been set to 1900 to 2008 (the latest date which the Ngram Viewer search en- gine will accept), the graphs have been made slightly smoother (smoothing set to 1), and only a portion of the resulting graph is shown.

When comparing the relative frequencies of 'light pollution' in the English 2012 with the English Fiction 2012[6] corpus, which is a subset of the former, it becomes evident that the bi-gram is relatively more frequent in general English than it is in fiction, but that the graphs correspond fairly well (Figure 2). Disregarding questions of statistical significance, and acknowledging that some degree of correspondence must be expected because one corpus is a subset of the other, I would read this as an indication that the frequency of the bi-gram in fiction is in some way linked to the growing frequency in general usage.

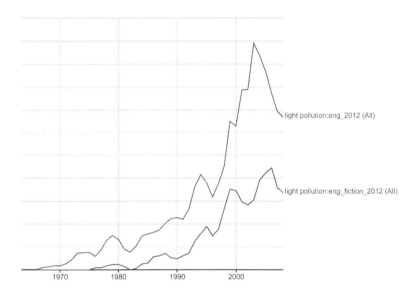

Figure 2: 'light pollution' in eng_2012 and eng_fiction_2012 corpora

There is some evidence, then, that the term light pollution has indeed entered literary discourse. At this stage, however, the question arises whether the bi-gram 'light pollution' consists of two nouns, or an adjective and a noun, in which case it would mean the opposite of 'heavy pollution' or 'strong pollution' and not light pollution as it has been discussed here. In principle the Google corpora do allow to differentiate between grammatical functions if the n-gram has

---

6 Version and file name googlebooks-eng-fiction-all-20120701.

been tagged accordingly, but unfortunately that appears not to be the case with 'light pollution'.

As a workaround, the relative frequency of the German compound noun 'Lichtverschmutzung' in the German 2012[7] corpus has been included in the analysis. 'Lichtverschmutzung' is the literal translation of light pollution in the sense of light constituting a form of pollution, and it is a term for the phenomenon in both scientific and public discourse in Germany today. The query yields a very similar curve (Figure 3) and, once again leaving aside questions of statistical significance, I would posit that this can be read as a strong indicator that the 'light' in the bi-gram 'light pollution' is a noun and not an adjective.

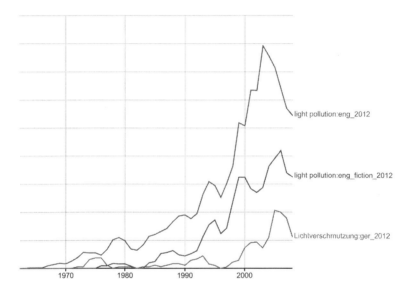

Figure 3: 'light pollution' and 'Lichtverschmutzung'

The question whether light pollution has entered literary discourse can thus be answered in the affirmative. In order to answer the question to what degree this is the case, the analysis must turn from relative frequencies to absolute numbers, which are not available via the Google Ngram viewer. Fortunately, the raw data of the various Google corpora does provide that information. Unfortunately, the

---

7 Version and file name googlebooks-ger-all-20120701.

files are of a format and size that cannot be handled by the standard software and office packages installed on most PCs. Shareware programmes that allow access to the raw data can be found via search engines, however, so the data can be retrieved, albeit by no means as comfortably as with the Ngram Viewer.

The English Fiction 2012 corpus is organised into several separate files, and the one containing the data for the bi-gram 'light pollution'[8] lists the first entry for the year 1977, in which the term occurred exactly once in one particular book, and the final one for the year 2009, when it occurred a total of 169 times in 151 separate books (Table 1). This means that in terms of absolute numbers, light pollution is mentioned explicitly only in a tiny fraction of fiction titles. Bowker LLC, a company specialising in providing bibliographical data and analytical services for the publishing industry, cites a figure of 48,738 new fiction titles and editions published in the United States in the year 2009 ("ISBN Output Report 2002–2013"). According to the raw data provided in Google's English Fiction 2012, the corpus contains 43,273 separate publications for that year, in which the ngram 'light pollution' occurs a total of 169 times in 151 separate volumes, i.e. roughly 0.35 percent of total volumes for that year.

It appears obvious that the next analytical step should be to identify which specific fiction titles contain a direct reference to light pollution. This information, however, is not encoded in the Ngram corpora. The naïve but obvious workaround which I have employed was to search for the term 'light pollution' manually via the standard Google Book Search interface. This, however, proved to be unreliable. Searching for the term 'light pollution' using the standard search field yielded both fiction and non-fiction titles, and included many apparent false positives. A further issue is that not all titles which have been digitised are fully accessible via Google Book Search. Titles in which the reference to light pollution was not accessible via the snippet or preview function could not be confirmed, and were disregarded in the following analysis. Ultimately, I was able to identify in Google Book Search 14 out of the 151 separate titles listed for 2009 in the Google Ngram English Fiction 2012 corpus, and a total of 103 titles in Google Book Search for the period 1977 to 2013.

My quantitative analysis stopped there. No doubt it would have been desirable to identify more titles with a greater degree of precision, to categorise them in terms of genre, to correlate the distribution across genres with the popularity of genres in the marketplace, and to consider the sales figures of individual titles, which in all likelihood would have yielded further indicators for the impact of light pollution on literary discourse. The resources required to follow up on

---

8 Version and file name googlebooks-eng-fiction-all-2gram-20120701.

Table 1: 'light pollution' in googlebooks-eng-fiction-all-2gram-20120701

Year	matches	volumes
1977	1	1
1979	1	1
1980	1	1
1985	4	2
1986	1	1
1987	7	7
1988	6	6
1989	3	3
1990	4	3
1991	6	4
1992	6	6
1993	8	8
1994	25	21
1995	22	17
1996	16	14
1997	8	8
1998	33	29
1999	62	55
2000	61	45
2001	48	44
2002	66	64
2003	76	75
2004	97	84
2005	159	116
2006	124	115
2007	164	145
2008	169	145
2009	169	151

these desiderata would have been considerable, and in excess of those available for the project. In summary, however, the quantitative analysis has clearly demonstrated that light pollution has no doubt entered literary discourse at this stage. While the frequency in which the concept is mentioned in literary texts is increasing, explicit references to light pollution are a very marginal occurrence in terms of absolute numbers, indeed. It is true that, not least due to the methodologically naïve approach, the results should be understood as indicators only and that their interpretation is tentative at best. They may nevertheless serve as a signpost pointing towards questions that require less of a quantitative and more of a qualitative approach.

In the following, then, I will turn from a distant to a closer reading of some of the texts in the light pollution corpus that the quantitative approach has yielded. The questions I would like to address are: What is the function of references to light pollution in literature? Which metaphoric and symbolic meaning, if any, does light pollution have when it is mentioned in a literary context? By necessity, the answers to these questions will have to assume the form of spotlights rather than providing a comprehensive overview.

I will begin this discussion with a quote from the introduction to a collection of essays and short stories entitled *Let There Be Night: Testimony on Behalf of the Dark* (2008). The editor, Paul Bogard, writes about how he invited contributions to the book:

> "As you may know," I wrote, "the light pollution blocking our view of the stars is only the most obvious result of artificial night lighting. Our lack of attention to the spread of these lights mirrors a lack of appreciation for night's ancient gifts of quiet, peace, and time to be with those we love. And, perhaps most seriously, as we've diluted the darkness, so have we negatively affected ecosystems in ways we're only beginning to understand." (Bogard 2008: 5)

Two rhetorical modes can be identified in the introduction. One is the rather stern warning about the ecological consequences of humanity's thoughtless actions, clearly focused on the ecological dimension of light pollution. The other one is a sense of nostalgia for the past when, apparently, less light at night signified a greater 'appreciation for night's ancient gifts of quiet, peace, and time to be with those we love'. It may be easy to take objection to the phrasing and, indeed, to the notion of nostalgia for a past in which everything was golden, but without a doubt, light pollution does have an impact on the cultural and the social dimension. Given the global scale of pressing ecological issues on the one hand, and how intricately nightly illumination is connected to the way in which contemporary industrialised societies are organised, a kind of ecological dread and a deep nostalgia anchored on the concept of light pollution are not surprising, and perhaps even to be expected. However, in most of the literary texts dealing explicitly with light pollution, the concept is functionalised quite differently.

In Mark Haddon's *The Curious Incident of the Dog in the Night-time* (2003), for example, light pollution is mentioned exactly once, in the following context:

> And later on, at 10:31 p.m., I went out onto the balcony to find out whether I could see any stars, but there weren't any because of all the clouds and what is called *Light Pollution* which is lights from streetlights and car headlights and floodlights and lights in buildings

reflected off tiny particles in the atmosphere and getting in the way of light from the stars. So I went back inside. (Haddon 2004: 247; emphasis in the original)

This is the voice of the novel's first person narrator, a 15-year old who describes himself as having some "Behavioural Problems" (59), which most likely are the result of Asperger's syndrome, or a similar condition.

What is the function of the reference to light pollution here? First, the fact that the term is capitalised and italicised draws attention to it, and marks it as unusual. This also serves to characterise the narrator, who happens to know about things 'normal people' like his parents and most of the people he meets have never heard about, and who feels the urge to share this knowledge, no matter whether people around him consider this information relevant or not. Knowing what light pollution is therefore sets the narrator and protagonist apart from other characters and, despite growing levels of public awareness, most likely in many instances the reader as well. Second, on a symbolic level, the idea of light pollution resonates with the narrator's condition. Light pollution is, amongst other things, an effect of the social organisation and functional differentiation of society and thus something he has no direct or even indirect control over. In a similar fashion, he fails to understand what motivates people because he cannot see through the emotional signals everyone around him is broadcasting all the time; again something he has no direct or even indirect control over. Light pollution thus serves the paradoxical two-fold function of setting the character apart while being bound up in inescapable social relations at the same time.

Referring to light pollution has a similar function of setting apart one of the characters in Ali Smith's 2005 novel, *The Accidental:*

> Astrid, the person is saying. Astrum, astralis. How does it feel to have such a starry name?
> Then she starts talking about stars. She says that because of light pollution from cities and streetlights, the night sky can't be seen properly any more and that all over the western world the sky now never gets properly dark. In more than half of Europe, in America, all over the world, people can't see the stars any more in the same way as they were able to in the past. (Smith 2006: 31)

The 'person' that is being referred to here is an uninvited guest to a family's holiday home, and this person will, in the course of the novel, essentially turn everyone's life around. In the passage quoted above, the daughter, Astrid, is the focaliser, and she knows nothing at all about light pollution. The fact that the 'person' does, sets her apart and again marks her as different or even slightly weird. But there is no doubt that she is going to have a profound effect on Astrid, as is evident a couple of pages later. I would argue that the reference to light pollution not only serves to set the 'person' apart, but that it also prefigures the influence she is going to exert. The girl Astrid is going through a teenage identity crisis, and through linking her name with the stars, light pollution becomes a metaphor for this crisis, for a notion of self which in the past was clear but has now become occluded. And, to varying degrees, this is true for the other members of the family as well, all of whom will be confronted with aspects of their identities which have become invisible to themselves (cf. Bach and Degenring 2015: 63).

Introspection is also a theme associated with light pollution in Monica Ali's *Alentejo Blue* (2006), which could be described as a collection of vignettes set in rural Portugal:

> It's warmer outside than in tonight and I'm sat out under the stars. I can see a few house lights. They look so far away, like you could walk all night and never reach them. Every now and then a little dot of silver slides across the black and disappears. It's a car going over the hill and down towards the sea. There are shooting stars as well. I've seen one tonight already. You never see them in England hardly because of all the light pollution. Some things you only see clearly in the dark. (Ali 2007: 198–199)

The focaliser in this section is an Englishwoman now living in Portugal, who is charged with illegally aiding her daughter to have an abortion there; a charge which in legal terms is comparable to one of murder. As a consequence, she has been thrown out of her house by her husband and is now living in a friend's caravan. Light pollution, or rather its marked absence, serves at least two different functions here. The final sentence of the passage quoted above – 'Some things you only see clearly in the dark' – is literally true, of course: you cannot see stars or even shooting stars very clearly in a bright sky. But the statement also plays with the close connections between words that describe light, seeing, etc. and the idea of knowledge and understanding in English. The darkness that surrounds her is a symbol for her social isolation; the next house lights seem very far away after all, and it is precisely this isolation which lets her think about her own situation, and perhaps even understand it.

But light pollution also serves a second function, which is as a marker of difference: In England you cannot see the stars because of light pollution, while in Portugal you can. You can even see shooting stars – a sign of hope and good fortune. And, indeed, it appears that things are resolved at the end of this episode and the narrator is reunited with her husband.

The presence or absence of light pollution functions as a marker for difference in quite a few of the texts which I have examined. Here is a straightforward example from *Gridlinked* (2001), a science fiction novel by Neal Asher:

> As the Lyric fell into orbit, leaving the station behind, Jarvellis sat and watched the advance of night. Unlike Earth the night side of the planet was almost completely black. Here was none of the huge light pollution igniting the sky from vast sprawls of cities. Only the occasional glow from the occasional small city. (Asher 2004: 258)

The absence of light pollution marks the planet the character observes from the spaceship as not-Earth, and also as less developed, if not outright backward. Light pollution, then, can serve to characterise a place through its presence, or through its absence. It is a marker for difference which is not limited to geographical distance, but also suggests oppositions such as urban vs. rural or artificial vs. natural. Consider the following two examples, both of which are set in the Los Angeles area. The first is from Sue Grafton's *O is for Outlaw: A Kinsey Millhone Mystery*, a 1999 crime novel:

> I crested the Camarillo grade and coasted down the far side into the westernmost perimeter of the San Fernando Valley. There were no stars in sight. The Los Angeles light pollution gave the night sky a ghostly illumination, like an aurora borealis underlaid by smog. (Grafton 1999: 161)

Light pollution is used here to establish a sense of place, and the effect described can actually be observed in the Los Angeles area. The reference is thus part of establishing a setting which corresponds very closely to an actual location.

T. C. Boyle's *The Tortilla Curtain* (1995) is set in the same geographical location, but here light pollution has a function beyond providing a detailed impression of the location:

> Delaney couldn't feel bad for long, not up here where the night hung close round him and the crickets thundered and the air off the Pacific crept up the hills to drive back the lingering heat of the day. There were even stars, a cluster here and there fighting through the wash of light pollution that turned the eastern and southern borders of the night yellow, as if a whole part of the world had gone rancid. To the north and east lay the San Fernando Valley, a single endless plane of parallel boulevards, houses, mini-malls and streetlights, and to the south lay the rest of Los Angeles, ad infinitum. (Boyle 1996: 63)

Light pollution is used here to create a sense of place, too. But it is not just a sense of place that is created: light pollution is used to semanticise space. The light from the urban and suburban areas which is turning the night a rancid yellow, signals that something awful is happening in southern California. Light pollution here evokes the economic and social structures that draw Mexican immigrants to the Los Angeles/San Fernando area and rely on their labour, yet also completely exclude them, thus effectively ruining their lives: a paradoxical, xenophobic capitalism taints the area just like light pollution spoils the night sky.

Quite frequently, light pollution marks space as civilised, but also as decadent, un-natural, dangerous. Characters trying to get away from light pollution might thus be attempting to escape from problems that result from their social and personal relationships. This is the case in Madison Bell's *The Colour of Night*, a 2011 novel whose protagonist is the victim of sexual abuse by her brother. In this passage from the beginning of the novel, she leaves the city limits of Las Vegas:

> I walked into the desert till the world began to curve, till the electric lights dropped behind the warp of the horizon. You can never get completely away from the light pollution of all those towns, but where I stopped the stars were brighter. Again, no moon. (Bell 2011: 39)

Here, the desire to get away from light pollution resonates with the narrator's desire to forget about her abuse. But just like she cannot walk away from light pollution, she cannot walk away from her personal history either. This is underlined by the marked absence of the moon, which would have provided a natural light source as a kind of counterpoint to artificial light pollution: there is no alternative, and what happened to the narrator cannot be undone.

Light pollution, then can be read as something that cannot be escaped from, as a kind of metaphorical trap. This is certainly the case in the next excerpt, which is from Joel Lane's queer vampire short story "Behind the Curtain", published in 2009:

> It was late May, but there was frost on the ground before it even got dark. A restless wind scratched the cars with litter. The pale clouds that had bleached the view this morning were stained with yellow as the hidden sun went down, trapping the city in a bell jar of its own light pollution. I felt almost too weak to satisfy my need, but knew if I didn't the next day would be even worse. (Lane 2009: 135)

The narrator here is not a vampire, as might be assumed, but someone who is addicted to being bitten by vampires. The narrator describes light pollution as a giant bell jar, a physical trap, from which escape is impossible. As in some of the texts discussed previously, light pollution here serves as a symbol of the narrator's isolation. Actually, the narrator is trapped and isolated in several ways: trapped by his addiction, trapped in the city because that is where the vampires are, and trapped at night-time because only then can he meet the creatures which will be able to satisfy his need. And the very term light pollution plays with imagery central to the vampire motif since Bram Stoker's days: the aversion to sunlight and the notion of degeneration and infection.

Concluding Remarks

The examples I have discussed are, of course, only a first step in answering the question of how the concept of light pollution is functionalised in literature. A more comprehensive answer would entail a number of additional steps: examining a much greater portion of the available corpus to begin with, and certainly a consideration not just of the passages where the term occurs but also of the light/darkness symbolism that may (or may not) inform the text as a whole. A comprehensive analysis would also attempt to identify and examine those texts in which the concept of light pollution can be traced without the actual term being used. Nevertheless, I hope to have shown that light pollution as a relatively new concept that originated predominantly in the context of astronomy has no doubt entered literary discourses at this stage. Its functionalisation is not limited to serving as a referent for the concept of light pollution itself; neither is it merely a placeholder for ecological awareness or an expression of nostalgia, even though it does fulfil these functions. Instead, light pollution is used as a means of characterisation, for example, or to evoke a sense of place, or to turn a place into semanticised space, and it can serve as a complex metaphor and symbol. It can be used in this fashion because it ties into the long tradition of the extended symbolic complex formed around light, night, and darkness. In bringing together two ostensibly contradictory terms, however, light pollution does add a genuinely new dimension to it. Nevertheless, in terms of absolute numbers, references to light pollution in literature remain quite rare. I would like to argue that in a context that is fraught with contradictions and paradoxes, it is precisely this combination of the widespread and the marginal that turns light pollution into such a rewarding subject of enquiry.

Works Cited

"ISBN Output Report 2002–2013". Bowker LLC, n.d. <http://www.bowker.com/documents/isbn-output-report-2002–2013.html> [accessed 26 May 2015].
"light pollution". Oxford English Dictionary Online, June 2013. <http://www.oed.com/view/Entry/108172?redirectedFrom=light+pollution#eid289962018> [accessed 26 May 2015].
Ali, Monica. *Alentejo Blue*. 2007. London: Black Swan.
Asher, Neal. *Gridlinked*. 2004. New York, NY: Tor.
Bach, Susanne and Folkert Degenring. 2015. "From Shakespearean Nights to Light Pollution: (Artificial) Light in Anglophone Literature". In: Josiane Meier, Ute Hasenöhrl, Katharina Krause, and Merle Pottharst (eds.). 2015. *Urban Lighting, Light Pollution and Society*. New York, NY: Routledge. 46–65.

Bazell, Robert J. 1971. "Star Bright, Street Light, Which Will They See Tonight?" *Science* 171.3970: 461.

Bell, Madison S. 2011. *The Color of Night*. New York: Vintage Books.

Bogard, Paul. 2008. "Introduction: Why Dark Skies?". In: Paul Bogard (ed.). *Let There be Night: Testimony on Behalf of the Dark*. Reno, NV: University of Nevada Press. 1–7.

Boyle, T. C. 1996. *The Tortilla Curtain*. New York, NY: Penguin.

Brox, Jane. 2010. *Brilliant: The Evolution of Artificial Light*. Boston, MA: Houghton Mifflin Harcourt.

Cho, Jounhong R., Eun Yeon Joo, Dae Lim Koo, and Seung Bong Hon. 2013. "Let There Be No Light: The Effect of Bedside Light on Sleep Quality and Background Electroencephalographic Rhythms". *Sleep Medicine* 14.12: 1422–1425.

Gallaway, Terrel. 2010. "On Light Pollution, Passive Pleasures, and the Instrumental Value of Beauty". *Journal of Economic Issues* 44.1.

Gangstad, John. 1968. "Voice of The People: Says Single Type of Lights Can't Serve all of City's Needs". *Madison Capital Times* 20 Jul: 28. <http://madison.newspaperarchive. com/madison-capital-times/1968–07–20> [accessed 26 May 2015].

Gooding, Paul. 2013. "Mass Digitization and the Garbage Dump: The Conflicting Needs of Quantitative and Qualitative Methods". *Literary and Linguistic Computing* 28.3: 425–431.

Grafton, Sue. 1999. *O is for Outlaw: A Kinsey Milhone Mystery*. New York, NY: Henry Holt and Company.

Green, Melanie C., Jeffrey J. Strange, and Timothy C. Brock (eds.). 2002. *Narrative Impact: Social and Cognitive Foundations*. Mahwah, NJ: L. Erlbaum Associates.

Haddon, Mark. 2004. *The Curious Incident of the Dog in the Night-time*. London: Vintage.

Haim, Abraham and Boris A. Portnov. 2013. *Light Pollution as a New Risk Factor for Human Breast and Prostate Cancers*. Dordrecht: Springer.

Hölker, Franz, Timothy Moss, Barbara Griefhahn, Werner Kloas, Christian C. Voigt, Dietrich Henckel, Andreas Hänel, Peter M. Kappeler, Stephan Völker, Axel Schwope, Steffen Franke, Dirk Uhrlandt, Jürgen Fischer, Reinhard Klenke, Christian Wolter, and Klement Tockner. 2010. "The Dark Side of Light: A Transdisciplinary Research Agenda for Light Pollution Policy". *Ecology and Society* 15.4: 13.

Jockers, Matthew L. 2013. *Macroanalysis: Digital Methods and Literary History*. Urbana, IL: Illinois University Press.

Juola, Patrick. 2013. "Using the Google N-Gram Corpus to Measure Cultural Complexity". *Literary and Linguistic Computing* 28.4: 668–675.

Koslofsky, Craig. 2011. *Evening's Empire: A History of the Night in Early Modern Europe*. Cambridge: Cambridge University Press.

Lane, Joel. 2009. "Behind the Curtain". In: Steve Berman (ed.). *Wilde Stories 2009: The Year's Best Gay Speculative Fiction*. Maple Shade, NJ: Lethe Press. 135–142.

Lin, Yuri, Jean-Baptiste Michel, Erez Lieberman Aiden, Jon Orwant, William Brockman, and Slav Petrov. 2012. "Syntactic Annotations for the Google Books Ngram Corpus". *Proceedings of the 50th Annual Meeting of the Association for Computational Linguistics:* 169–174.

Longcore, Travis and Catherine Rich. 2004. "Ecological Light Pollution". *Frontiers in Ecology and the Environment* 2.4: 191–198.

Meier, Josiane, Ute Hsenöhrl, Katharina Krause, and Merle Pottharst (eds.). 2015. *Urban Lighting, Light Pollution and Society*. New York, NY: Routledge.

Melbin, Murray. 1987. *Night as Frontier: Colonizing the World After Dark*. New York, NY: Free Press.

Michel, Jean-Baptiste, Yuan Kui Shen, Aviva Presser Aiden, Adrian Veres, Matthew K. Gray, William Brockman, The Google Books Team, Joseph P. Pickett, Dale Hoiberg, Dan Clancy, Peter Norvig, Jon Orwant, Steven Pinker, Martin A. Nowak, and Erez Lieberman Aiden. 2010. "Quantitative Analysis of Culture Using Millions of Digitized Books". *Science* 331.6014: 176–182.

Moretti, Franco. 2007. *Graphs, Maps, Trees: Abstract Models for Literary History*. London: Verso.

Narisada, Kohei and Duco Schreuder. 2004. *Light Pollution Handbook*. Dordrecht: Springer.

Richter, Tobias, Markus Appel, and Frank Calio. 2014. "Stories Can Influence the Self-concept". *Social Influence* 9.3: 172–188.

Riegel, Kurt W. 1973. "Light Pollution: Outdoor lighting is a growing threat to astronomy". *Science* 179.4080: 1285–1291.

Schivelbusch, Wolfgang. 1988. *Disenchanted Night: The Industrialisation of Light in the Nineteenth Century*. Berkeley, CA: University of California Press.

Smith, Ali. *The Accidental*. 2006. London: Penguin.

Stevenson, Robert L. 1881. "A Plea for Gas Lamps." *Virginibus Puerisque: And Other Papers*. London: C. Kegan Paul & Co. 288–296.

Index

About the Contributors

Susanne Bach is Professor of English Literature at the University of Kassel, Germany. She has published, among other topics, on modern British Drama, 19th-century novels, spirituality and transcendence, light pollution, medicine and literature, intertextuality, gender studies, and cultural criticism.

Stella Butter is Teaching Centre Coordinator at the International Graduate Centre for the Study of Culture, Justus Liebig University, Giessen, Germany. She has published on contingency and literature in the process of modernisation, cultural functions of literature, literary representations of home, as well as on gender and subjectivity.

Folkert Degenring is an independent scholar and holds a doctoral degree in English literature. His research interests include identity in fiction, intersectionality, literature and gender, and literature and science.

Robert Gillett is Reader in German and Comparative Cultural Studies at Queen Mary University of London. He has a special interest in the German queer author Hubert Fichte, but has published very widely on English, French, German, Austrian, and Swiss authors of the last three centuries.

Paul Goetsch is Emeritus Professor of English and American Literature at the University of Freiburg, Germany. He has published widely on English, American, and Canadian Literature as well as on New Literatures in English; the most recent publications focus on the treatment of Faust in English Literatures and on motifs and themes in modern British and American Poetry.

Lars Heiler is Associate Professor of English and American Literature at the University of Kassel, Germany. He has published on regression in modern British fiction, taboo, transgression and censorship, myth and femininity, gender and violence, and on contemporary American drama.

Richard Leahy is Visiting Lecturer and PhD candidate at the University of Chester, England. He has published on the works of Elizabeth Gaskell and Emile Zola, and his research interests include 19th-century literature, technology and literature, and critical theory.

Laura E. Ludtke is a D. Phil. Candidate in English Literature at St Anne's College, Oxford. Her research, supported by a Doctoral Fellowship from the Social Sciences and Humanities Research Council of Canada, focuses on the literary influence of artificial light in British fiction set in London from 1880 to 1950.

Jarmila Mildorf is Senior Lecturer for English Literature and Culture at the University of Paderborn. Her research interests are in narratology, dialogue studies, medicine and literature and stylistics.

Maria Peker is Visiting Lecturer of English Literature at the University of Kassel, Germany. She is currently completing her monograph on the interdependence of gender and time in the Victorian novel. Her research interests include gender and sexuality in Victorian literature, and the modern Anglo-Jewish novel.

Murat Sezi is Assistant Professor of English Literature at the University of Kassel, Germany. His research interests include genre theory, narratology and space, and literature and knowledge.

Isabel Wagner is an independent researcher with a PhD from Queen Mary University of London. Her thesis focuses on self-reflexivity and music in Wolfgang Hildesheimer's work, and her current research interests include intermediality, comparative literature, and capitalism and the arts.

Made in the USA
Middletown, DE
01 May 2023

29806170R00146